Arvinder Singh Chawla

Asset Liability Management in Banks

Harpreet Kaur Kohli
Arvinder Singh Chawla

Asset Liability Management in Banks

A Study of Performance and Profitability of Banks

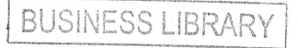
LAP LAMBERT Academic Publishing

Impressum / Imprint

Bibliografische Information der Deutschen Nationalbibliothek: Die Deutsche Nationalbibliothek verzeichnet diese Publikation in der Deutschen Nationalbibliografie; detaillierte bibliografische Daten sind im Internet über http://dnb.d-nb.de abrufbar. Alle in diesem Buch genannten Marken und Produktnamen unterliegen warenzeichen-, marken- oder patentrechtlichem Schutz bzw. sind Warenzeichen oder eingetragene Warenzeichen der jeweiligen Inhaber. Die Wiedergabe von Marken, Produktnamen, Gebrauchsnamen, Handelsnamen, Warenbezeichnungen u.s.w. in diesem Werk berechtigt auch ohne besondere Kennzeichnung nicht zu der Annahme, dass solche Namen im Sinne der Warenzeichen- und Markenschutzgesetzgebung als frei zu betrachten wären und daher von jedermann benutzt werden dürften.

Bibliographic information published by the Deutsche Nationalbibliothek: The Deutsche Nationalbibliothek lists this publication in the Deutsche Nationalbibliografie; detailed bibliographic data are available in the Internet at http://dnb.d-nb.de.
Any brand names and product names mentioned in this book are subject to trademark, brand or patent protection and are trademarks or registered trademarks of their respective holders. The use of brand names, product names, common names, trade names, product descriptions etc. even without a particular marking in this works is in no way to be construed to mean that such names may be regarded as unrestricted in respect of trademark and brand protection legislation and could thus be used by anyone.

Coverbild / Cover image: www.ingimage.com

Verlag / Publisher:
LAP LAMBERT Academic Publishing
ist ein Imprint der / is a trademark of
AV Akademikerverlag GmbH & Co. KG
Heinrich-Böcking-Str. 6-8, 66121 Saarbrücken, Deutschland / Germany
Email: info@lap-publishing.com

Herstellung: siehe letzte Seite /
Printed at: see last page
ISBN: 978-3-8383-5453-8
ᴸ100ᵞ0109S1
Zugl. / Approved by: Patiala,PunjabiUniversity,PhD Thesis,2008

MANAGEMENT OF ASSETS & LIABILITIES IN RELATION TO PERFORMANCE & PROFITABILITY OF COMMERCIAL BANKS

ACKNOWLEDGEMENT

Research is an arduous task and no research work can be completed without invoking the blessings of the Almighty.

I pronounce with reverence, my deep sense of gratitude and indebtedness to my guide, Dr. A.S. Chawla, Professor, School of Management Studies and Registrar, Punjabi University, Patiala, for his resolute guidance and abiding interest   throughout my research work. A meticulous supervision by him has helped me discover faster and more efficient ways to reach to my research objectives and present my thesis in its present form.

I would like to offer my sincere thanks to Mr. Rakesh K. Dawra, Technical Assistant, Department of Advanced Centre for Technical Development of Punjabi Language, Literature, Punjabi University,   Patiala for his technical guidance in the course of publication and enabling me to submit the dissertation in time.

I place on record my sincere gratitude to Lambert Publishing House, Germany, for encouraging me in publication of my thesis.

I am highly grateful to my husband, Mr. Gurpreet Singh, and my parents for inspiring me and providing me moral support throughout the course of the study. I would also acknowledge the contribution of my loving son, Hariansh, and daughter, Jasmine who have truly shared in the gestation of the present study.

(HARPREET KAUR KOHLI)

CONTENTS

LIST OF TABLES

LIST OF FIGURES

CHAPTER – 1

INTRODUCTION

The Banking Sector in India consists of a vast and diversified network operating at several tiers, linked operationally to the international/multilateral financial organizations, national government machinery and other sectors of the economy at various other points (Bhatnagar, 2000). Over the last three decades, however, the role of banking in the process of financial intermediation has undergone complete metamorphosis due to the changes in the Global Financial System. It is now clear that a thriving and vibrant Banking System requires a well-developed Financial Structure with multiple intermediaries operating in markets with different risk profiles (Bhushan et al.,2002).

The present Banking System in India was evolved to meet the financial needs of trade and industry and also to satisfy the credit needs of the institutions of the country.

Over the last five decades since independence, Indian Banking System has passed through five distinct phases, viz:

A. Evolutionary Phase (Prior to 1950)

B. Foundation Phase (1951-1968)

C. Expansion Phase (1969-1984)

D. Consolidation Phase (1985-1990)

E. Reformatory Phase (1991 onwards)

1.1 GROWTH OF BANKING SECTOR

1.1.1 Pre-Reforms Era

A. Evolutionary Phase (Prior to 1950)

The sudden boom of investments in the 1900s led to the emergence of leading joint stock banks such as the Punjab National Bank (1907), Bank of Baroda (1909), Central Bank of India (1911), and Union Bank of India (1919). The three Presidency Banks: Bank of Bombay, Bank of Madras, Bank of Bengal were amalgamated into the Imperial Bank of India in 1921.

In 1926, the Royal Commission on Indian Currency and Finance (The Hilton Young Commission) which was appointed to study the currency and finance situation in India and to make the necessary recommendations, recommended the establishment of a Central Bank. The Reserve Bank of India was established in 1935. While the RBI became a state owned institution from January 1, 1949 the Banking Regulation Act was enacted in 1949 providing a framework for regulation and supervision of commercial banking activity (Reddy, 2002).

The United Bank of India was formed in 1950 by the merger of four existing commercial banks. The number of Scheduled Banks rose to 81 out of which 23 were either liquidated or merged, leaving 58 Indian Scheduled Banks (Srivastava and Nigam, 2005).

B. Foundation Phase (1951-1968)

During this period, a sound banking system was emphasized. The Rural Credit Survey Committee recommended the establishment of State Bank of India by amalgamating with the Imperial Bank, the major State associate banks. Consequently, on July 1, 1955 the Imperial Bank was taken over by the Government and renamed as the State Bank of India. The State Bank of India has seven subsidiaries: -

(1)   State Bank of Bikaner and Jaipur;

(2)   State Bank of Hyderabad;

(3)   State Bank of Indore;

(4)   State Bank of Mysore;

(5)   State Bank of Patiala;

(6)   State Bank of Saurashtra and

(7)   State Bank of Travancore.

By the 1960s, the Indian Banking System had made considerable progress, both functionally and in terms of geographical coverage, nevertheless, there were still several semi-urban and urban areas which were not served by banks, while banks had hardly penetrated into the rural interior.

The Government initiated the scheme of social control over banks in December 1967 with a view to ensure that bank credit was distributed equitably and purposefully among different sectors of the economy.

With the egalitarian goals of achieving a wider spread of bank credit, the scheme of social control over Banks was introduced in 1967.

C. Expansion Phase (1969-1984):

The scheme of social control initiated by the Government in December 1967 was found to be unsatisfactory and inadequate by the Government. Eventually, on July 19, 1969, 14 major Indian Scheduled Banks (with deposits over Rs. 50 crore) were nationalized by the Government with a view to serve better the needs of the development of the economy according to national priorities and objectives.

The nationalization of 14 major commercial banks marked a turning point in the history of the Banking System in India. Credit Authorization Scheme was introduced in 1965 as part of the Reserve Bank's Credit policy.

The Lead Bank Scheme introduced by the Reserve Bank in December 1969 was a major step towards the implementation of the two-fold objective of the mobilization of deposits on a massive scale throughout the country and of stepping up lending by the banking system for the growth of the economy.

In 1970, nearly 85 per cent of bank deposits and credit of Scheduled Commercial Banks was accounted for by public sector banks and Public Sector Banks accounted for nearly 80 percent of total branches (Ajit and Bangar, 2003).

As part of the scheme of social control, the Government appointed the Banking Commission in 1969, with Shri R.G. Sariya as its Chairman to conduct an enquiry into the financial needs, policies and practices of the Banking System.

Recommendations of the Banking Commission:

1. The Commission suggested the scheme of restructuring the banks in the Public Sector. The Commission felt that the nationalized banks should be reorganized into two or three all India Banks and five or six other banks each specializing in developing Banking services in a broad region.

2. The Commission suggested that in places where there are excessive branches of Public Sector Banks, the number should be reduced through a process of inter-bank exchange of staff.

3. The concept of 'Banking' should include acceptance of all kinds of deposit regardless of their mode of withdrawal.

4. Definition of 'deposit' should cover borrowings by way of loans also except certain specified categories of loans.

5. Rural banking should be encouraged by expediting the statutory framework.

6. Banks should be allowed to diversify into other avenues like buying machinery and leasing them.

7. Constant monitoring of the Banking laws should be done to ensure that socio-economic objectives are being attained by the Banking Sector.

Arising out of those recommendations of the Commission, which were acceptable to the Government and to the Bank, certain statutes governing banks were amended, viz. Banking Regulation Act and State Bank of India Act.

In 1974, RBI appointed a study group under Shri P.L. Tandon to frame guidelines for the follow-up of bank credit. The Group was therefore asked to make suggestions as to the extent to which the current assets i.e. assets which are of a short-term character, should be normally financed by the banks.

To restrain further expansion of credit to the industry, RBI again constituted a Working Group under the Chairmanship of Shri K.B. Chore in 1979. The primary aim of setting up this committee was to look into the operation of cash credit system and to find alternative ways of controlling the flow of credit to industry, particularly to the medium and large borrowers, in order to establish a link between output and credit needs.

This period also witnessed the birth of Regional Rural Banks (RRBs) in 1975, which has priority sector as its target sector.

Second Phase of Nationalization:

By an Ordinance issued on April 15th 1980, the Government nationalized six more commercial banks whose demand and time liabilities in each case exceeded Rs. 200 crore as on March 14, 1980.

As such over 90 percent of the banking activity in the country was brought into the public sector.

The goals of nationalization were presumed to be achieved through:

(i) Considerable spread of branch network to all parts of the country not confined to urban and metropolitan areas only;

(ii) Mobilization of funds from all sections of the society by framing deposit schemes tailored to suit its different segments;

(iii) Deployment of funds in all productive endeavours, big or small, so that production effort becomes broad-based; and

(iv) Particular attention to credit needs of hundreds and thousands of people engaged in agriculture and small business whose production and distribution efforts contribute substantially to the national cake (Chawla, 1987).

D. Consolidation Phase (1985-1990)

To achieve the objectives of nationalization, policy makers followed credit rationing approach and high-directed credit obligations. Performance of a bank began to be evaluated in terms of growth of advances, deposits and quality was sacrificed to achieve these targets.

Banks functioned in a regulated environment with restrictions on credit flows and pre-emption of significant proportion of funds for the priority sectors. These resulted in sub-optimal use of credit, low levels of investment and growth, decline in productivity and profitability.

The malaise in the Banking Sector paved the way for consolidation of banks. After achieving a phenomenal expansion in branch network during the first decade and half of bank nationalization at nearly 2400 branches per year, the Scheduled Commercial Banks entered a consolidation phase in the mid-1980s.

In 1985, the Chakravarty Committee was set up to review the working of the Monetary System. The Committee recommended a more liberal approach to interest rates, including a selective approach to concessional interest rates and a hike in coupon rates on government borrowing. For the first time, serious attention was

6

paid to improving house-keeping, customer services, staff productivity and profitability of banks and concrete steps were taken to rationalize the rates of bank deposits and lending (Srivastava and Nigam, 2005).

To bring about a qualitative and quantitative improvement in the banks' lending operations in the rural areas, Service Area Approach (SAA) was introduced from April 1989. Under this scheme, the commercial banks were entrusted with the coordination between credit institutions, on the one hand and field level agencies, on the other, on an on-going basis, for the effective implementation of credit plans.

1.1.2. Reforms Era (1991 onwards)

By the end of 1990, the economic situation became highly critical. Exchange reserves were at rock bottom, inflation had crossed the double-digit level and was moving higher and the fiscal deficit was sharply widening. In mid-1991, the total incremental pre-emption of bank deposits was as high as 63.5 per cent, comprising CRR of 15 percent, incremental CRR of 10 per cent and SLR of 38.5per cent (Kanagasabapathy, 2001).

Interest rates on both sides of the balance-sheet were highly regulated. Banks had limited access to financial markets and strict entry barriers were imposed for the private banks and foreign banks.

Manpower planning and development received little attention, concern for profitability and productivity was less. Against this backdrop, Narasimham Committee was constituted in 1991 to examine all aspects of the financial system so as to create a more diversified and vibrant banking system. The underlying philosophy was to make the banking system more market-oriented and to that end, engender a shift in the role of the RBI from micro-management of bank's operations to macro-governance (Das et al., 2005).

The Committee's observation was that the deterioration in the financial health of the system has reached a point where unless remedial measures are taken soon, it could further erode the real value of and return on the savings entrusted to them and have an adverse impact on depositor and investor confidence (Kumar, 2000).

In view of the extremely critical situation, the Narasimham Committee was set up under the Chairmanship of Shri M. Narasimham, Governor of Reserve Bank of India, in 1991 to address the problems and suggest corrective measures.

Narasimham Committee-I Recommendations:

The major recommendations of this committee were:

1. Progressive reduction in Statutory Liquidity Ratio (SLR) and Cash Reserve Ratio (CRR) so as to increase the lending capacity of the banks.

2. Allowing entry of new private sector banks and permitting Foreign banks to open branches under terms and conditions applicable to domestic banks.

3. The regulated interest rate should be rationalized and simplified.

4. The nationalized banks were to be allowed direct access to capital markets to mobilize funds from the public.

5. Introduction of Prudential Norms relating to Income recognition, Asset Classification and soundness of the Financial System to impart greater transparency and accountability in operations. For this, introduction of a formal Asset-Liability Management was emphasized.

6. Improving operational autonomy and accountability of Bank management with regard to internal management, credit and investment decision and speeding up computerization in banks.

7. Branch licensing policy should be liberalized.

8. The Recovery of Debts due to Banks and Financial Institutions Act, 1993 was enacted to set up dedicated tribunals for expeditious adjudication and recovery of debts.

Progress during 1991-98

The Narasimham Committee recommendations have created metamorphosis in the banking industry. The major recommendations of the Committee are:

The SLR was brought down from its peak level of 38.5 per cent on April 3, 1992 to 31.5 per cent on net demand and time liabilities (NDTL) as on September, 30, 1994, and to 25 per cent on Oct 25, 1997(Kanagasabapathy, 2001). CRR was also reduced from 15 per cent to 14 per cent during April-May, 1993.

All Indian banks with international presence had to achieve a Capital to Risk Assets Ratio of 8 percent by March 31, 1994. By 1997, almost all Public Sector Banks had achieved the minimum Capital Adequacy norm of 8 per cent (Raj, 2002).

Securities and Exchange Board of India (SEBI), which was set up in 1988, was given statutory powers in 1992 in relation to matters affecting Capital market.

Realizing the importance of customer satisfaction in banking industry, the Goiporia Committee was also appointed to make recommendations to bring about an improvement in customer service. With a view to further improve customer service; the RBI framed the Banking Ombudsman Scheme in 1995 to provide speedy redressal of customers' grievances in respect of complaints on matters covered by the scheme.

Narasimham Committee-II Recommendations:

After seven years of economic liberalization, there was a coming of the Narasimham Committee with the following recommendations for the second phase of reforms in 1998:

- **Capital Adequacy:**

The Committee recommended that Capital Adequacy Ratio be raised from 8 per cent to 9 percent by March, 2000 and 10 per cent by 2002.There should be a 5 per cent weight for market risk for Government and approved securities. The Committee suggested that commercial risk weight of 100 percent be assigned to Government-guaranteed advances which were previously treated as risk free.

- **Asset quality:**

Banks should adopt a more general approach of Asset-Liability Management to modify their liability in accordance with the desired asset structure. It was recommended that Government guaranteed irregular accounts should be classified as Non-Performing Assets (NPAs) and accounted for. The Committee redefined priority sector and suggested that allocation of funds under priority sector be reduced from the existing 40 per cent of the aggregate advance to 10 per cent in a phased manner. **Industry Structure:**

The Committee recommended that strong banks should not be merged with weak banks as the asset quality of the strong banks will be deteriorated due to the unhealthy weak banks. Mergers should be driven by market and business considerations and should not be imposed by regulators. Banks should focus on non-fund or fee-based business such as advisory and consultancy services, guarantees and custody services. The Committee strongly recommended the combination of operational flexibility and global competition for improving the functioning of the Public Sector Banks. For this the minimum Government shareholding was to be reduced from 55 percent to 33 per cent for State Bank of India and 51 per cent for other Public Sector Banks.

- **Regulation and Supervision:**

Banking regulation and supervision should be progressively delinked from the monetary policy. It was suggested that Board for Financial Regulation and Supervision should be constituted with statutory powers. Greater emphasis was suggested on public disclosure as opposed to disclosure to regulators.

- **Khan Committee Recommendations:**

Another committee which needs to be mentioned is the Khan Committee, which was constituted by the Reserve Bank of India in 1997 to examine the harmonization of the role and operations of development financial institutions (DFIs) and banks.

The major recommendations of this Committee were a gradual move towards Universal Banking along with exploring the possibility of gainful mergers as between banks, and banks & financial institutions.

1.2 PROGRESS SINCE REFORMS

Banking Sector Reforms constituted an integral part of the Financial Sector Reforms in India. These reforms have infused competition in the banking system. The reforms were aimed to strengthen the banking sector through Prudential Income Recognition and Asset classification norms along with harmonizing the role of the banks and DFIs.

- **Capital Adequacy:**

As at end March 31, 2002, all Scheduled Commercial Banks(except five)recorded Capital to Risk-weighted Asset Ratios (CRARs) in excess of the stipulated nine per cent with as many as 53 SCBs posting CRAR between 10 per cent and 15per cent , while for another 30 SCBs, CRARs were in excess of 15 per cent.

The majority of SCBs (Scheduled Commercial Banks)74 out of 97 banks as on 31st March 2002, recorded net NPAs within 10 per cent of their net advances(RBI's Annual Report,2001-02).

- **Deregulation of Interest Rates:**

Rationalization of the Interest Rate structure has been carried out gradually to achieve total deregulation of interest rates. The lending rates on advances above Rs. 2 lakh have been deregulated. Banks have been allowed to evolve a Prime Lending Rate (PLR) which will be the rate offered to the first class clients of the bank and the rates to be offered to other clients will be based on this rate. Pressures of competition and intensity of demand for funds and to the borrower to source his requirements will determine what rate would be appropriate (Janakiraman, 1995).

- **Reduction in Statutory Pre-emption:**

Financial repression through statutory pre-emptions was lowered, as at March end 2003, the Cash Reserve Ratio (CRR) stood at 4.75 percent (legal minimum is 3 percent) and Statutory Liquidity Ratio (SLR) at 25 percent (legal minimum)(Das et al.,2005).

- **Delicensing:**

The commercial banks were given the freedom to open branches without the prior sanction of the RBI. The Committee on Financial System, headed by Mr. M. Narasimham, recommended that the entry of new private sector banks be permitted. It further recommended that freedom of entry into the financial system should be liberalized and the Reserve Bank should now permit the establishment of new banks in the private sector, provided they conform to the minimum start-up capital and other requirements and the set of prudential norms with regard to accounting, provisioning and other aspects of operations. (Sreekantaradhya, 2004).

In all, nine Private Sector Banks were established in 1995:Indusind Bank Ltd., Global Trust Bank Ltd., UTI Bank Ltd., ICICI Bank Ltd., HDFC Bank Ltd., Times Bank Ltd., Centurion Bank Ltd., IDBI Bank Ltd., and Bank of Punjab.

However, many of the above banks went in for mergers, i.e. HDFC Bank and Times Bank Ltd., UTI Bank and Global Trust Bank Ltd., and Bank of Punjab Ltd. and Centurion Bank Ltd. reducing the number to seven as on 31st March 2007.

- **Priority Sector Credit:**

The definition of priority sector has been enlarged. Though the stipulation that 40 per cent of total bank credit should be reserved for priority sector continues, the target is not rigid. If the target is not reached, an amount equivalent to the shortfall should be invested in NABARD/SIDBI so as to prevent the banks from investing in commercially non-viable activities.

- **Banking Regulation and Supervision :**

Recent efforts at improving the regulatory and supervisory system are based on the recommendations of the Basel Committee on Banking Supervision. This Committee has been functioning since 1975. Though it is essentially an advisory group of G-10 countries, some non-G-10 countries are also consulted in the formulation of standards.

The Basel Committee drew up 25 core Principles for Effective Banking Supervision in 1997. As a result, Board for Financial Supervision (BFS), comprising the Governor of RBI as Chairman, one of the Deputy Governors as Vice Chairman and four directors of the Central Board of RBI as members was constituted in 1994 for supervision and inspection in relation to the banking companies, financial institutions and non-banking companies. The periodical inspections as also the targeted appraisals by the RBI are now supplemented by off-site surveillance which particularly focuses on risk profile of a bank, its capital adequacy, Asset Quality including credit and investment, level of NPAs, credit concentration and group exposures, connected lending management changes etc(Talwar,2002). A process of rating of banks on the basis of Capital Adequacy, Asset Quality, Management, Earnings, Liquidity and systems and control (CAMELS), in respect of Indian banks and Capital, Asset Quality, Compliance, Systems and Control (CACS) in respect of foreign banks has been instituted.

Following the adoption of international Financial standards and codes, the RBI has put in place a system of Prompt Corrective Action (PCA) which will help in addressing fiscal distress in banks in a pro-active manner (Radhakrishan, 2004). Three main parameters have been proposed viz. Capital to Risk Asset Ratio (CRAR), Net NPAs and Return on Assets (ROA). Trigger points have been set under the three parameters and for every trigger point, a set of mandatory and discretionary preventive correlative actions have been prescribed.

- **Prudential Regulations**

A major element of the Financial Sector Reforms has been the application of Prudential norms and regulations aimed at ensuring the safety and soundness of the Financial System and at the same time encouraging markets to play increasing role. Prudential norms introduced in India relate to Income Recognition, Asset Classification, and Provisioning for bad and doubtful debts and Capital Adequacy. Prudential norms required the banks to make 100% provisions for all non-performing assets.

The practice of taking Income into account only on actual basis and not accrual basis and the practice of classifying assets into standard, sub-standard, doubtful and loss assets were brought in.

14

Various amendments are being announced in Income Recognition and Asset Classification (IRAC) norms by RBI through its policy initiatives every year.

Introduction of Prudential norms on Income Recognition, Asset Classification and Provisioning during 1992-93 and other steps initiated apart from bring transparency in the loan portfolio of banking industry have significantly contributed towards improvement of the pre-sanction appraisal and post-sanction supervision which is reflected in the lowering of the levels of fresh accretion of NPAs of banks after 1992(Siddiqui et al., 2002).

- **Debt Recovery Tribunals**

Recovery of Debts due to Banks and Financial Institutions Bill, 1993 was passed in August 1993 for establishment of Debt Recovery Tribunals (DRTs) to expedite adjudication and recovery of debts due to banks and financial institutions. The main purpose of setting up these tribunals is to help clean up balance-sheets of banks from the burden of Non-performing Assets so as to improve the liquidity position of banks.

- **Opening up of the Financial Sector**

In terms of the agreement arrived at under the aegis of the World Trade Organization, India is committed to permitting the opening of 12 new branches by foreign banks per year in the country. 32 foreign banks now operate 217 branches in India and during 2003-04 permission was granted to 5 foreign banks to open 18 new branches according to RBI Annual Report 2003-04.

As per this Annual Report, 10 banks were given in- principle approval to open 14 overseas banking units (OBUs) in Special Economic Zones (SEZs). Of these, 6 banks, viz. State Bank of India, Bank of Baroda, and Union Bank of India, ICICI Bank and Punjab

National Bank have begun operations in the Santa Cruz Electronics Export Processing Zone, Mumbai and Canara Bank in Noida (U.P.).

1.3 RISK MANAGEMENT AND ALM

Risk is the potentiality that both the expected and unexpected events may have an adverse impact on the bank's capital or earnings. It is essential to have an understanding of the risks faced by the banks so as to effectively manage and control them.

As per the RBI guidelines issued in 1999, there are three major types of risks encountered by the banks:

1. **Credit Risk:** It is the risk related to the possibility of a default in the repayment obligation by the borrowers of funds.

2. **Market Risk:** It is defined as the possibility of loss to a bank caused by the changes in the market variables i.e. movements in equity and interest rate markets, currency exchange rates and commodity prices.

(a) **Liquidity Risk:** Liquidity risk originates from the potential inability of a bank to generate cash to cope with any decline in liabilities or increase in assets.

(b) **Interest Rate Risk:** - It is the gain/loss that arises due to sensitivity of the interest income/interest expenditure or values of assets/liabilities to the interest rate fluctuations.

(c) **Foreign Exchange Risk:** It is the risk that relates to the gains/losses that arise due to fluctuations in the exchange rates.

3. **Operational Risk:** The Basel Committee on Banking Supervision (BCBS) published the Capital Accord in 1988 which was to be adopted by 1992. This accord focused mainly on credit risk and operational risk was not explicitly addressed. Financial innovations and complexity of financial transactions called for a review of the capital adequacy framework. Operational risk is the risk of loss arising from various types of technical or human error or failed internal process, legal hurdles, fraud, failure of people and systems or from external agencies.

The complexity of financial risk, no doubt, argues a strong case for an identifiable and dedicated risk management function in a bank's organization, which should be comprehensive to include asset, liability and off-balance-sheet risks.

Deregulation and integration have led Indian Banks and financial institutions into competition both on Assets side as well as Liabilities side of the Balance-sheet, forcing them to assume greater and newer risks in their quest for higher returns. Asset Liability Management (ALM) has grown up as a response to the problem of managing modern day business which is subject to a wider range of risks in an environment where interest rates, exchange rates and economic conditions are subject to changes and at times volatile movement (Khurana, 2000).The maturity mismatches and disproportionate changes in the levels of assets and liabilities cause both liquidity risk and interest-rate risk (Kamath, 1996).

Though the ALM process is too complex to practice, it is perhaps the only solution for banks to survive in this rapidly changing environment where the composition, duration and risk profile of their assets and liabilities have an important bearing on their growth and profitability (Vij, 2005).

While most of the banks in other countries conceptualized ALM as early as 1970s, the Indian banks remained oblivious of it due to the highly regulated and protected environment till the 1980s. Banks are now free to determine on their own, interest rates on deposits and advances in both domestic and foreign currencies on a dynamic basis.

The Narasimham Committee Reports on the Banking Sector Reforms highlighted the weaknesses in the Indian Banking system and suggested reforms based on the Basel norms.

Recognizing the need for a strong and sound banking system, the Reserve Bank of India came out with its guidelines on Asset Liability Management System in banks in February 1999. These guidelines were to be implemented with effect from April 1, 1999.

The final guidelines have been formulated to serve as a benchmark for those banks which lack a formal ALM system. Banks which have already adopted more sophisticated systems may continue their existing systems but they should ensure to fine-tune their current information and reporting system so as to be in line with the ALM system suggested in the Guidelines. Other banks should examine their existing Management Information System (MIS) and arrange to have an information system to meet the prescriptions of the new ALM system. To begin with, banks should ensure coverage of at least 60% of their liabilities and assets. As for the remaining 40% of their assets and liabilities, banks may include the position based on their estimates. By April1, 2000 it was necessary for banks that set targets in the interim, for covering 100 per cent of their business.

1.3.1 Asset-Liability Management (ALM) System in Banks- RBI Guidelines 1999

Under the guidelines, the initial focus of the ALM function would be to enforce the risk management discipline viz. managing business after assessing the risks involved.

The ALM process rests on three pillars:

1.3.2 ALM Information Systems

- Management Information System
- Information availability, accuracy, adequacy and expediency

Information is the key to the ALM process. Varied business profiles of banks in the public and private sector as well as those of foreign banks do not make the adoption of a uniform ALM system for all banks feasible. The problem of ALM needs to be addressed by following an ABC approach i.e. analyzing the behaviour of asset and liability products in the sample branches, accounting for significant business and then making rational assumptions about the way in which assets and liabilities would behave in other branches.

1.3.3 ALM Organization

- Structure and responsibilities
- Level of top management involvement

Successful implementation of the risk management process would require strong commitment on the part of the senior management in the bank, to integrate basic operations and strategic decision making with risk management. The Board should have overall responsibility for management of risks and should decide the risk management policy of the bank and set limits for liquidity, interest rate, foreign exchange and equity price risks.

The Asset-Liability Committee (ALCO) consisting of the bank's senior management including CEO should be responsible for ensuring adherence to the limits set by the Board as well as for deciding the business strategy of the bank in line with the bank's budget and decided risk management objectives.

1.3.4   ALM Process

- Risk parameters
- Risk identification
- Risk measurement
- Risk management
- Risk policies and tolerance limits.

The scope of ALM function can be described as follows:

- Liquidity risk management
- Management of market risks
- Trading risk management
- Funding and capital planning
- Profit planning and growth projection.

Measuring and managing liquidity needs are vital for effective operation of commercial banks. The importance of liquidity transcends individual institutions, as liquidity shortfall in one institution can have repercussions on the entire system. Banks management should measure not only the liquidity position of banks on an ongoing basis but also examine how liquidity requirements are likely to evolve under crisis scenarios.

Thus, an ALM function must strive to include:

- ALM process must preserve and enhance the net worth of the institution.
- ALM is a quantification of the various risks in the balance-sheet.
- ALM function must streamline the management of regulatory capital.
- ALM should provide liquidity management within the institution ALM should actively and judiciously leverage the balance-sheet (Ong, 1998).

REFERENCES

Ajit, D; and Bangar,R.(2003), "Banks in Financial Intermediation-Performance and Issues," in A.Vasudevan (ed.), *Money and Banking-Select Research Papers by the Economists of Reserve Bank of India*, Academic Foundation, New Delhi, p.244.

Bhatnagar, Amitabh(2000),*Reengineering Millennium's Indian Banking Sector*, Anmol Publications Pvt. Ltd., New Delhi, p.12.

Bhushan,Sanjay; Mani, Saurabh;and Sharma, S.K.(2002),"Strategic Focus on Executive Development- Genesis of Banking Sector Reforms: A study of selected Commercial Banks of India," *South Asian Journal of Socio-Political Studies*, Vol. 3, No. 1, July Dec,p.56.

Chawla, A.S. (1987), *Nationalisation and Growth of Indian Banking*, Deep & Deep publications Pvt. Ltd. New Delhi,p.18.

Das, Abhiman; Nag, Ashok; and Ray,Subhash (2005), " Liberalization, Ownership and Efficiency in Indian Banking-A Non-parametric Analysis, " *EPW*, Vol. XL, No. 12, March 19, p.1191.

Dharmarajan, S. (2004),"ALM Model for Managing Liquidity and Interest Rate Risks in Cooperative Banks," *Vinimaya,* Vol. XXV, No.1, April- June.

EPW Research Foundation (2004)," Scheduled Commercial Banks in India: A 30 year Data Base, "*Economic and Political Weekly*, Vol. XXXXIX, No. 12, March.20-26. p.1331.

Janakiraman, R. (1995),"Indian Banking by 2000 A.D.- Challenges Ahead," in N.Vinayakam (ed.),*Indian Banking by 2000 A.D.*, Kanishka Publishers, Distributors, New Delhi, p.21.

Kamath, M.V.(1996), " ALM in Banks," *CanBank Quarterly Review*, Vol. VI No. 4 & Vol. VII No. 1, October - March p.9.

Kanagasabapathy,K.(2001),"Monetary Policy Underpinnings: A Perspective," *Economic & Political Weekly*, Vol. XXXVI, No. 4 Jan. 27-Feb. 2, pp.305-306.

Khurana,S.K.(2000),*Asset Liability Management,* Skylark Publications, New Delhi.

Kumar, RaviT.(2000), "Banking Sector Reforms-Shackled Liberation, " in Ravi Kumar T.(ed.), *Indian Banking System in Transition-Issues and Challenges*, ICFAI Vision Series, Finance, p.138.

Mithani, D.M.(2004), *Money, Banking, International Trade and Public Finance*, Himalaya Publishing House, Mumbai.

Ong,K. Michael.(1998), "Integrating the Role of Risk Management in ALM,"in *Asset & Liability Management: A Synthesis of New Methodologies*, Risk Books, Kamakura Corp., London, p.3.

Pathak, V. Bharati.(2004),*Indian Financial System*, Pearson Education Pvt. Ltd., Delhi edition,p.399.

Radhakrishan, R.(2004), " A Decade of Financial Sector Reforms in India," in M.P. Srivastava & S.R. Singh (eds.), *Indian Banking in the New Millennium*, Anmol Publications Pvt. Ltd., New Delhi, edition, p.107.

Raj, Dev(2002)," Financial Sector Reforms in India: Functional Realities and Prospects, " in Amalesh Banerjee and S.K. Singh (eds.), *Banking, and Financial Sector Reforms in India* Deep & Deep Publications Pvt. Ltd., New Delhi,p. 62.

RBI(2001-02 & 2003-04),Financial Regulation and Supervision, Annual Reports.

Reddy, Y.V.(2002),"Public Sector Banks and the Governance Challenge-the Indian Experience," *http://www.rbi.org.in.com*.

Siddiqui, A.Q, Rao A.S., and Thakkar R.M. (2002), " Some Aspects and Issues Relating to NPAs in Commercial Banks," in P.

Mohana Rao and T.K. Jain (eds.), *Management of Banking and Financial Institutions*, Deep & Deep Publications Pvt. Ltd, New Delhi, p.163.

Sreekantaradhya, B.S. (2004), *Banking and Finance -Perspectives on Reform*, Deep & Deep Publications Pvt. Ltd., New Delhi,p.13.

Srivastava, R.M.;and Nigam, Divya(2005),*Management of Indian Financial Institutions*, Himalaya Publishing House, Mumbai .

Talwar, S.P.(2002), "The Changing Dimensions of Supervision and Regulations," in P. Mohana Rao and T.K. Jain (eds.) *Management of Banking and Financial Institutions*, Deep & Deep Publications Pvt. Ltd., New Delhi, p.224.

Vij, Madhu(2005),"Asset Liability Management,"in S.K. Tuteja (ed.), *Management Mosaic*, Excel Books, New Delhi, p.334.

CHAPTER – 2
REVIEW OF LITERATURE AND RESEARCH METHODOLOGY

One of the major imperatives of the Financial Sector Reforms has been to strengthen the Banking Sector by improving the financial health of banks through better capital adequacy and asset quality. The traditional face of banks as mere financial intermediaries has since altered and risk management has emerged as the defining attribute.

With the initiation of the reforms, banks were required to evolve strategies rather than ad hoc fire-fighting solutions. These strategies are executed in the form of ALM practices. ALM involves quantification of risks and conscious decision-making with regard to Asset-Liabilities structure in order to maximize interest earning within the framework of perceived risks. ALM is the only solution for banks to survive in this rapidly changing environment where the composition, duration and risk profile of a bank's assets and liabilities have an important impact on their growth and profitability.

Many studies have been conducted in India and abroad to investigate the major structural changes in the field of banking and the relevance of ALM for commercial banks in maintaining their interest spreads and profitability. In this context, the present chapter is an attempt to review the studies already done and draw some important conclusions that can serve as a guide mark for the study. The following review of the studies has been divided thematically into three sections. The first section deals with studies on Asset Liability Management. The second section deals with the studies on profitability performance of banks. The third section reviews the studies on lending policies of banks.

2.1 REVIEW OF LITERATURE

(A) Studies on Asset Liability Management

Sinkey (1992), in his work discussed the various aspects and tools of ALM. He opined that Asset Liability Management (ALM) refers to the coordinated management of a bank's balance-sheet to allow for alternative interest-rate and liquidity scenarios. The vital variable of ALM in the short-run is net interest income (NII) or its ratio form or, net interest margin (NIM=NII/earning assets). In addition to the planning aspect of ALM, direction and control of the levels, changes (flows) and mixes of assets, liabilities and capital are integral parts of over all balance-sheet management. In this broader context, six policies have been advocated to achieve both the short and long-run objectives of ALM: Spread Management, Control of Net Non-interest Income/Burden, Liquidity Management, Capital Management, Tax Management, Management of the off-balance-sheet activities.

Patheja (1994), in her research work analyzed the importance of Asset Liability Management and Spread Management in Punjab National Bank. According to her, ALM is the management process of developing and evaluating overall objectives, policies and strategies based upon the environmental conditions, opportunities in the market place, risk preferences and risk-reward characteristics. The researcher concluded that Spread Management is a function of cost reduction and return maximization and in the context of banking; it involves efficient assets management, especially of credit portfolio and liability management in terms of deposits and capital funds.

Subrahmanyam (1995), in her research article studied Asset Liability Management as a tool to enhance income and control risk exposure of bank's activity in the light of the liberalized environment created by the banking sector reforms. She believed that the basic purpose of ALM is to control interest sensitive funds at the disposal of banks. An efficient ALM policy consists of devising requisite strategies for managing bank funds which has enabled banks to gain control over asset growth, liquidity and profitability by offering competitive interest rates on purchased funds to match the available yields on money market instruments.

Ammannya(1996), in his article on Asset Liability Management Strategy for banks has emphasized that the core objective of asset liability management is to ensure and increase profitability and long- term viability. He stressed that Asset Liability Management is essentially a planning function designed to move the organization in the direction of its long range plan while maintaining flexibility to adapt to short-run changes. Therefore, it is important to adopt an approach that requires coordination of various specific functions such as planning, directing and controlling the levels, changes and mixes of various balance-sheet items. He emphasized that a sound investment policy, market timing and securities selection have become crucial for investment decisions in banks.

Das (1996), in his research paper attempted to identify the relationships and structural changes, including hedging pattern, between asset-liability variables of the commercial banks in India by using statistical techniques at two different points of time representing pre- and post-liberalization periods. He found that Public Sector Banks, in spite of their large size and greater access to money market sources, have performed relatively poor in terms of portfolio matching compared to the small sized foreign banks. Foreign banks showed a better hedging pattern in their assets and liability management of interest rate risks. However, some marginal changes were noticeable on the portfolio matching behaviour of Public Sector Banks in the post-reform period, the reform process did not make a significant impact on the interest rate risk management of these banks.

Agarwal (1998), studied the asset portfolio and liability profile of the Indian banking system over a period of 13 years with 1990-91 as median year. The linking of the interest rates on government borrowing to market rates with the simultaneous opening up of the economy to regain competition has resulted in a downgrading of credit in the risk return approval framework of banks. He concludes that in order to free the borrower for infrastructure and agrarian development, it is imperative to redirect flow of credit to the private economy. This would help in provisioning for NPAs and also imposing quantitative limits on the banks' investments.

Chawla (1998), in his article on Asset Liability Management in banks has highlighted its importance in the liberated environment created by the economic reforms. The banks have been given freedom to manage their balance-sheet, but the knowledge and organizational changes required to manage it, particularly the banking risks, are still lacking. He advocates requirements to implement ALM in these banks in the stated order; Developing a better understanding of ALM concepts and setting up ALM decision-making process (ALM Committee/ALCO).The Private Sector Banks have made headway in this area but the Public Sector Banks need to focus on ALM which would provide the necessary framework to define, measure, monitor, modify and manage interest-rate risk.

Mehta (1998), in her article tried to highlight the importance of managing asset-liability mix in the deregulated interest rate environment that has evolved after liberalization. In her opinion, the

ALM system is not only a management information system, but also an advance warning system of the bank's sensitivity to adverse changes in the environment. Thus, an effective risk management process requires that banks maintain their interest rate risk within prudent limits. She concluded that the adoption of sophistication in ALM would go a long way in strengthening the entire banking sector, which will positively affect the banks' profitability.

Ong (1998), in his research paper tried to draw attention to non-traditional ways of conducting the ALM function in an integrated and enterprise-wise risk management framework. According to him, ALM involves the trade-off between risk and reward. It is about taking risk in innovative ways to achieve the desired reward. He highlighted such innovations as Value-at-risk, Asset Securitization and Credit Derivatives. An Asset Liability Management function must preserve and enhance the net worth of the institution. It must streamline the management of regulatory capital, and provide liquidity management within the institution. He advocated that the single most important function of ALM is to preserve and enhance the net worth of an institution through whatever means are available to it.

Kumar (2000), in his work on Asset Liability Management has discussed the ALM in different models. According to him, ALM is basically a hedging response to the risk in financial intermediation. With ALM in place, managers can evaluate the impact of alternative decisions on the future risk profiles. Managing the spread income and controlling the risks associated with generating the spread are the crucial part of the ALM process for any bank. He concluded that intense competition for business on the asset and liabilities side, coupled with increasing volatility in both domestic interest rates and foreign exchange rate is putting pressure on the management of banks to maintain spreads, profitability and long term viability. He further concluded that to remain competitive Indian financial institutions cannot afford to remain aloof and they should evolve necessary systems for the adoption of ALM.

Das and Singh (2001), in their empirical study on maturity pattern of assets & liabilities of Public Sector Banks tried to investigate whether there exists any maturity mismatch between assets and liabilities of such banks and to measure the extent of concentration of assets (loans/ advances and investment securities) and liabilities (deposit and borrowings) in various maturity buckets. They concluded that the Public Sector Banks exhibit asset-liability mismatch in terms of their maturity pattern. This is more pronounced in the long-term category indicating that short and medium-term funds are being utilized for financing long-term assets. A part of the mismatch has been due to the predominance of investment in the government securities, which, in general, have longer maturities. Another reason is that banks are ordinarily not allowed to raise long-term deposits. They suggested that banks be allowed to accept long-term deposits, particularly, when commercial banks are keen to enter to into infrastructure financing, which are long-term in nature.

Joshi and Joshi (2002), in their work on the management of Indian Banks emphasized the importance of ALM in the planning process. According to them, ALM focuses on the net interest income of the institution. The principal purpose of ALM has been to control the size of the net interest income. To achieve transparency a bank must provide accurate, relevant and sufficient disclosure of qualitative and quantitative information that would enable users to make a proper assessment of an institution's activities and risk profile. In the light of the recommendations of the Basel Committee, the balance-sheet must truly highlight the state of the bank's health. They concluded that banks should take some amount of risk in their asset/liability management, but it should never be on interest rate predictions, as in a globally competitive environment, Indian banks need to build on their strengths and reach the desired standards as soon as possible.

Rajwade(2002), in his article discussed various issues of Asset Liability Management and pricing of liabilities. He attempted to provide a base for pricing of liabilities. According to him, the basic objective of pricing should be to achieve the desired return on shareholders' funds, which has to be quantified at the board level. After setting this, a target for the net interest income, factoring in the bank's non-interest income and non-interest expenditure has to be set. The desired net interest income then becomes the base number for considering the pricing of assets and liabilities. If a bank is already having higher than needed SLR investments, the cheaper way of generating resources needed for lending is to liquidate the surplus investments than to pay higher than government security yields to depositors.

Sehgal and Kher (2002), in their research paper stressed on the objectives and aspects of Asset Liability Management (ALM) in the bank, and to some extent, on the broader aspects of risk management. They viewed that a sound ALM system for the bank should encompass review of interest rate outlook, fixation of interest, product pricing of both Assets and Liabilities, review of credit portfolio and credit risk management of foreign exchange operations and management of liquidity risk. In the present context, the ALM exercise should comprise of prudential management of funds with respect to size and duration, minimizing undesirable maturity mismatch to avoid liquidity problem and reducing the gap between

30

rate sensitive assets and rate sensitive liabilities with the given risk taken capacity.

Kumar (2003), in her research article emphasized on the need to have a mechanism for a stringent and standardized supervision of banks for proper regulation of their business parties. The current supervisory process adopted by the Department of Banking Supervision is applied uniformly to all supervised institutions. The process is based on CAMELS (applicable to all domestic banks/CALCS applicable to India) approach where Capital Adequacy, Asset Quality, Management Aspects Earnings, Liquidity and System and Control are examined keeping in view the requirements of section 22 of the Banking Regulation Act, 1949. While concluding, she expressed her satisfaction over the move towards risk based supervision in the emerging financial front.

Debasish (2004), in his research paper investigated the evidence of market discipline in the Indian banking sector over the period 1995-2003. He concluded that deposit growth in private sector banks is directly driven by capitalization and negatively driven by non-performing assets. In the case of public sector banks, deposit growth is directly related to GDP growth. In the case of foreign banks, neither the asset quality, capital ratio nor earnings are decisive in harnessing deposit growth. Only liquidity plays a vital role in influencing deposit, hinting at the possibility that depositors take limited cognizance of the overall soundness of foreign banks in entrusting their deposits.

Dharmarajan(2004), in his research paper tried to emphasize on the importance of funds management in banks and the concepts, significance and objectives of ALM. It also covers the framework of ALM system in general and the need for implementing the system in cooperative banks. The article mainly discusses the implementation procedure viz. ALM Information System, ALM Process – Management of Interest Spread/Liquidity Gap Management / Management of Interest Rate Risk, ALM Committee and Duties and Responsibilities of ALM Committee. He concludes that it is high time the Cooperative Banks adopt the ALM system to ensure their financial discipline and also fulfil the mandatory provisions coming into force in the near future.

Raghavan(2004), in his research paper discussed the implications of Basel II Accord on the Capital Structure of banks. The purpose of Basel II is to introduce a more risk-sensitive capital framework with incentives for good risk management practices. Under Basel-II approach, capital requirements will increase for those banks that hold high risk assets (low quality assets) and those with low risk assets (high quality assets), a balanced portfolio as well as effective risk management control systems may need less capital requirements. He concluded that the financial system has to cope constantly with changes in the broader environment in which it operates and face new challenges that those developments impose on it.

Thimmaiah(2004), in his research article discussed Asset Liability Management in the light of Post Indian Banking Sector Reforms. He has focused on the importance of Asset Liability Management, and to some extent, on the broader aspects of risk management. He stated that a sound Asset Liability Management system should encompass: review of interest ate out-look; fixation of interest product pricing of both assets and liabilities; review of credit portfolio and credit risk management; review of investment portfolio and risk management and management of liquidity risk.

With the gradual rise in the ratio of current investment to permanent investment by RBI, banks have shown greater willingness to value major portion of their investment as ''mark to market''. While this will expose the investment portfolio to potential market risks, steps for countering the adverse impact of interest rate changes or other market risk variables can be initiated through proper ALM only.

Bagchi(2005), in his article attempted to study operational risk and analyzed its likely impact on Indian Banking operations. Operational Risk Management in banking will need new skill sets aided and supported by an articulated operational Risk Policy of each Bank due to the implications of Basel-II Accord released in June 2004. He has suggested for the convergence of Capital Measurement and standards in Operational Banking. He suggested that each bank should prepare an Operational Risk Policy which would enable the identification, measurement, monitoring and control of its Operational Risk areas. He concluded that Basel II Accord on Operational Risk will strengthen the business orientation and focus of Indian Banking.

Ghosh and Das(2005), in their research paper tried to analyze how market forces may motivate banks to select high capital adequacy ratios as a means of lowering their borrowing costs. The paper attempts to examine whether market forces can act as a substitute for capital adequacy requirements by explicitly considering both market forces (interest rate on deposits) and government intervention (deposit insurance). They concluded that better capitalized banks experienced lower borrowing costs. Bank competition cannot substitute capital adequacy regulation because of substantial systemic effect. Thus competition motivates banks to select higher capital adequacy ratios than otherwise.

Sinha(2005), in his article attempted to highlight the importance of Asset Liability Management in the current deregulated scenario. He observed that the Indian banks have to realize that ALM is an important mechanism for profit planning in a scientific way. ALM is an integrated approach towards effective balance sheet management which can be achieved through proper restructuring of the asset and liability portfolio from time to time. He stressed that the scope of ALM has to be enlarged in Indian banks and Asset Liability Management Committee (ALCO) has to be achieved to undertake a comprehensive management of the balance-sheet. Greater sophistication will be ushered in when the banks will hedge the interest-rate risk by entering into contracts of swap, futures and options as is being practiced in developed financial markets.

Vij (2005), in her research paper on Asset Liability Management focused on developing a dynamic interest rate risk management programme and the importance of derivatives as a tool for asset liability management. The participation by banks in the derivative markets has risen sharply in recent years and one of the major concerns facing regulators at present is the increased risk of the individual banks and of the banking system as a whole. She suggested that banks can systematically estimate the economic value of changes to market interest rates by calculating the duration of each asset, liability and Off-Balance-Sheet position and weigh each of them to arrive at the weighted duration of assets, liabilities and Off-Balance-Sheet items.

Sharma and Kulkarni(2006), in their article emphasized that Asset Liability Management should ensure a proper balance between funds mobilization and their deployment with respect to their maturity profiles, cost, yields and risk exposures. For this, Indian banks need to reorient their credit deployment strategies. They suggested that banks should diversify the portfolio suitably between the large and small borrowers as this will help in reducing risks. Banks should withdraw their exposure to sunset industries as their loans may turn into NPAs. Banks should think in terms of loan exposures to different regions in the country. It is highly essential to look at credit deployment in terms of managing credit portfolio and its diversification, both geographically and industry-wise, which helps them to reduce the portfolio risk of credit.

Bhasin(2007), in her article endeavoured to discuss the important concepts in task management as applicable to banks against the backdrop of Basel II. The article aims to develop a basic understanding on major risks surrounding a bank institution as also the more popular means of managing them. She concluded that risk management calls for consolidating on the techniques and structures already built rather than going haphazardly for new techniques as efforts have been made already to create an environment for all market participants in terms of regulation, infrastructure and instruments.

Sy (2007), in his research paper discussed the management of interest rate risk of Indian banks' portfolio. He has attempted to review the recent changes in the regulation of the market risk of Government Securities holdings and suggests possible avenues for policy-makers. He suggested that banks could manage interest rate risk by reducing the duration of their assets by selling long-dated government securities and by increasing their loan books by building on the recent high growth in consumer credit and infrastructure and the contribution of fee-based income to operating income. Widening of the investor base for government securities could also reduce the reliance on banks as the main investors in the market.

(B) Studies on Profitability

Bhalerao (1984), in her article analyzed the causes of declining profitability of the Scheduled Commercial Banks during the post-nationalization in India. The important factors contributing to the decline in profitability are: continuous rise in statutory liquidity reserve and cash reserve ratio; increasing incidence of industrial sickness; persistent emphasis on social goals i.e. thrust on priority sector; unfavourable deposit mix; mounting over dues and declining recovery; continued accent on massive rural network expansion; increased burden due to salary revision of staff; and declining spread between interest earned and interest paid. She suggested certain steps to arrest these trends: emphasized the need for recycling of banks' funds, increasing income through levy of service charges, reducing operating costs, improving the quality of lending and streamlining the operations of overseas branches.

Sundaram(1984), attempted to find out the causes of falling profitability of banks. According to him, the main causes are: branch expansion particularly in the remote areas, priority sector advances, mounting overdues, mainly due to priority sector advances and financing sick units. This has been due to the fact that profit planning had taken back seat in view of over emphasis on social objectives. The profitability of banks depends not only on interest spread but on conscious and innovative search for profitable avenues of business, measures to improve labour productivity and cost control measures. He suggested that banks should expedite recovery of loans. Remission of penal interest may be considered for defaulting borrowers only in genuine cases. In branches where overdues are high, fresh advances may be considered on a low key.

Satyamurthy (1987), in his research paper attempted to clarify the concepts of profits, profitability and productivity applicable to the banking industry and extend the technique of ratio analysis to evaluate the profit and profitability performance of banks. He suggested that endeavours should be made to improve the spread performance through better funds management, cash management, recycling of funds through better recovery, exploring new avenues for increasing non-fund business income and above all cost effectiveness and control. Banks need to manage these functions successfully replete with significant economic, competitive and technological challenges in order to improve their profitability and productivity.

Mazumdar(1996), in her research paper on profitability and productivity in Indian banking took a critical look at the Indian banking while comparing them with their counterparts elsewhere. She analyzed the performance of Indian banks in post-liberalization era. She observed that Indian banks have higher spreads than banks abroad; Indian banks have higher operating costs than foreign countries; and Indian banks have higher risk provision levels .She suggested certain strategies for improving profitability: the banks should move from deposit orientation to profit orientation; turnover strategies, income-oriented and cost-oriented strategies should be spelt out from time to time. Banks need to put effective asset-liability management systems in place.

Kannan et al. (2001),in the their econometric study on determinants of Net Interest Margin under regulatory requirements sought to identify the factors influencing spreads of Scheduled Commercial Banks in India. Spreads that are unduly high can impinge on the saving and investment potential of an economy. Their analysis reveals that size does not necessarily correlate with higher spread and higher fee- income enables banks to tolerate lower spreads. With regard to regulatory requirements, they found that capital plays an important role in affecting spreads of public sector banks and non-performing assets are uniformly important across all bank groups in influencing spreads.

Chandan and Rajput(2002), carried out their research on profitability analysis of banks in India. A Multiple Regression Approach was followed to determine empirically the factors influencing the profitability of Banks in India. They concluded that interest spread is still the major source of income across all Bank categories. Problem of NPAs is prominent in the case of Public Sector Banks. Non-Interest income is becoming important in the revenue streams of Foreign Banks and Private Sector Banks. Foreign Banks and Private Banks are spending heavily to upgrade their technology in the light of stupendous growth in information technology which has increased their operating expenditures. Public Sector Banks need more funds to invest in technology upgradation which will augment data management and quicker flow of information.

Cheema and Agarwal (2002), in their research paper studied the productivity in Commercial Banks. A Data Envelopment Analysis (DEA) Approach was followed to make a comparative study of performance of Public Sector Banks, Indian Private Sector Banks and Foreign Banks. They found that the excessive amount of owned funds i.e. capital and retained earning was the root cause of inefficiency of the Public Sector Banks. Spread was their main source of income and very few of them had concentrated on activities other than advancing loans. The Private Sector Banks, on the other hand, raised funds mainly from deposits. Very few of them used the owned funds as the main source of financing. The main source of inefficiency of Foreign Banks was the borrowings. They were depending less on the owned funds and deposits and more on the borrowings for raising finances.

Mahadevan (2002), in his study discussed the avenues for non-interest income and strategies to develop remittance of funds. According to him, the profitability of the banks can be increased by increasing the interest spread and reducing the burden through cost-control measures and increasing fee-based incomes. In the wake of interest deregulation and strict prudential accounting norms, the banks can improve their profitability by reducing the burden only. Burden can be reduced only to a small extent by cost-control methods. The advantage of fee-based income is that it does not increase the risk weighted asset while contributing to the profitability of the bank and it is not affected much by the vagaries in the market conditions.

Jain (2003), in his article studied the progress of the banking system since the initiation of financial reforms. Integration of banking and financial institutions across the globe has posed many challenges, viz. the high level of non-performing assets, low level of customer satisfaction and integration of financial markets across the globe. He suggested that for the Banking system to become vibrant, markets should acquire depth and liquidity. Rigidity in market structure should be supported by necessary legal changes to strengthen the enforceability of contracts and continuous improvements in technological infrastructure be made.

Kapil et al. (2003) in their study reviewed the benchmarking performance of Indian Public Sector Commercial Banks in the wake of Banking Sector Reforms. The viability of the 27 Public Sector

Banks has been assessed on the basis of off-site supervisory exam model, i.e. CAMEL model (C for Capital Adequacy, A for Asset Quality, M for Management, E for Earnings, L for Liquidity). According to this model, majority of the PSBs have been rated as non-viable and need immediate attention and Government support. Majority of the Indian PSBs are still plagued with the problems of low profitability, liquidity, Capital adequacy and high non-performing assets.

Qamar (2003), in his research paper attempted to identify the difference in terms of endowment factor, risk factor, revenue diversification, profitability and efficiency that may exist between the different types of banks so as to identify the determinants of efficiency and profitability of banking institutions in the country. In fact, there are significant variations in performance parameters within each category of banks. Much of this difference in the profitability performance of the banks is attributed to the human resources efficiency as measured in terms of business per employee and the future prospects of the Public and old Private Sector Banks seems to be impinging on their ability to improve productivity of their human resources.

Gurumoorthy (2004), in his article attempted to analyze the income, expenditure and operating profit of public sector banks, foreign banks, old private sector banks and new private sector banks. The new private sector banks have been in the stage of branch expansion and recruitment and have spent for full-fledged internet banking. Thus, the percentage rise in expenditure of the new private sector banks has been greater than that of the other banks. As far as operating profits are concerned, new private sector banks stand first, followed by old private sector banks, public sector banks and foreign banks. In this competitive environment, efficient asset-liability management, project appraisal and recovery mechanism will help to earn the interest income substantially.

Mohan and Ray (2004), in their paper attempted a comparison of performance among three categories of Banks: Public, Private and Foreign using physical quantities of inputs and outputs and comparing the revenue maximization efficiencies of Banks during the period 1992-2000. They found that Public Sector Banks performed significantly better than Private Sector Banks but not differently from Foreign Banks on this measure. The superior performance of the Public Sector Banks is ascribed to higher technical efficiency.

Ramasastri et al. (2004), in their research paper tried to assess whether Non-Interest Income has helped in stabilizing the total income of Scheduled Commercial Banks in India from 1997 to 2003. The study concluded that the Net Interest Income of Scheduled Commercial Banks declined during the said period though the Non-Interest income increased. This trend is more prominent in the case of Foreign Banks.

Chandan and Rajput (2005),in their research paper attempted to analyze the performance of Individual banks on the basis of 'Z'score analysis. According to them, Public Sector Banks which include Nationalized Banks and SBI Group are largely owned by the Government and the functioning of these banks is generally influenced by the policies of the Government from time to time. They have large network of branches throughout India and assume the national character. Foreign banks are owned by foreign entities and are working solely for profit. Their operations are concentrated in metropolitan and urban areas with high net worth client. Similarly, old Private Banks presumed the local character and their operations are limited to single state. New Private Banks are the latest entrant in the banking business. Customers' attraction and subsequently, their retention is an important objective of these banks.

Mohan (2005), in his research paper tried to analyze the impact of the Economic Reforms on the Banking Sector in India. He observed that from the position of net loss in mid-1990 to recent years, the share of Public Sector Banks in the profit of the Commercial Banking System has become broadly commensurate with their share in assets, indicating a broad convergence of profitability across various bank groups. He concluded that the increasing sophistications, flexibility and complexity of products and servicing offerings make the effective use of technology critical for managing risks associated with banking business.

Ramathilagam and Preethi(2005), in their article focused on the viability and performance of commercial banks in the period of liberalization from 1992 to 2001.They found that the proportion of bank deposits to national income has improved. Deposits continue to account for around 80% of the total bank liabilities in the post-reform period. On the assets side, the share of investments increased. While the share of loans and advances declined in 1990s, it recovered in recent years. Despite the large decline in statutory liquidity reserves (SLR) in the 1990s, the sharp increase in investments by banks is reflective of their attempt to evolve treasury operations into profit centres.

Shetty (2005), in his research article analyzed the factors affecting interest rate movements and made suggestions to mitigate interest rate risk. The factors affecting interest rate movements are domestic factors like inflation and liquidity position. With the integration of domestic and international financial markets, interest rates abroad also influence the domestic interest rates. The structural factors like fiscal deficit, operating cost, NPA levels in the banking sector,and wage structure also influence the interest rate levels. He concluded that total elimination of interest rate risk may not be practical in the Indian banking scenario, however, being conscious of its existence, magnitude and impact and managing it well is the essence of risk management function.

Srivastava (2006), in his article attempted to evaluate the efficiency of banks in terms of intermediation function, productivity, profitability, financial soundness and customer service. He has analyzed that Indian banks are offering a bouquet of customized products through multiple channels to a wide spectrum of customers. Productivity of commercial banks in terms of operating costs to total assets has increased for all bank groups except foreign banks. The interest spread has declined due to competitive pricing, growing macro-economic stability and healthy policy environment. In order to sustain this growth, banks must expand their market base by penetrating into untapped but highly potential rural markets, lending greater support to boost production, entrepreneurial innovation and infrastructure sector and providing better satisfaction to the customers.

Datar and Banerjee (2007), in their research paper titled, "Simultaneity between Bank Profitability and Regulatory Capital," have attempted to study the relationship between bank profitability and regulatory capital. According to them, the factors affecting demand for regulatory capital are likely to be uniform across banks but the sources of supply of regulatory capital are likely to be different among ''good" and ''bad" banks. Good banks would, generally, augment their regulatory capital by way of ploughed back profits which augment reserves. The impact of capital on

43

profitability would depend on the advantage better capitalized banks would get in attracting better and safe clients. If better capitalized banks can raise funds at relatively low rates and these are offered on attractive terms to better rated, safe clients, better capitalized banks could earn higher profits.

Uppal and Kaur (2007), in their article attempted to study the impact of falling interest rates on the profitability of banks. Due to the fall in the interest rates in the banks, interest margins are coming down spreads decrease, NPAs mount up and thus, profitability reduces. They suggested that spread may be increased by providing better market strategies and observing strict cost control.

(C)Studies on Lending Norms

Upadhyay (2003), in her study on financial sector reforms has attempted to analyze the impact of these reforms on the credit regulatory mechanism after the implementation of the Narasimham Committee recommendations.In keeping with international practices and for providing further flexibility, banks have been allowed to lend at interest rates below their respective PLRs to creditworthy borrowers, including exporters on the basis of a transparent policy approved by the respective boards. Financial sector reforms, initiated during 1991-92 have enhanced commercial banks' opportunities in extending credit facilities to commercial sector by way of non-SLR investments. On the other hand, cost of funds as represented by return on advances, continued to be another dominant factor determining credit demand in India.

Roy (2006), in her research paper on bank lending to priority and retail sectors attempted to study the changing face of bank lending. Banks have to fulfil the prescribed directed credit in the Indian banking system, which takes the form of priority sector credit, wherein the Reserve Bank of India mandates a certain type of lending on the banks operating in India, including foreign banks. She suggested that there is a need to look at strengthening credit analysis and collection processes; and from customer's perspective, there is a need to make the customer aware of the cost of unsecured credit.

Sinha (2008), in his empirical study on attempted to compare select public and private sector commercial banks in respect of priority sector lending for the period 2000-01 to 2004-05. He concluded that the observed private sector commercial banks have performed better than the observed public sector commercial banks. Even in a market-oriented economy, the importance of priority sector lending cannot be undermined. Therefore, according to him, it is essential that the priority sector lending behaviour of these banks be closely monitored in the national interest.

2.2 RESEARCH METHODOLOGY

The present study is an attempt to study the two aspects of the banking sector, viz. Asset Liability Management and its impact on the Profitability.

2.2.1 Rationale of the Study

On the threshold of the new millennium, the Indian Banking Sector is waking up to the concept of Asset Liability Management. The uncertainty of interest rate movements gave rise to interest rate, risk, thereby causing banks to look for processes to manage their risk. In the wake of interest rate risk, came liquidity risk and credit risk as interest components of risks for banks. The recognition of these risks has brought Asset Liability Management to the centre-stage of financial intermediation. With the RBI framing up a regulatory framework to monitor the ALM from March 31, 1999, the Asset Liability Management has attained tremendous importance in the banking sector.

Banks are now operating in a fairly deregulated environment and are required to determine on their own, interest rates on deposits and advances on a dynamic basis. Managing the spread income and controlling the risks associated with generating the spread is a vital area of Asset Liability Management as it requires simultaneous decisions about the asset/liability mix and maturity structure of the institution.

Majority of the studies on Asset-Liability Management have discussed the theoretical framework of ALM without discussing the management of the vital assets and liabilities in detail. A limited number of studies have been carried out on the various aspects of ALM, viz. liquidity management, loan portfolio management, reserves position management, investment management and their impact on the profitability performance of banks in the light of the Guidelines issued by RBI on ALM in 1999 and afterwards. There is a need to study the various aspects of ALM that directly affect profitability because commercial viability is essential for the existence and growth of banks. The management of assets and liabilities in tandem can prevent the situation of asset-liability mismatch and save the banking system from embarrassment. In the light of a plethora of risks confronting banking business, proper risk management becomes vital, which is an integral part of Asset-Liability Management. Thus, an attempt is made to analyze the factors affecting Asset Liability Management and to assess the improvement in profitability performance of the banks after the adoption of ALM techniques.

The present study aims to analyze the importance of Asset Liability Management for banks and its impact on the profitability performance of banks. Management of Net Interest Margin is one of the most important means of earning of banks. The choice of asset portfolios of banks is expected to be influenced by the kinds of liabilities held by them and vice versa. In this context, a bank has to identify its asset and liability structure which is not only compatible but also capable to generate net interest revenue that helps in attaining the earnings objective.

2.2.2 Objectives of the Study

The present research attempts to undertake a comprehensive study on the various areas of asset liability management and their impact on profitability performance of banks. The specific objectives of the study are:

- To analyze the growth and development of banks over the last two decades since consolidation started.
- To study the extent to which banks have effectively managed their Assets and Liabilities during the period under study.
- To examine the profitability trends in the light of changed policies after privatization.
- To examine the change in lending policies of banks.
- To suggest the future strategy for assets and liabilities of banks.

The present study relates to the impact of Asset Liability Management as part of the Banking Sector Reforms, on the profitability and performance of the selected banks. The impact of Asset Liability Management (which was implemented by RBI in 1999) may be studied in two ways. The first way is to analyze the change in the pattern of development of all those activities which banks had been pursuing prior to the reforms, e.g. branch expansion, deposit mobilization, credit deployment and profitability. This would require a study of the performance of the banking activities prior to the reforms. The second way is to probe the performance of banks in the light of the objectives of the reforms, viz. ensuring capital adequacy of banks, improved profitability, lending on commercial considerations and avoidance of mismatch between assets and liabilities.

The study aims at analyzing the pattern and profitability of banking from the period of consolidation of banks, i.e. from December 1985 to March 2007, so as to compare the performance of banks during the pre and post-reforms era, after the introduction of Asset Liability Management.

2.2.3 Chapter Scheme

The study has been divided into eight chapters as stated below:

Chapter-1 includes the introduction, structure and growth of banking sector divided into various phases along with the advent of the economic reforms and the importance of Asset Liability Management in banking sector.

Chapter-2 has been divided into two parts. The first part consists of the reviews of the selected studies that are relevant for the study. The second part deals with Research Methodology used for the present study. It includes the sources of data, data analysis and limitations of the study.

Chapter-3 traces the trends and progress of the banking system from 1985 to 2007 in terms of branch expansion, credit-deposit ratio and deposit mobilization. It also studies the growth of the selected banks on the basis of various parameters, viz. credit-deposit ratio, deposit mobilization, loans and advances, investments, branch expansion, spread as percentage to total assets, share of priority sector lending in total advances etc.

Chapter-4 studies the various aspects of Asset Management of the selected banks, viz. Reserve Position Management, Investment Management and Liquidity Management. It also discusses the asset-liability mismatch (Gap) position of the banks from the year 2000 to

2007 on the basis of Gap Statements of the selected banks prepared as per RBI Guidelines.

Chapter-5 highlights the management of the liabilities of the selected banks, viz. the Capital Adequacy Position since 1995, and composition of deposits mobilized by the banks (both from other banks and customers), borrowings and current liabilities.

Chapter-6 studies the trends in profitability of the selected banks. It deals with the composition of Interest Income, Non-Interest Income and their share in the Total Income of the banks. The trends in Spread, Burden in relation to Average Working Funds have been analyzed in detail.

Chapter-7 is based on the Loan Portfolio Management of the banks. The lending norms have been discussed along with the impact on priority sector lending. The various forms in which banks grant loans are discussed, viz. Bills Purchased and Discounted, Cash credit, Overdraft and loans payable on demand, Term loans and the proportion of each in the total advances.

Chapter-8 highlights the major findings of the study. Further, various suggestions have been given for better asset liability management and improving the profitability performance of banks.

2.2.4 Data Collection

The study is based on secondary data obtained from various sources, viz. IBA Bulletin, IBA's Performance Highlights of Public Sector and Private Sector Banks, RBI's Report on Trends and Progress of Banking in India, RBI's Statistical Tables Relating to Banks in India, RBI's Basic Statistical Returns of Scheduled Commercial Banks in India, Economic Surveys, various RBI Reports, and Economic and Political Weekly and the websites of Reserve Bank of India and Indian Banks Association.

2.2.5 Period of Study

The study covers the period from December 1985 to March 2007. (Data from 1985-1987 pertains to December end and March end for the remaining years). This is the period when consolidation of banking industry was initiated and major policy shift was brought about in banking industry in India.

2.2.6 Scope and Methodology

The study covers State Bank of India Group, Punjab National Bank, ICICI Bank and Centurion Bank of Punjab. The purpose of this is to concentrate on two largest banks, one each from public and private sector and two banks having strong presence in Punjab, one each from the public and private sector. In the course of the analysis, the performance on various parameters has been recorded in terms of Trend growth rate.

(I) Growth Rate

Trend Growth Rate: It is calculated for a period on the basis of the value of a variable for all the years. The exponential equation used is:

$$Y_C = ab^t \quad \cdots\cdots\cdots\cdots\cdots\cdots\cdots (1)$$

Where,

$$b = 1 + \frac{g}{100} \quad \ldots\ldots\ldots\ldots\ldots(2)$$

Y_C is the computed value of the concerned variable, a and b are the parameter estimates, t is the time period and g is the growth rate. In the semi-logarithmic form, the equation (1) takes the form:

$$Log\ Y_C = \log a + \log b \ldots\ldots\ldots\ldots\ldots (3)$$

Since the variable Y_C on the left hand side of the equation (3) is in the log form, this equation is known as semi-logarithmic equation. The trend growth rates have been computed for three periods, viz. Period I i.e. Pre-reforms period, (from 1985 to 1994-

95); Period II, i.e. Post-reforms period (from 1995-96 to 2006-07); and Period I&II,i.e. (from 1985 to 2006-07, covering the growth rate for the entire period under study).

Then, the 't' test is applied for finding out whether the calculated growth rate is significant at five percent level of significance.

The correlation coefficient 'r' is calculated between the various performance parameters and t, the time variable.

$$r = \frac{N\sum XY - \left(\sum X\right)\left(\sum Y\right)}{\sqrt{\left[N\sum X^2 - \left(\sum X\right)^2\right]\left[N\sum Y^2 - \left(\sum Y\right)^2\right]}}$$

Where, N is the number of observations and N-2 gives the degrees of freedom.

The 't' value for 'r' is $t = r\sqrt{\dfrac{N-2}{1-r^2}}$

We compare this computed value of 't' with its table value at five per cent level of significance for N-2 degrees of freedom. If the computed value of 't' is greater than its theoretical value, then the growth is significant.

(II) Coefficient of Variation: It is applied to find out and compare the variability in terms of the various parameters (e.g. branch expansion, credit growth, deposit mobilization etc.) among the different banks during the period under study.

$$C.V. = \frac{\sigma}{\overline{X}} \times 100$$

Where, σ stands for Standard Deviation and $\overline{X}$ stands for Mean.

(III)Simple Average: Average of relevant ratios over the period of study (i.e. from 1985 to 2007) is one of the commonly used tools of analysis due to their comparability and relevance of the various relationships established among variables.

(IV) GAP Method: The objective of this method is to immunize a banks net interest income (NII). Gap is defined as the difference between rate sensitive assets (RSAs) and rate sensitive liabilities (RSLs) in a particular period.

GAP=RSAs-RSLs

GAP Ratio=RSAs-RSLs/RSAs

If RSAs>RSLs= Positive GAP

If RSAs<RSLs= Negative GAP

The Statement of structural Liquidity is prepared by placing all cash inflows and outflows in the maturity ladder according to the expected timing of cash flows. A maturing liability will be a cash outflow while a maturing asset will be cash inflow. The Maturity Profile on the basis of liquidity has been prescribed by RBI for measuring the future cash flows of banks in different time buckets as under:

(i)   1 to 14 days;

(ii)   15 to 28 days;

(iii)   29 days and up to 3 months;

(iv)   Over 3 months and up to 6 months;

(v)   Over 6 months and up to 1year;

(vi)   Over 1year and up to 3years;

(vii) Over 3 year and up to 5years;and

(viii) Over 5 years

With in each time bucket there would be mismatches defending on cash inflows and outflows. The Statement of Structural Liquidity of the selected four banks from 2000-01 to 2006-07 have been prepared to find out the Gap situation.

2.2.7 Limitations of the Study

The present study has some limitations considering the objectives of the study and its coverage in terms of the formidable time span. Some of the major unavoidable limitations of the present study are:

- ICICI Bank was merged with ICICI Corporation in 2002 and Bank of Punjab merged with Centurion Bank in 2005.After the merger both the banks have registered remarkable improvement in most of the parameters. Thus, it is difficult to separate the performance of merged firms from the normal growth factors.

- Financial information collected for the present study is entirely secondary in nature. In such a case, the study carries all the limitations inherent with the secondary data.

- The data of some indicators was not available from 1985 to 1990-91, due to which the trend growth rate for the pre-reforms period could not be computed. The data pertaining to income from sale of investment for all the four banks was not available for 1995-96 also as data under this head was not available independently.

- The basic data of the various assets and liabilities could not be given in the Statements of structural liquidity of the selected banks as it was making the study voluminous. Hence, the Gap position and mismatch between the assets and liabilities has been presented in percentages.

REFERENCES

Agarwal, Som(1998), "Assets &Liabilities of Indian Banks- The Long and Short of Credit, " *The Economic Times*, September 28, p. 9.

Ammannya, K.K. (1996), "Asset Liability Management Strategy for Banks," *The Banker*, Vol. 43 (8), October 1996, pp.28-29.

Bagchi, S.K. (2005), "BaseI II: Operational Risk Management need for a Structured Operational Risk policy for banks,"*The Management Accountant*,Vol.40,No.1,January,pp.32-34.

Bhalerao,Asha(1984), "Post-Nationalization Trends in Profitability of Commercial Banks in India, " *Banking Finance*,Vol. 1(4),April,pp.11-13.

Bhasin, Aastha (2007), "Understanding Risks in Banking: A Note, " *Vinimaya*,Vol.XXVII,No. 4,January-March,pp.23-30.

Chandan, C.L.;Rajput;and Pawan Kumar(2002), "Profitability Analysis of Banks in India:A Multiple Regression Approach, " *Indian Management Studies Journal,*Vol. 6,No.2,October, pp.119-129.

Chandan, C.L.; and Rajput, P.K. (2005), "Performance of Individual Commercial Banks-A 'Z' Score Analysis, "*Indian Management Studies Journal*,Vol. 9,No.2, Oct,pp.71-81.

Chawla, O.P. (1998), "Asset Liability Management," *The Financial Express*, February7, p.7.

Cheema, C.S.; and Agarwal, Monika (2002), "Productivity in Commercial Banks:A DEA Approach, "*The Business Review*,Vol. 8,No. 1&2, pp.15-28.

Das, Abhiman (1996), "Structural Changes and Asset-Liability Mismatch of Scheduled Commercial Banks," *Reserve Bank of India Occasional Papers*, Vol. 17,No. 4, December, pp.305-330.

Das,M.R.;and Singh, Balwant (2001), "Maturity Pattern of Assets and Liabilities of Public Sector Banks: An Empirical Investigation," *SBI Monthly Review*, Vol. 40,No.7, July, pp.334-347.

Datar, M.K.; and Banerjee, Saumya Sankar (2007), "Simultaneity Between Bank Profitability and Regulatory Capital, "*Prajnan*, Vol.XXXVI,No.1,April-June,pp.31-46.

Debasish, Satya Swaroop (2004), "Investigating the Evidence of Market Discipline in the Banking Sector, " *Journal of Management Studies and Research*,Vol. II,No 2,April – September,pp.54-66.

Dharmarajan, S. (2004), "Asset Liability Management Model for managing Liquidity and Interest Rate Risk inCooperative Banks," *Vinimaya*,Vol. XXV,No 1,April-June,pp.31-40.

Ghosh, Saibal.;and Das, Abhiman(2005), "Market Discipline,Capital Adequacy and Bank Behaviour," *Economic and Political Weekly*,Vol.XL,No.12,March19, pp.1210-1215.

Gurumoorthy, T.R. (2004), "Analysis of Income and Expenditure in Banks," *Business and Economic Facts For You*, June, pp.27-31.

Jain, A.K.(2003), "Challenges before the Banking and Financial Sectors in the context of Globalisation," *Indian Journal of Economics*, Vol.XXXIV, No.332,July,pp.183-187.

Joshi, C.Vasant.;and Joshi C.Vinay(2002),*Managing Indian Banks-The Challenges Ahead*,Response Books, New Delhi.

Kannan,R.;Narain,Aditya.;and Ghosh, Saibal(2001), "Determinants of Net Interest Margin under Regulatory Requirements-An Econometric Study, "*Economic and Political Weekly*,Vol.XXXXVI,No. 4,January 27, pp.337-344.

Kapil, Sheeba; Kapil, Kanwal Nayan; and Nagar, Kailash(2003), "Benchmarking Performance of Indian Public Sector Banks, " *Indian Journal of Accounting*, Vol.XXXIV, December, pp.24-28.

Kumar, Ranjana(2003), "Move Towards Risk Based Supervision of Banks:The Role of the Central Banker and the Market Players," *Vinimaya*,Vol.XXIV,No.1, pp.5-12.

Kumar, Ravi T.(2000),*Asset Liability Management*, Vision Books Pvt. Ltd., New Delhi.

Mahadevan, K.(2002), "Non-Interest Income: Our Potential and Strategies to Increase its Share, "in P. Mohana Rao and T.K. Jain (eds.), *Management of Banking and Financial Institutions*,Deep and Deep Publications Pvt.Ltd.,pp59-69.

Mazumdar, Tanushree(1996), "Profitability and Productivity in Indian Banking, "in T RaviKumar(ed.)*Indian Banking in Transition-Issues and Challenges*, ICFAI Vision Series, 1996, pp.73-83.

Mehta, Sangita(1998), "Defusing Time Bombs Ticking in the Books, " *Business Standard*,September 24,p.10.

Mohan, Rakesh(2005), "Financial Sector Reforms in India-Policies and Performance Analysis," *Economic and Political Weekly*,Vol.XL,No12,March19 ,pp.1106-1121 .

Mohan, Ram T.T; and Ray, C. Subhash(2004),"Comparing Performance of Public and Private Sector Banks-A Revenue Maximization Efficiency Approach,"*Economic and Political Weekly*,Vol. XXXIX,No. 12,March 20,pp.1271-1276.

Ong,K. Michael(1998), "Integrating the Role of Risk Management In ALM,"in *Asset &Liability Management-A Synthesis of New Methodologies*, Risk Books, Kamakura Corporation, London, pp.1-20.

Patheja, Anju(1994), *Financial Management of Commercial Banks*,South Asia Publications, New Delhi.

Qamar, Furquan(2003), "Profitability and Resources Use Efficiency in Scheduled Commercial Banks in India; A Comparative Analysis of Foreign, New Private Sector, Old Private Sector Banks," *Synthesis*,Vol. 1,No. 1,July –December ,pp.1-16

Raghavan, R.S. (2005), "Risk Management-An Overview, "in S.B. Verma (ed.) *Risk Management*, Deep &Deep Publications Pvt Ltd,New Delhi, pp.3-21.

Rajwade, A.V. (2001), " Issues in Asset Liability Management- V, Pricing of Liabilities, " *Economic and Political Weekly*,Vol. XXXVII, No. 5,February 2,pp.1186-1187.

Ramasastri, A.S.;Samuel, Achamma and Gangadaran S.(2004), "Income Stability of Scheduled Commercial Banks-Interest vis-à-vis Non-Interest Income, "*Economic and Political Weekly*,Vol. XXXIX,No. 12,March 20,pp.1311-1318.

Ramathilagam, G;and Preethi, S.(2005), "Efficiency of Indian Commercial Banks in the Post-Reform Period, "*Business and Economic Facts For You*,November,pp.36-40.

Roy, Mohua(2006), "A Review of Bank Lending to Priority and Retail Sectors, "'EPW Vol.XLI,No.11,pp.1035-1040.

Satyamurthy(1987), "Profitability and Productivity in Banks-Concepts and Evaluation, " *IBA Bulletin*,Vol.9 (11), Nov, pp.270-275.

Sehgal, Madhu and; Kher, Rajni(2002), "Asset Liability Management in the Indian Banks, "in P.Mohana Rao and T.K.Jain (eds.), *Management of Banking and Financial institutions*,Deep & Deep Publications, Pvt Ltd, New Delhi, pp.90-100

Sharma,Kapil and Kulkarni, P.R.(2006), "Asset Liability Management Approach in Indian Banks:A Review and Suggestions, " *The Journal of Accounting and Finance,*"Vol. 20,No. 2,April-September,pp3-14.

Shetty,V.P. (2005), "Interest rate risk in Investment Portfolio and its impact on the Profitability of banks, " *IBA Bulletin,*Vol. XXVII.No. 2, February, pp.6-8.

Sinha, R.P.(2005), "Asset Liability Management :Relevance for Indian Banks, "in Sugan Jain.C, Priti Gupta and N.P. Agarwal, (eds.) Accounting and Finance for Banks, Raj Publishing House,Jaipur,pp.319-328.

Sinha,RamPratap(2008), "Priority Sector Lending of Indian Commercial Banks: Some Empirical Results, "*Prajnan*, Vol. XXXVI, No. 4,Jan-March,pp.291-306.

Sinkey,Jr.F. Joseph(1992), *Commercial Banks Financial Management in the Financial Services Industry,*"MacMillan Publishing Co,Nu York.

Srivastava, R.M.(2006), "Indian Commercial Banks on Path Towards Competitive Efficiency, "*Vinimaya,*Vol.XXVII,No.3,

Subrahmanyam, Ganti(1995), " Asset Liability Management for Banks in a Deregulated Environment, "*Prajnan*, Vol.XXIII, No. 1, pp11-27.

Sundaram, Satya(1984), "Banks:Improving Productivity and Profitability, " *The Journal of Indian Institute of Bankers,*Vol.1,No 55(30),July-September,pp.155-160.

Sy, Amadou(2007), "Indian Banks' Diminishing Apetite for Government Securities, " *Economic and Political Weekly*, Vol. XLII,No. 13,pp.1211-1218.

Thimmaiah, G.(2004), "Asset Liability Management in Post Indian Banking Sector Reforms, "in M.P. Shrivastava and S.R. Singh (eds.) *Indian Banking in the New Millennium*, Anmol Publications, New Delhi,pp.293-300.

Upadhyay, Saroj(2003), "Financial Sector Reforms:New Norms have Reduced Credit Supply to Commercial sector, " *The Management Accountant*,Vol.38,No.3,March pp.176-178.

Uppal, R.K.;and Kaur, Rimpi(2007), "Falling Rate of Interest in the Banks:Bank Spreads,Profitability Comes Under Pressure, "in R.K.Uppal and Rimpi Kaur (eds.)*Banking in the New Millenium*,Mahamaya Publishing House,New Delhi, pp.352-359.

Vij, Madhu(2005), " Asset Liability Management, "in S.K.Tuteja (ed.), *Management Mosaic*, Excel Books,New Delhi,pp.333-367.

CHAPTER-3

PROGRESS AND DEVELOPMENT
OF COMMERCIAL BANKING

The expansion of Indian banking in the post-nationalization era is unprecedented in the annals of banking across the globe (Mazumdar,1996). The post-nationalization period has witnessed an unprecedented, phenomenal, geographical and spatial expansion of the Scheduled Commercial Banks over 90% of which has been in the public sector(Bhalerao,1988).

The process of reforms that had started with the nationalization of the State Bank of India in 1955, which was further consolidated in 1969 by nationalizing a large number of Scheduled Commercial Banks, completed a phase with the last nationalization in 1980. During these three decades, the banking sector on the one hand witnessed rapid expansion in the number of bank branches, deposit mobilization and priority sector lending, while on the other, it also experienced equally rapid decline in the profitability and productivity of the banking institutions(Qamar,2003).

For a greater part of the twentieth century, the role of the financial system was perceived as mobilizing the massive resource requirements for growth. The financial system is no longer viewed as a passive mobilizer of funds.

3.1 Structure of Banking in India

Among the banking institutions in the organized sector, the commercial banks are the oldest institutions in having a wide network of branches, commanding utmost public confidence and having the lion's share in the total banking operations. Figure3(a) presents the structure of banking in India.

Fig.3(a) Structure of Banking in India

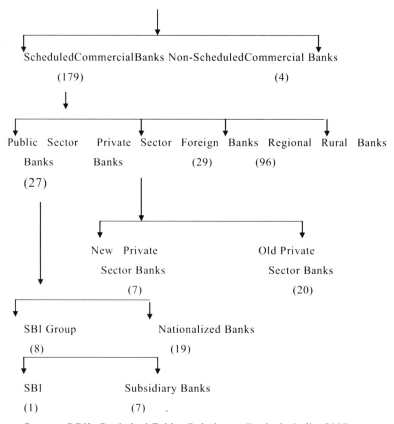

Source: RBI's Statistical Tables Relating to Banks in India, 2007.

Scheduled Commercial Banks are those whose names are included in the 2nd schedule to the Reserve Bank of India Act.

Under Section 42(6) of the Reserve Bank of India Act, a banking institution can claim for its name being included in the schedule, if:

(1) it satisfies the Reserve Bank that its affairs are not being conducted in a manner detrimental to the interests of its depositors; and

(2)Its paid-up capital and reserves have an aggregate value of not less than Rs. 5 lakh; and

(3)It must either be a company as defined in section 3 of the Indian Companies Act, 1956, or a corporation, or a company incorporated by or under any law in force in any place outside India, or an institution notified by the Central Government or a state cooperative bank.

The Central Government is empowered under section 42 (6) of the RBI Act to notify an institution as a Scheduled Bank.

Non-Scheduled Banks:

These are the banks whose names do not appear in the list of Scheduled Banks maintained by the Reserve Bank.

Public Sector Banks:

These include banks which are owned by the Central Government either directly or through the Reserve Bank of India. They are classified as:

a) State Bank Group

b) Nationalized Banks

(a) The State Bank Group consists of State Bank of India and its seven subsidiaries. It was established under the State Bank of India Act, on July 1, 1955, by nationalizing Imperial Bank of India. SBI together with its subsidiaries is the largest commercial bank in India in terms of its branch network, resources and manpower.

(b) Nationalized Banks: These banks were established under two acts i.e. Banking Companies (Acquisition and Transfer of Undertakings) Act, 1970; and Banking Companies (Acquisition and Transfer of Undertakings) Act, 1980. These banks are owned by the Government of India.

(c)Foreign Banks: These banks are incorporated outside India but have a place of business in India. These banks have established their branches in big cities.

(d)Regional Rural Banks: These banks have been established under the Regional Rural Banks Act, 1976. The major objective of the RRBs is to develop the rural economy by providing credit and other facilities for agriculture, trade, industry and other productive activities in rural areas, particularly to the small and marginal farmers, agricultural labourers, artisans and small entrepreneurs. The RRBs are sponsored by Scheduled Banks, usually by Public Sector Banks. In order to improve the operational viability of Regional Rural Banks and take advantage of the economies of scale, the route of amalgamation of Regional Rural Banks was suggested taking into account the views of the stakeholders(Vyas Committee 2004).

(e)Private Sector Banks: Indian banking under the liberalization process has recognized the significance of Private Sector Banking in the market economy. The Private Sector Banks can be broadly grouped as:

- **Old Private Sector Banks**: The banks which were established in the Private Sector before independence and after independence were free from the conditions of nationalization fall under this category. The number of these banks was 20 as on 31st March 2007.

- **New Private Sector Banks:** The Narasimham Committee on Financial Sector Reforms (1991) suggested the establishment of Private Sector Banks in India. There were seven New Private Sector Banks as on 31st March 2007(according to RBI's Basic Statistical Returns of Commercial Banks in India, 2007). The banks included in this category are: Centurion Bank of Punjab Ltd., IndusInd Bank Ltd., ICICI Bank Ltd., HDFC Bank Ltd.,UTI Bank Ltd., Kotak Mahindra Bank Ltd., and Yes Bank Limited.

3.2 Progress of Banks during the Post-Nationalization Period and After

Table 3.1 provides an overview of the progress of Commercial Banking in India. From 1985 to 2007, the total number of Commercial bank branches rose from 51,385 to 73,836. From 1985 onwards, Indian Banking Sector entered the consolidation phase due to which there was a slow-down in the programme of branch expansion, which is reflected in the marginal increase in the number of branches from 53,287 in 1986, to 53,859 branches in 1987 and so on. The number of commercial banks also reduced from 268 in 1985 to183 in 2007.The number of Regional Rural Banks also reduced from183 in 1985 to 96 in 2007 as a result of the merger of Regional Rural Banks.

The aggregate deposits of Scheduled Commercial Banks soared up from Rs. 77,075 crore in 1985 to Rs. 26,08,309 crore in 2007 registering approximately thirty-four times increase. Similarly, the credit of Scheduled Commercial Banks also increased from Rs. 50,921 crore in 1985 to Rs. 19,28,913 crore in 2007.

The credit-deposit ratio was 66.10% in 1985 and it increased to 73.95% in 2007. However, it was lowest in 1999 at 51.07% and showed minor fluctuations from 1985 to 2007.

As far as population served per office is concerned, it was 15,000 in 1985 and rose to 16000 persons in 2007.

One of the objectives of bank nationalization was to extend banking services to all geographical regions and to extend credit to socially important segments of the economy like agriculture, small-scale industries, etc.

Table 3.1: Progress of Commercial Banking at a glance (1985 to 2007)

Indicators	June 1985	June 1986	June 1987	June 1988	June 1989	March 1990	March 1991	March 1992	March 1993	March 1994	March 1995
Number of Commercial Banks	268	276	279	278	278	274	276	276	276	276	284
Scheduled Commercial Banks	264	272	275	274	274	270	272	272	272	272	281
of which Regional Rural Banks	183	193	196	196	196	196	196	196	196	196	196
Non-Scheduled Commercial Banks	4	4	4	4	4	4	4	4	4	4	3
Number of Bank Offices in India	51385	53287	53859	55410	57699	59752	60220	60570	61169	61803	62367
Population per office (in thousands)	15	14	15	14	14	14	14	14	14	15	15
Aggregate deposits of Scheduled Commercial Banks in India(in Rs. crore)	77075	91828	107898	126323	147854	173515	201199	237566	274938	323632	386859
Credit of Scheduled Commercial banks in India (inRs. crore)	50921	57229	64213	72436	89080	105450	121865	131520	154838	166844	211560
Credit-Deposit Ratio	66.10	62.32	59.51	57.34	60.25	60.77	60.57	55.36	56.32	51.55	54.69

Table 3.1 (Contd)

March 1996	March 1997	March 1998	March 1999	March 2000	March 2001	March 2002	March 2003	March 2004	March 2005	March 2006	March 2007
293	299	300	301	299	301	298	294	291	288	222	183
291	297	299	301	297	296	294	289	286	284	218	179
196	196	196	196	196	196	196	196	196	196	133	96
2	2	1	1	2	5	4	4	5	4	4	4
63026	63550	66408	67157	67868	67937	68195	68512	69220	70440	71685	73836
15	15	15	15	15	15	15	16	16	16	16	16
429003	499763	598485	722203	851593	989141	1131188	1311761	1504416	1700198	2109049	2608309
254015	278401	324079	368837	454069	529272	609053	746432	840785	1100428	1507077	1928913
59.17	55.71	54.15	51.07	53.32	53.51	53.84	56.90	55.89	64.72	71.46	73.95

Source: RBI's Basic Statistical Returns of Scheduled Commercial Banks in India, Various Issues.

A significant feature of banking development after nationalization has been the increasing tempo of branch expansion with more offices opened in unbanked areas, thus further reducing the regional disparities in provision of banking facilities (Jha, 1986).

3.3 A Brief Profile of the Selected Banks

(1) Centurion Bank of Punjab Ltd: Bank of Punjab Ltd., a vision of Dr. S. Inderjit Singh who always used to believe in "Coming together is beginning, keeping together is progress, and working together is success," is one of India's leading tech-savvy new generation Private Sector Banks established in April 1995(Kumar,2005). However, it faced serious liquidity problems due to which it went for merger with Centurion Bank in October 2005.Now, the merged entity is functioning under the name Centurion Bank of Punjab and has a wide network of branches ranging from the north to the south of the country. Centurion Bank of Punjab provides the entire range of banking and financial products like Global-e-Bank Debit cum ATM cards, Anywhere banking and Multichannel banking through ATMs, Mobile Phones, Tele-banking, Phone banking and Internet banking.

(2)ICICI Bank Ltd: It was incorporated in 1994 with its corporate office in Mumbai. It provides a wide spectrum of financial activities, with its presence in almost all areas of financial services, right from lending, investment and commercial banking, venture capital financing, consultancy and advisory services to on-line stock broking, mutual funds and custodial services. In a way to reach customers, it has used multiple delivery channels including conventional branch outlets, ATMs, telephones call centers and also through internet. The Reserve Bank of India approved the merger between ICICI Ltd. and ICICI Bank as on 26th April, 2002 which has made it the one of the leading Private Sector Banks in India. The merged entity has now access to low cost deposits, higher income and participation in the payments system, entry into new business segments, and higher market share in various segments especially in fee-based services and the vast talent pool of ICICI and its subsidiaries which in turn, would enhance the value for ICICI Bank shareholders.

Public Sector Banks:

(1)State Bank of India and its Associates: The Public Sector Commercial banking in India started with the setting up of the State Bank of India, in 1955, by taking over the Imperial Bank of India.

SBI together with its subsidiaries is the largest commercial bank in India in terms of its branch network reserves and manpower.

(2)Punjab National Bank: It is one of the 19 nationalized banks in the country. The nationalization was effected by an Ordinance which was later replaced by an Act of Parliament, known as the Banking Companies (Acquisition and Transfer of Undertakings) Act, 1970.

Over the years, backed by a long tradition of sound and prudent banking, Punjab National Bank is today among the premier banking institutions in the country and ranks among the top 500 banks in the world (Raghuraman, 2006).Punjab National Bank has been making rapid strides in supporting the development of the rural economy and promotion and growth of the small scale industry.

3.4 Credit-Deposit Ratio:

C/D ratio indicates the total advances as a percentage of total deposits. It is a measure of the utilization of resources by banks and has a direct bearing on the size and the loan portfolio. This ratio indicates the bank's aggressiveness to improve income.

Although the deployment of credit and the time-path of C/D ratio, in general, are influenced by the structural transformation of the economy, the role of credit culture and bank's lending policy have an inherent impact on the size of the ratio (RBI's RTPBI, 2004-05).

Table 3.2 highlights that the Credit-Deposit Ratio rose for SBI Group in the pre-reform period i.e. from 59.72% in 1985 to 60.94% in 1995-96 and declined from 53.21% in 1985 to 46.75% in 1995-96 for PNB.

Table 3.2 : Trends in Credit-Deposit Ratio

Year	SBI Group	ICICI Bank	PNB	CBoP
1985	59.72	-	53.21	-
1995-96	60.94	89.42	46.75	79.49
2006-07	76.15	84.97	69.06	75.49
Trend GR Period I	-0.67	-	2.27	-
Period II	1.51	6.38	3.54	2.45
Period I&II	-0.98	-	1.45	-
C.V.	15.87	44.43	13.85	22.98
T-value	1.83	1.51	4.23*	1.16
Average Ratio	60.31	76.29	51.58	55.52

Source: Performance Highlights of Public Sector and Private Sector Banks, Various Issues, published by IBA, Mumbai.

Note: (i)GR stands for growth rate in all the tables.
(ii)* denotes significance at five percent level in all the tables.
(iii)C.V. stands for Coefficient of Variation

Despite a reduction in the Statutory Liquidity Ratio, Cash Reserve Ratio and falling spread in the Public Sector banks, the overall credit deployment did not pick up in the desired direction in the post-reform period (Sooden and Bali, 2004).

The two Private Sector Banks also suffered a decline in this ratio. The ratio reduced from 89.42% in 1995-96 to 84.97% in 2006-07 for ICICI Bank and from 79.49% to 75.49% for CBoP, during the same period. The rise in this ratio has been significant at 5% level for PNB only.

Bank-wise analysis reveals that the Credit-Deposit Ratio has been the highest, on an average, for ICICI Bank (76.29%),followed by SBI Group(60.31%),CBoP (55.52%)and PNB(51.58%).

The explosion in credit growth since 2004 as much as the tardy pace of credit growth earlier together paint a flattering picture of Public Sector Banks, they suggest that the Public Sector Banks are indeed taking the right credit decision based on a proper evaluation of the underlying risks(Bhattacharya and Ray,2007). When economic conditions were adverse, the Public Sector Banks invested in government securities and when conditions improved, they tilted towards credit.

During period I, (from 1985 to 1994-95), the rise in Credit-Deposit ratio has been greater for PNB (2.27) than that for SBI Group (-0.67). However, ICICI Bank has the highest Trend Growth Rate (6.38),followed by PNB(3.54),CBoP(2.45) and SBI Group(1.51) during Period II, i.e. the post-reforms period(1995-96 to 2006-07).If we compare the overall trend growth rates of the two Public Sector Banks, i.e.from1985 to 2006-07,then the growth rate of PNB has been greater(1.45) than that of SBI Group(-0.98).The growth rate has improved after the reforms for both the Public Sector Banks probably due to aggressive lending activities followed by the banks as an aftermath of reforms.

The Coefficient of Variation in respect of Credit-Deposit Ratio has been the highest for ICICI Bank (44.43%),indicating maximum volatility, followed by CBoP (22.98%), SBI Group(15.87%) and PNB(13.85%).

Credit management ensures adequate and reasonable balance between liquidity and safety of funds and profitability of operations.

71

While the surge in financial intermediation is generally associated with increased growth and efficiency, excessive credit often leads to some erosion in credit quality.

3.5 Loans and Advances

Loans and advances represent that part of customers' deposits, which the bank considers may be safely lent, while the remainder is in the form of cash and other assets. Loans and advances include working capital and term finance to different types of borrowers on unsecured basis in various forms of bank lending by way of loans (demand loans and term loans) and advances overdrafts, cash credit, letters of credit and bill finance.

Over the years, loans and advances have increased significantly (at five per cent level) for all the four banks under study as shown in Table 3.3.

Table3.3: Trends in Loans & Advances

(Amount in Rs. crore)

Year	SBI Group	ICICI Bank	PNB	CBoP
1985	21,369	-	3,359	-
1995-96	78,126	651	12,679	221
2006-07	4,82,426	1,95,866	96,596	11,221
Trend G.R. Period I	13.71	-	18.31	-
Period II	17.37	79.45	20.41	35.13
Period I&II	14.42	79.45	16.86	35.13
C.V.	95.02	127.02	103.82	125.03
T-value	7.71*	6.26*	7.78*	4.00*

Source:Performance Highlights of Public Sector and Private Sector Banks, Various Issues, published by IBA, Mumbai.

During Period I, i.e. from 1985 to 1994-95, the rise in Loans and Advances has been greater for PNB (18.31) while for SBI

Group, the trend growth rate has been lower (13.71). However, ICICI Bank has the highest Trend Growth Rate (79.45),followed by CBoP (35.13),PNB(20.41) and SBI Group(17.37) during Period II, i.e. the post-reforms period(1995-96 to 2006-07).If we compare the overall trend growth rate of the two Public Sector Banks i.e.from1985 to 2006-07,then the growth rate of PNB has been greater (16.86) than that of SBI Group (14.42).The growth rate has increased after the reforms for both the Public Sector Banks due to the phased reduction of Cash Reserve Ratio and Statutory Liquidity Ratio, which has made more assets available to the banks for lending.

The Coefficient of Variation has been the highest for ICICI Bank (127.02%), indicating maximum volatility followed closely by CBoP (125.03%), PNB(103.82%) and SBI Group(95.02%).

Improved atmosphere for recovery created in the recent years coupled with greater awareness about market risks associated with large holding of securities portfolio seem to have induced banks to put greater efforts in extending loans (Mohan, 2005).

3.6 Deposit Mobilization

Deposits are the vital sources of funds for commercial banks, which are used in rendering credit services to their customers. In fact, one of the greatest strength of a bank is its level of customer deposits, which also enables it to achieve a lower cost of funds than the cost of alternative sources of funds. The growth rate has increased after the reforms for both the Public Sector Banks due to greater deposit mobilization by the banks as the rates on deposits have been deregulated with only the rate on savings being mandated by the RBI as depicted in Table 3.4.

During period I, (from 1985 to 1994-95), the rise in Deposits, as shown by its trend growth rate, has been greater for PNB (15.69) than that of SBI Group(14.44). However, ICICI Bank has the

highest Trend Growth Rate (68.69),followed by CBoP (31.90), PNB
(16.29) and SBI Group(15.63) during Period II, i.e. the post-reforms
period(1995-96 to 2006-07).If we compare the overall trend growth
rates of the two Public Sector Banks i.e. from 1985 to 2006-07,then
the growth rate of SBI Group has been slightly greater (15.58) than
that of PNB (15.19).

Table3.4: Trends in Deposits

(Amount in Rs. crore)

Year	SBI Group	ICICI Bank	PNB	CBoP
1985	35,782	-	6,313	-
1995-96	1,28,432	730	27,123	278
2006-07	6,33,476	2,30,511	1,39,860	14,863
Trend GR Period I	14.44	-	15.69	-
Period II	15.63	68.69	16.29	31.90
Period I&II	15.58	-	15.19	-
C.V.	85.69	130.32	87.93	99.87
T-value	12.36*	5.67*	10.49*	4.84*

Source: Performance Highlights of Public Sector and Private Sector
Banks, Various Issues, published by IBA, Mumbai.

After the nationalization of these banks, as a favourable
response to social obligations, their managements devised various
schemes of deposits mobilization and started providing many
facilities to their deposits as to create interest and evince more
interest in them for saving their funds in these banks (Padmavathi,
2006).

The Coefficient of Variation has been the highest for ICICI
Bank (130.32%), indicating maximum volatility, followed by CBoP
(99.87%), PNB (87.93%) and SBI Group (85.69%).Statistically, the
growth in Deposits has been significant for all the four banks at five
percent level of significance.

3.7 Investments

Investments are vital assets of a bank and an important parameter to gauge the growth and development of banks. All the four have experienced substantial rise in investments as shown in Table3.5

The reduction in Cash Reserve Ratio and improved inter-office adjustments in a substantially computerized and networked environment, inter alia, did free up substantial amounts of bank resources, which enabled banks to concentrate on investment operations with greater vigor (Mohan, 2005).

During period I, from 1985 to 1994-95, the rise in Investments, as shown by its trend growth rate, has been greater for SBI Group (22.61) than that of PNB (19.25).

However, ICICI Bank has the highest Trend Growth Rate (74.05),followed by CBoP (27.18), SBI Group(15.84) and PNB(14.19),during Period II, i.e. the post-reforms period(1995-96 to 2006-07).

If we compare the overall trend growth rates of the two Public Sector Banks i.e.from1985 to 2006-07,then the growth rate of SBI Group has been greater (18.39) than that of PNB (15.83).The growth rate has decreased after the reforms for both the Public Sector Banks due to lesser investment in approved securities. The Coefficient of Variation has been the highest for ICICI Bank (107.83%), indicating maximum volatility, followed by SBI Group (89.22%), PNB (82.67%) and CBoP(79.90%).

Statistically, the growth in investments has been significant for all the four banks at five percent level of significance.

However if we study the trends in investments as percentage of Total Assets, in the case of the two Public Sector Banks, the share grew from 18.76% in 1985 to 33.53% in 1995-96 for SBI Group and from 33.58% in 1985 to 37.91% for PNB during the same period. The ratio decreased to 26.27% and 27.82%for SBI Group and PNB respectively in 2006-07.

Table 3.5: Trends in Investments

(Amount Rs. crore)

Year	SBI Group	ICICI Bank	PNB	CBoP
1985	7660 (18.76)	-	2,336 (33.58)	-
1995-96	55,627 (33.53)	262 (22.59)	11,936 (37.91)	90 (19.31)
2006-07	2,11,664 (26.27)	91,258 (26.48)	45,189 (27.82)	4,632 (25.09)
Trend GR Period I	22.61	-	19.25	-
Period II	15.84	74.05	14.19	27.18
Period I&II	18.39	-	15.83	-
C.V.	89.22	107.83	82.67	79.90
T-value	11.77*	8.63*	12.81*	5.07*

Source: Performance Highlights of Public Sector and Private Sector Banks in India, IBA Mumbai, Various Issues.
Note: (i) Figures given in parentheses denote growth in percentage share of Investments in Total Assets.

The two Private Sector Banks also improved their share of investments in the total assets from 22.59%in 1995-96 to 26.48%in 2006-07 and from 19.31% to 25.09% for ICICI Bank and CBoP respectively, during the same period.

While in the 1990s, greater orientation towards investment activities and aversion to credit risk exposure may have deterred banks from undertaking their 'core function' of providing loans and advances, banks seem to have struck a greater balance between investment and loans and advances in recent years(Mohan,2005).

3.8 BRANCH EXPANSION

Since nationalization, Public Sector Banks have grown enormously, especially in unbanked and under-banked areas, in terms of the number of branches, volume of deposits, credit and priority sector advances.

3.7.1 Trends in Rural Branch Expansion

Though the reform process of the 1990s did not prevent the banks from expanding rural branch network and in fact, the Narasimham Committee did specifically emphasize the importance of rural institutions and branch banking, in reality quite the contrary has happened. Until banking reforms began in the early 1990s, the Reserve Bank of India, as a policy enforced slowdown in branch expansion in metropolitan areas. On the other hand, steady increases particularly in the number of rural branches were encouraged on the consideration that the Scheduled Commercial Banks had a role to play in branch banking in the process of institutionalization of rural savings. After the expiry of the five year Branch expansion programme of 1990-95, the subject of opening rural branches was left to the commercial judgement of banks.

Banks were allowed to convert their non-viable rural branches into satellite offices or even closure of bank branches at rural centres served by two commercial banks. As a consequence, the number of urban and metropolitan branches has increased rapidly.

Table 3.6 shows that the share of rural branches in the total branch network of SBI Group has reduced from 48.20% in 1985 to 45.41% in 1995-96.The share of rural branches of PNB has increased from 46.81% to 53.59% during the same period. The two Private Sector Banks did not open any branch in rural area in1995-96.However,the share of rural branches was (12.67%)for ICICI Bank and (2.57%)for CBoP in 2006-07.Later on, the share declined to 37.42% for SBI Group and 47.51% for PNB in 2006-07.

Table3.6: Trends in Rural Branch Expansion of Banks

Year	SBI Group	ICICI Bank	PNB	CBoP
1985	5,280 (48.20)	-	1,020 (46.81)	-
1995-96	5,880 (45.41)	-	2,001 (53.59)	-
2006-07	5,289 (37.42)	90 (12.67)	1,957 (47.51)	7 (2.57)
Trend GR Period I	1.79	-	7.37	-
Period II	-0.80	64.36	-0.02	-42.36
Period I& II	-0.05	-	2.24	-
C.V.	4.74	100.19	16.11	246.87
T-value	0.34	6.13*	5.65*	1.80

Source: Performance Highlights of Public Sector and Private Sector Banks, Various Issues, published by IBA, Mumbai.
Note: (i) Figures given in parentheses denote percentage share in total branches.

During period I, from 1985 to 1994-95, the rise in rural branches, as shown by its trend growth rate, has been greater for PNB (7.37), while for SBI Group, the trend growth rate has been lower (1.79). However, only ICICI Bank has the highest Trend Growth Rate (64.36) indicating maximum growth in rural branches. The share of rural branches has declined for all the other bank,the decrease being the most for CBoP(-42.36),followed by SBI Group(-0.80) and PNB(-0.20),during Period II, i.e. the post-reforms period(1995-96 to 2006-07).If we compare the overall trend growth rate of the two Public Sector Banks, i.e. from 1985 to 2006-07, then the growth rate of rural branches of PNB has been greater (2.24) than that of SBI Group (-0.05).The growth rate has decreased after the reforms for all the three banks   due to   concentration of banking activities in metropolitan areas.

The Coefficient of Variation in respect of rural branches has been the highest for CBoP (246.87%) indicating maximum volatility, followed by ICICI Bank (100.19%), PNB (16.11%) and SBI Group (4.74%). Statistically, the   growth in rural branches has been significant only for PNB and ICICI Bank at five per cent level of significance.

3.7.2. Trends in Semi-urban Branch Expansion

The share of Semi-urban Branches decreased   from   31.59% in 1985   to   28.29% in 1995-96 for SBI Group and from 20.65% to 17.03% for PNB   during the same period.

Table 3.7: Trends in Semi-urban Branch Expansion of Banks

Year	SBI Group	ICICI Bank	PNB	CBoP
1985	3,461 (31.59)	-	450 (20.65)	-
1995-96	3,664 (28.29)	-	636 (17.03)	6 (40.00)
2006-07	4,120 (29.15)	185 (26.05)	816 (19.81)	64 (23.53)
Trend GR Period I	0.57	-	3.23	-
Period II	0.96	44.49	2.43	24.90
Period I& II	1.16	-	3.12	-
C.V.	7.83	95.81	19.91	80.93
T-value	15.10*	7.27*	22.59*	6.57*

Source: Performance Highlights of Public Sector and Private Sector Banks, Various   Issues, published by IBA, Mumbai.
Note: (i) Figures given in parentheses denote percentage share in total branches.

The share reduced from 40.00% in 1995-96 to 23.53%   in 2006-07   for CBoP, and was   26.05% for ICICI Bank in 2006-07.

The share increased to 29.15% and 19.81% for SBI Group and PNB respectively in 2006-07.During period I, from 1985 to 1994-95, the rise in   semi-urban branches, as shown by its trend growth rate, has   been greater for PNB   (3.23), while for SBI Group, the trend growth rate has been lower (0.57).   However, ICICI Bank has the highest Trend Growth Rate (44.49) indicating maximum growth in semi-urban branches, followed by CBoP(24.90),PNB(2.43) and SBI Group(0.96),during Period II, i.e. the post-reforms period(1995-96 to 2006-07).If we compare the overall   trend growth rates of the two Public Sector Banks i.e.from1985 to 2006-07,then the growth rate of semi-urban branches of PNB has been   greater (3.12) than that of SBI Group (1.16).

The Coefficient of Variation in respect of semi-urban   branches has been the highest for ICICI Bank (95.81%) indicating maximum volatility, followed by CBoP (80.93%), PNB (19.91%) and SBI Group (7.83%). Statistically, the growth in semi-urban branches has been significant for all the four banks at five per cent level of significance.

3.7.3 Trends in Urban Branch Expansion

Rapid applications of new technology and significant changes in the Indian economy including the growth of the services sector and acceleration in urban orientation and sophistication in consumption have provided an expanding space for high-street banking.

The share of urban branches   increased from 12.09% in 1985 to   16.39% in 1995-96 for SBI Group, but reduced from 20.60% to 18.77% for PNB during the same period. The share increased to 18.31% and 19.54% for SBI Group and PNB respectively in 2006-07.

The share reduced from 36.36% in   1995-96 to 27.75% in

2006-07 for ICICI Bank and from 40.00% to 37.13% for CBoP, during the same period.

Table 3.8: Trends in   Urban Branch Expansion of   Banks

Year	SBI Group	ICICI Bank	PNB	CBoP
1985	1,325 (12.09)	-	449 (20.60)	-
1995-96	2,123 (16.39)	4 (36.36)	701 (18.77)	6 (40.00)
2006-07	2,588 (18.31)	197 (27.75)	805 (19.54)	101 (37.13)
Trend GR Period I	4.44	-	4.48	-
Period II	1.32	46.97	1.51	28.74
Period I& II	2.55	-	2.99	-
C.V.	16.08	91.85	19.11	89.97
T-value	17.15*	9.70*	14.56*	5.69*

Source: Performance Highlights of Public Sector and Private Sector Banks, Various Issues, published by IBA, Mumbai.
Note: (i) Figures given in parentheses denote percentage share in total branches.

During period I, from 1985 to 1994-95, the rise in   urban branches, as shown by its trend growth rate, has   been   slightly greater for PNB (4.48) than that of SBI Group (4.44). However, ICICI Bank has the highest Trend Growth Rate (46.97) indicating maximum growth in urban branches, followed by CBoP (28.74),PNB(1.51) and SBI Group(1.32),during Period II,   i.e. the post-reforms period(1995-96 to 2006-07).If we compare the overall trend growth rates of the two Public Sector Banks i.e. from1985 to 2006-07,then the   growth rate of urban branches of PNB has been greater   (2.99) than that of SBI Group   (2.55).The growth rate has decreased after the reforms for both the Public Sector banks due to concentration of banking activities in metropolitan areas.

The Coefficient of Variation in respect of urban branches has been the highest for ICICI Bank (91.85%) indicating maximum volatility, followed by CBoP (89.97%), PNB (19.11%) and SBI Group (16.08%). Statistically, the growth in urban branches has been significant for all the four banks at five per cent level of significance.

3.7.4 Trends in Metropolitan Branch Expansion

The 1990s have also seen a rapid expansion of high-street Banking promoted by new private sector banks and foreign banks. As a consequence, the rural branches have stagnated or declined in number and number of and metropolitan branches have galloped for all the four banks under the study as shown in Table 3.9.

The share of metropolitan branches increased from 8.09% in 1985 to 9.89% in 1995-96 for SBI Group, but reduced from 11.93% to 10.60% for PNB during the same period. The share reduced from 63.64% in 1995-96 to 33.52% for ICICI Bank in 2006-07, though it rose from 20.00% to 36.76% for CBoP, during the same period. The share increased to 15.11% and 13.13% for SBI Group and PNB respectively in 2006-07.

During period I, from 1985 to 1994-95, the rise in metropolitan branches, as shown by its trend growth rate, has been greater for PNB (4.00), while for SBI Group, the trend growth rate has been lesser (3.09).

However, CBoP has the highest Trend Growth Rate (40.85) indicating maximum growth in metropolitan branches, followed by ICICI Bank(38.40), SBI Group(4.40) and PNB(0.93),during Period II, i.e. the post-reforms period(1995-96 to 2006-07).

Table 3.9: Trends in Metropolitan Branch Expansion of Banks

Year	SBI Group	ICICI Bank	PNB	CBoP
1985	887 (8.09)	-	260 (11.93)	-
1995-96	1280 (9.89)	7 (63.64)	396 (10.60)	3 (20.00)
2006-07	2135 (15.11)	238 (33.52)	541 (13.13)	100 (36.76)
Trend GR Period I	3.09	-	4.00	-
Period II	4.40	38.40	0.93	40.85
Period I& II	3.50	-	3.51	-
C.V.	23.84	90.58	24.89	88.99
T-value	12.94*	9.41*	7.64*	9.21*

Source: Performance Highlights of Public Sector and Private Sector Banks, Various
Issues, published by IBA, Mumbai.
Note: (i) Figures given in parentheses denote percentage share in total branches.

If we compare the overall trend growth rates of the two Public Sector Banks, i.e.from1985 to 2006-07,then the growth rates of metropolitan branches have been similar for both PNB(3.51) and SBI Group (3.50).The trend growth rate of metropolitan branches has increased after the reforms for SBI Group, while it has reduced for PNB.

The Coefficient of Variation in respect of metropolitan branches has been the highest for ICICI Bank (90.58%) indicating maximum volatility, followed by CBoP (88.99%), PNB (24.89%) and SBI Group (23.84%). Statistically, the growth in metropolitan branches has been significant for all the four banks at five per cent level of significance.

The New Private Sector Banks are less inclined to open branches in regions where scope of business and profits are less. These banks are concentrating only in big industrial and commercial cities. The commercial viability of opening a branch is the sole criterion of the New Private Sector Banks. Concurrently, the bank's reach for the rural population and the informal sectors seems to have suffered a set back which, however, has turned out to be an unintended fall-out of banking reforms.

This concentration of banking activities reflects another dimension that banks' lending activities have increasingly shifted in favour of retail activities in metropolitan and some important urban centers.

3.9 Priority Sector Advances

Priority Sector Advance is an important element of social banking. Bank-wise analysis reveals that over the period under review, the advances to Priority sector as a percentage to total advances have increased for the two Private Sector Bank and decreased for the two Public Sector Banks as depicted in Table 3.10.

The share of priority sector advance in total advances declined from 40.46% in 1985 to 27.38% in 1995-96 for SBI Group and from 44.45% to 32.27% for PNB during the same period. The share, however, increased later on, to 32.66% for SBI Group and 37.81%for PNB in 2006-07.A redeeming feature of the Priority Sector Lending of the two Private Sector Banks has been the rise in the share from 11.69% in 1995-96 to 28.22% in 2006-07 for ICICI Bank and from 19.00% to 31.23% for CBoP, during the same period.

On an average, PNB leads all other three banks in Priority Sector Lending, (39.92%) followed by SBI Group, (31.65%) ICICI Bank (21.04%) and CBoP (19.27%). The Private Sector Banks need to realize their social responsibility by increasing advances to the priority sector.

Table 3.10: Trends in Priority Sector Advances to Total Advances

Year	SBI Group	ICICI Bank	PNB	CBoP
1985	40.46	-	44.45	-
1995-96	27.38	11.69	32.27	19.00
2006-07	32.66	28.22	37.81	31.23
Average rate	31.65	21.04	39.92	19.27
Trend GR Period I	-5.60	-	-3.36	-
Period II	1.42	3.21	3.24	1.11
Period I& II	-0.93	-	-0.40	-
C.V.	14.76	40.10	13.38	35.95
T-value	2.38*	0.91	0.95	0.87

Source: Performance Highlights of Public Sector and Private Sector Banks,Various Issues,published by IBA, Mumbai.

The concept of priority sector lending is mainly intended to ensure that the assistance from the banking system flows in an increasing measure, to those sector of the economy which, though significant proportion of the national product, have not received adequate support of institutional finance in the past (Padmavathi and Hemachandrika, 2006).

During period I, from 1985 to 1994-95, the Priority Sector Lending, as shown by its trend growth rate, has reduced for both the Public Sector banks, the decline being more pronounced for SBI Group (-5.60) than that of PNB(-3.36). However, PNB has the highest Trend Growth Rate (3.24) indicating maximum growth in Priority Sector Lending, followed by ICICI Bank(3.21), SBI Group(1.42) and CBoP(1.11),during Period II, i.e. the post-reforms period(1995-96 to 2006-07).If we compare the overall trend growth rates of the two Public Sector Banks, i.e. from 1985 to 2006-07,then the growth rate of Priority Sector Lending has again reduced for both the Public Sector Banks, the rate being (-0.40) for PNB and (-0.93) for SBI Group. The growth rate has increased after the reforms for the two Public Sector Banks due to the operational flexibility that the reform process has provided while attaining social objectives.

The Coefficient of Variation in respect of Priority Sector Lending has been the highest for ICICI Bank (40.10%) indicating maximum volatility, followed by CBoP (35.95%), SBI Group (14.76%) and PNB (13.38%). Statistically, the decline in Priority Sector Lending has been significant only for SBI Group at five per cent level of significance.

The rise in priority sector lending since the initiation of reforms reflects greater flexibility provided to banks to meet such targets. Currently, if a bank fails to meet the priority sector lending target through direct lending, the bank can invest the shortfall amount with the apex organizations dealing with the flow of funds towards agriculture and small scale industries. While adherence of banks to the norms on priority sector is desirable, the current arrangement reflects the operational flexibility that the reform process has provided while attaining social objectives.

Thus, the banks can extend loans on commercially viable terms. Though these changes are welcome from the point of view of enabling banks to operate on commercially viable terms, availability of bank loans for agriculture, small scale Industries and weaker sections is bound to suffer (Sreekantaradhya, 2004).

Share of priority sector advances to total advances of both Private Sector Banks has increased gradually, i.e. from 11.69% in

1995-96 to 28.22% in 2006-07 for ICICI Bank and from 19.00% in 1995-96 to 31.23% in 2006-07 for CBoP.

In spite of the rise, the two banks are lagging far behind the target of 40 per cent lending to priority sector. The private sector banks have promoted high-street banking by being urban-centric and technology savvy. As a result, they did not open many branches in rural areas but targeted at the metropolitan and urban areas only. The priority sector, thereby, got neglected.

Thus, as far as priority sector lending is concerned, all   the four banks under study fall short of the target of priority sector lending, though PNB is close to the target. The Private Sector Banks have, in the recent years, increased lending to the priority sector due to the reforms in the priority sector lending.   It is high time that the Private Sector Banks fulfil the targets of priority sector lending or else the banks reach for the rural population and the informal sector will suffer.

3.10 Net Interest Margin

Spread management is a function of cost reduction and return maximization and in the area of banking it boils down to efficient assets management, especially of credit portfolio and liability management in terms of deposits and capital funds apart from operational aspects in terms of branches and personnel spread (Patheja,1994).

Spread Management emphasizes the difference between the return on assets and the cost of liability overtime (also known as NIM) (Vij, 1991).

Due to the liberalization of the banking sector and the resultant competition and soft interest rates prevalent in the Indian economy, risks arising out of the traditional banking business are on the increase (Ramasastri et al., 2004).

Table 3.11: Trends in Net Interest Margin

Year	SBI Group	ICICI Bank	PNB	CBoP
1985	1.92	-	2.11	-
1995-96	3.05	2.67	3.27	4.51
2006-07	2.79	1.93	3.39	3.08
Average rate	2.73	1.89	2.92	2.79
Trend GR Period I	6.91	-	5.62	-
Period II	-0.81	-4.63	0.02	0.16
Period I& II	1.86	-	2.75	-
C.V.	19.39	39.53	19.84	24.60
T- value	2.74*	1.89	5.91*	0.17

Source: Performance Highlights of Public Sector and Private Sector Banks, Various Issues, published by IBA, Mumbai.

The NIM initially increased for both the Public Sector Banks; from 1.92% in 1985 to 3.05% in 1995-96 for SBI Group and from 2.11% to 3.27% for PNB during the same period. However, later on, NIM reduced to 2.79% for SBI Group, but increased to 3.39% for PNB in 2006-07 as given in Table 3.11.Initially, the two Private sector Banks, ICICI Bank and CBoP had higher spreads which reduced gradually over the years due to the increasing competition with the entry of new banks and deregulated interest rates. Later, the spreads declined substantially for both the Private Sector Banks i.e. from 2.67% in 1995-96 to 1.93% in 2006-07 for ICICI Bank and from 4.51% to 3.08% for CBoP during the same period. Customer attraction and their retention has been an important objective of these banks. Initially, these banks were able to earn higher spreads, which reduced gradually over the years due to the increasing competition with the entry of new banks and deregulated interest regime.

However, the increased competition improves the efficiency of banks which gets reflected in narrowing down the "spread."

Bank-wise analysis reveals, that, on an average, PNB has highest spread ratio (2.92%) followed closely by CBoP (2.79), SBI Group,(2.73) and ICICI Bank (1.89%).

During period I, from 1985 to 1994-95, the rise in Net Interest Margin, as shown by the trend growth rate, has been higher for SBI Group (6.91) than that for PNB (5.62). However, CBoP has the highest Trend Growth Rate (0.16) indicating maximum growth in NIM, followed by ICICI Bank(0.02), SBI Group(-0.81) and CBoP(-4.63),during Period II, i.e. the post-reforms period(1995-96 to 2006-07).If we compare the overall trend growth rates of the two Public Sector Banks i.e.from1985 to 2006-07,then the growth rate of NIM has again reduced for both the Public Sector Banks, the rate being (2.75) for PNB and (1.86) for SBI Group .

The Coefficient of Variation in respect of NIM has been the highest for ICICI Bank (39.53%) indicating maximum volatility, followed by CBoP (24.60%), PNB (19.84%) and SBI Group (19.39%). Statistically, the growth in NIM has been significant for SBI Group and PNB, at five per cent level of significance.

Too large a spread in a deregulated environment indicates the absence of competition within the banking system and is perhaps reflective of the existence of a certain degree of monopoly power on the part of the financial intermediaries (Kannan et al., 2001). In this competitive environment efficient asset-liability management, project appraisal and recovery mechanism can help to earn the interest income substantially.

3.11 Non–Interest Incomes

Non-interest income, also known as fee-based income, has become an important source of income for Banks. The non-interest income consists of income from commission, exchange and brokerage transactions and other miscellaneous incomes. This stream of revenues is not dependent on the banks' capital adequacy and consequently, potential to increase this transaction is immense. For all the banks, this income has increased over the years. In the post-liberalization era, Public Sector Banks have diversified to non-traditional activities such as mutual funds, merchant banking, venture capital funding and other para-banking activities such as leasing, hire purchase, factoring and so on.

Table3.12: Trends in Non-Interest Income as % to Total Income

Year	SBI Group	ICICI Bank	PNB	CBoP
1985	11.83	-	5.99	-
1995-06	16.78	17.73	10.48	15.15
2006-07	12.16	20.50	8.28	24.21
Average rate	14.10	20.84	10.58	20.53
Trend GR Period I	2.49	-	4.74	-
Period II	0.40	2.87	0.73	2.76
Period I& II	1.66	-	4.01	-
C.V.	17.42	19.97	34.91	25.39
T-value	3.63*	1.79	4.33*	1.30

Source: Performance Highlights of Public Sector and Private Sector Banks, Various Issues, published by IBA, Mumbai.

Bank-wise analysis shown in Table3.12 indicates that on an average, Non-interest income as percentage of total income has been highest for ICICI Bank (20.84%) followed closely by CBoP, (20.53%) then SBI Group (14.10%) and least for PNB (10.58%).

CBoP has adopted technology in banking and is offering various services to its customers, thereby generating fee-based income. PNB, on the other land has been rather slow in adopting the latest technology, thereby relying more on the traditional sources of income.

During period I, from 1985 to 1994-95, the rise in non-interest income as a percentage to total income, as shown by the trend growth rate, has been higher in the case of PNB (4.74) than that of SBI Group (2.49). However, ICICI Bank has the highest Trend Growth Rate (2.87) indicating maximum growth in non-interest income as a percentage of total income, followed closely by CBoP(2.76), PNB(0.73) and SBI Group(0.40),during Period II, i.e. the post-reforms period(1995-96 to 2006-07).If we compare the overall trend growth rates of the two Public Sector Banks i.e. from1985 to 2006-07,then the growth rate of non-interest income as a percentage to total income has again reduced for both the Public Sector Banks, the rate being higher for PNB (4.01) than that of for SBI Group(1.66). The growth rate of non-interest income as a percentage of total income has decreased after the reforms for the two Public Sector banks due to greater competition generated by the Private Sector banks in fee-based sources of income.

The Coefficient of Variation in respect of non-interest income as a percentage to total income has been the highest for PNB (34.91%) indicating maximum volatility, followed by CBoP (25.39%), ICICI Bank (19.97%) and SBI Group (17.42%). Statistically, the growth in non-interest income as a percentage to total income has been significant for SBI Group and PNB at five per cent level of significance.

The two Private Sector Banks have tapped the sources of fee-based income and have adopted technology in a big way. PNB has not fully explored the new avenues of fee-based income and has been rather slow in adopting information technology.

3.12 CONCLUSIONS

All the four banks under study have registered a significant rise in deposits, investments and loans and advances. However, the rate of growth of deposits, investments and loans and advances has been higher for both the Private Sector Banks as compared to their Public Sector counterparts and ICICI Bank has the highest growth in these parameters. The most discernible feature is that, both SBI Group and ICICI Bank have major share in all the segments of banking whether these are deposits, advances, priority sector lending or number of branches. However, the branches of both ICICI Bank and CBoP are concentrated in metropolitan and urban areas. Priority sector has also been neglected by these banks due to their urban orientation, which proved a bane for the reforms.

The Private Sector Banks are riding the bandwagon of technology and are providing consumer-centric services to the urban elite. This has led to high fee-based incomes for both ICICI Bank and CBoP. They are leveraging on technology and have entered greatly into para-banking activities which have provided them higher non-interest income. The Public Sector Banks have been rather slow in technology upgrading and are concentrating more on conventional banking business. The higher spread of SBI Group and PNB explains this fact.

With the diversification of banks' portfolio, other income comprising trading income and fee-based income has evolved as an important source of income for banks over the last few years. This reflects greater diversification of banks into non-fund based business and also emergence of off-balance-sheet activities as profit centers for Indian banks.

To compete effectively with non-banking entities, banks have been permitted to undertake para-banking activities like investment banking, securities trading and derivatives trading. Thus, the changing face of banking has led to the erosion of margins on traditional banking business and this has encouraged banks to search for newer activities to augment their fee-based incomes. Increase in the fee-based activities would also go a long way in enhancing the financial position of banks.

REFERENCES

Ajit, D; and Bangar, R.D(2003)," Banks in Financial International, Performance and Issues," in A.Vasudevan (ed.),*Money and Banking Sector Research papers by the Economists of Reserve Bank of India*, Academic Foundation, New Delhi, p. 254.

Bhalerao, Asha(1988), "Post-Nationalization Trends in profitability of Commercial Banks in India," *Banking Finance*,Vol.1,No.4, April, p.11.

Bhattacharya, Indernil;and Ray, Partha(2007), "How do we Assess Monetary Policy Stance ?" *EPW*, Vol. XLII, No. 13, p. 1205.

EPW Research Foundation (2004), "Scheduled Commercial Banks in India, " March. 20, *EPW*,Vol. XXXIX, No. 12 p. 1331.

EPW Research Foundation (2006), " Increasing Concentration of Banking Operations-Top Centers & Retail Loans, " EPW, Vol. XLI, No. 11, March. 18, p. 1113.

Gurumoorthy, T.R. (2004),"Analysis of Income & Expenditure in Banks," *Business and Economic Facts for You*, June.

Jha, Kumar Pramod(1986), "Commercial Banking and Economic Growth, " in. S. Subrahmanya (ed.), *Trends and Progress of Banking in India,* Deep & Deep Publications Pvt. Ltd., New Delhi, p.88.

Kannan, R; Narain, Aditya;and Ghosh, Saibal(2001), "Determinants of Net Interest Margin under Regulatory Requirements" *EPW*, Vol. XXXVI, No. 4, p.337.

Kumar, Parmod(2006), " *Banking Sector Efficiency in Globalised Economy*, " Deep & Deep Publications Pvt. Ltd., New Delhi.

Kumar, Pawan (2005), *Indian Banking Today-Impact of Reforms*, Kanishka Publishers, Distributors, New Delhi.

Mazumdar,Tanusree(1996),*Indian   BankingSystem   in Transition:Issues & Challenges*, ICFAI Vision Series, p. 72.

Mohan, Rakesh(2005), " Financial Sector Reforms in India-Policies and Performance Analysis, " *EPW*, Vol. XL., No.12, March 19-25, p.1110.

Padamavathi,A;and HemaChandrika,G.(2006), *Public Sector Banks in India*, Global Research Publications, New Delhi.

Pathak, V.Bharati,(2004), *Indian Financial System*, Pearson Education Pvt. Ltd., New Delhi.

Patheja, Anju(1994), *Financial Management of Commercial Banks*, South Asia Publications, New Delhi.

Qamar, Furquan(2003), " Profitability and Resources Use Efficiency in Scheduled Commercial Banks in India: A Comparative Analysis of Foreign, New Private Sector, Old Private Sector & Public Sector Banks," *Synthesis,* Vol. 1, No.1, July- December, p.1.

Raghuraman, K (2006), "Corporate Social Responsibilities," The Indian Banks, *IBA Bulletin*, August. Vol. 1 No. 8, p. 11.

Ramasastri, A.S; Samuel, Achmma;and Gangadaran,S. (2004), "Income Stability of Scheduled Commercial Banks: Interest vis-a-vis Non-Interest Income," *EPW*, March 20,p.1311.

RBI (2004-05) Report on Trends & Progress of Banking in India.

RBI's Basic Statistical Returns of Scheduled Commercial banks in India, various years.

Sooden, Meenakshi;and Bali, Manju(2004),"Profitability in the Public Sector Banks in India in the Pre and Post-Reform Period," *Indian Management Studies Journal*, Vol. 8 No. 2, Oct, p. 72.

Sreekantaradhya, B.S. (2004), *Banking & Finance: Perspectives on Reform*, Deep & Deep Publications Pvt. Ltd., New Delhi.

Suneja, H.R. (1992), Management *of Bank Credit*, Himalaya Publishing House, Mumbai.

Vashisht, A.K. (1991), *Public Sector Banks in India*, H.K. Publishers & Distributors, New Delhi.

Vij, Madhu(1991),*Management of Financial Institutions in India*, Anmol Publication Pvt. Ltd., New Delhi.

CHAPTER- 4
ASSETS MANAGEMEMT

The introduction of Financial and Banking Sector Reforms has brought some major policy measures like disintermediation, deregulation, decontrol, liberalizing of control in trade/ foreign exchange etc.(Dharmarajan,2004).

In the process of financial intermediation, banks are exposed to severe competition compelling them to encounter various types of financial and non-financial risks, viz. credit, interest rate, foreign exchange liquidity, equity price, commodity price, legal, reputational, brand equity risk etc.(Raghavan,2005). The volatile nature of the bank's operating environment aggravates the effect of risks.

Prior to deregulation, bank funds were obtained from relatively stable demand deposits and from small time deposits (Joshi and Joshi,2002). Core deposits were the major sources of funds and volatility of interest rates was less. Interest rates on deposits as well as on advances were fixed by the Reserve Bank of India and uniformly implemented in all the banks. Spreads between the deposit and lending rates were very wide also; these spreads were more or less uniform among the commercial banks and were changed only by the RBI(Chawla,1998). The economic reforms initiated in the 1990s brought deregulation of the banking sector.

The process of deregulation was further strengthened by the following factors:

- Erosion in the traditional role of financial institutions;
- Development of many types of financial instruments;
- Technological changes;
- Globalization and competition from overseas banks (Joshi and Joshi,2002).

Recognizing the need for a vibrant and sound banking system, the Reserve Bank of India came out with its guidelines on Asset Liability Management system in Banks in February 1999. These guidelines were to be implemented with effect from April, 1990.

Fig.4(a):   MAJOR COMPONENTS OF RISK

Market Risk Management

- Interest rate sensitivity
- Hedging and trading port folio

Prepayment risk Loss

Credit Risk Management

*Credit policy and loan
   portfolio management

* Expected and
      unexpected loss

*Expected default frequency

* Internal risk ratings

* Counterparty credit   exposure

* Collateralization

Capital adequacy

* Regulatory reporting
   requirement

* Off-balance sheet items

* BIS Risk-based capital
   guidelines

* "Window dressing "   of
Financial statements

Liquidity Risk Management

* Funding Sources

* Cost of funds

* Investment portfolio

*Gap analysis

**Operational and business risk
Management**.

         * Return and performance measures

         * Legal and compliance matters

         * Business strategy

         * Projected net interest income

         * System and reporting

         * Business interruptions

Source:Ong,K.Michael(1998) " Integrating the role of Risk Management" in *Asset & Liability Management: A Synthesis of New Methodologies*, Risk Books, Kama Kura Corporation, London, p.4.

With this, the RBI launched the second phase of Banking Sector Reforms in the country, after the Capital Adequacy and Prudential norms, to ensure systemic endurance to liquidity, interest rate and currency risks involved in banking operations. The guidelines are mainly concerned with recording the liquidity and interest rate risks which banks run in their day to day operations and then putting prudent limits on such risks.

As per the Reserve Bank of India Guidelines issued in October 1999 (in relation to the BCBS consultative paper on New Capital Adequacy Framework in June 1999) there are three major risks encountered by the bank.

- Credit Risk
- Market Risk
- Operational Risk.

Mismatch of assets and liabilities is the cause of many risks. Banks need to address these risks in a structured manner by upgrading their risks management and adopting more comprehensive ALM practices than has been done earlier. As per RBI Guidelines Dated 10th Feb. 1999, issued to all Scheduled Commercial Banks, ALM is also concerned with risk management and provides a comprehensive and dynamic framework for measuring, monitoring and managing liquidity, interest rates, foreign exchange, equity and commodity price risks of a bank that needs to be closely integrated with the bank's business strategy. The focus of ALM should be the bank profitability and long-term operating viability(Subrahmanyam,1995). Thus, an Asset Liability Management function should achieve the following objectives:

- To ensure adequate liquidity of banks by analyzing the short-term maturity profile of assets and liabilities;
- To improve profit through the effective management of

interest spread;

- To manage and reduce risks such as, Credit Risk, Interest Rate, Liquidity Risk and Operational Risk;

- To strengthen the solvency of banks by ensuring the fulfilment of prescribed Capital Adequacy Norms (Nag,1998).

Fig. 4(b):   FUNDAMENTAL OBJECTIVES OF ALM

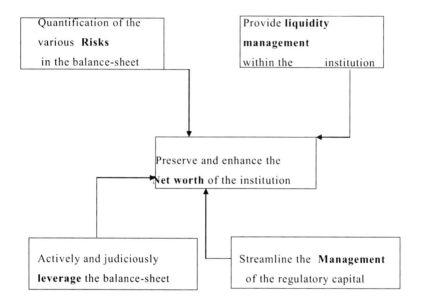

Source: Ong,K. Michael.(1998) "Integrating the Role of Risk Management in ALM,'' in *Asset & Liability Management- A Synthesis of New Methodologies*, Kama Kura Corporation, London,p.3.

Purpose of ALM

An efficient ALM technique aims to manage the volume, mix, maturity, rate sensitivity, quality and liquidity of assets and liabilities as a whole, so as to earn a predetermined acceptable risk/ reward ratio (Vij,2005).

The purpose of ALM, thus, is to enhance the asset quality, quantify the risks associated with assets and liabilities and to control and manage them. Commercial bank assets may be divided into four basic categories: assets, security investments, loans and fixed assets. The problem of asset management centres primarily on the allocation of funds among and within the first three categories, management is normally not involved on a day-to-day basis with the investment in buildings and equipments(Reed and Gill,1989). In the above light, areas of Asset Management cover:

(i)Reserve Position Management;

(ii)Investment Management;

(iii)Liquidity Management;

(iv)Loan Port-folio Management.

4.1 RESERVE POSITION MANAGEMENT

Reserve Position Management is based on the Statutory Reserve Requirements along with maintenance of working reserves for operational needs. The primary objective of Reserve Position Management is minimizing risks and maximizing returns by achieving an optimum risk-reward ratio.

4.1.1 Primary Reserves

The first priority in the allocation scheme is to establish the proportion of funds that will be allocated to primary reserves. This category of assets is a functional category that does not appear on the balance-sheet of a commercial bank. The aggregate of cash holdings by a bank with itself and with the Central Bank and other commercial banks is designated as the primary reserve.

Three loss categories can arise from Reserve Position Management risk:

(a)Opportunity Cost Losses: These are associated with excess reserves positions. Reserves are a sterile asset and therefore

101

holding excess reserve involves opportunity costs and a reduction in bank profits.

(b)Penalty Rate Losses: Failure to meet legal reserve requirement involves strict penal provisions. If a bank manages the reserve position too aggressively then it may have to borrow money from call market at very high rates to avoid high penalty rates.

(c)Surveillance Losses: Continued abuse of legal reserve requirement may lead to greater surveillance by the banking authorities. The latter is not a costless activity since the time that bank officers have to spend explaining their "reserve-mismanagement" to the regulators means that they have less time to do their jobs which tends to reduce the efficiency of a bank's operations, this is how "surveillance losses" arise(Patheja,1994).

4.1.2 Constituents of Primary Reserves

Primary Reserves consist of cash in hand, the balance with Central Bank and demand deposits with other banks. The main purpose of Primary Reserves is to ensure liquidity in the bank so that the demands of the depositors are satisfied. Thus, it serves as the first-line of defence in meeting the withdrawals of depositors. Primary reserves may be:

(i) Legal Reserves: Legal reserve is that constituent of Primary reserve which a bank is statutorily required to maintain. These reserves are based on the average deposits outstanding on the banks' books over a short-period of one or two weeks. These reserves comprise of Cash Reserve Ratio. In terms of Section 42(1) of the RBI Act, 1934, Scheduled Commercial Banks are required to maintain with RBI an average cash balance, the amount of which shall not be less than 3 percent of the total of the Net Demand and Time Liabilities (NDTL) in India, on a fortnightly basis. RBI is empowered to raise the said rate of CRR to such higher rate not exceeding 20 percent of the NDTL.

(ii) Working Reserve : The legal reserve cannot be relied upon at all times for meeting liquidity crises. This is the reason why commercial banks have to maintain Cash reserves in excess of the legal reserves to meet unforeseen contingencies. This additional cash reserve maintained by the banks to meet the working business needs is known as working reserve. Its main constituents are:-

a) Cash in their own vaults;

b) Current a/c deposits, demand deposits with other banks; and

c) Excess reserve with Central Bank.

The proportion of deposit liabilities to be maintained as working reserves involves a trade-off between liquidity and solvency. Cash in hand is a non-earning asset but banks need to maintain adequate cash to meet the routine as well as unforeseen demands of the customers. A multitude of factors affect the amount of reserves to be maintained by a bank.

4.1.3 Internal Factors affecting Primary Reserves

- **Profile of Deposits :** In case of a bank having a major portion of its total deposits as fixed deposits and savings accounts, small cash holding will suffice. Conversely, a bank having majority of its deposits as current account will have to maintain greater amount of working reserves.

- **Scale of Operations of the Bank:** With the growth in the size of business of a bank, a lower ratio of cash needs to be maintained as it is subject to lesser deposit variability.

- **Location of Bank:** Location of a bank influences the amount of cash a bank has to hold in its vault. Banks located in far-flung areas of the country away from the banking centres require to hold more cash as compared to banks situated near banking centres.

- **Size of Deposit Accounts:** - If the number of depositors is less but the amount deposited is large, then a bank has to maintain larger cash reserve as compared to a bank having greater number of depositors with numerous small accounts.

- **Ownership of Deposit Accounts :** The class to which the deposit holders belong has an important influence on the cash reserve to be maintained. If current accounts are held by businessmen and shareholders, then their balances will be affected by the fluctuations in the prices of commodities and Bullion. On the other hand, if a large share of the current account holders holds the current account then fluctuations in the amount withdrawn will be lesser.

- **Magnitude of Secondary Reserves:** The amount of Working Reserve is also influenced by the size of the Secondary Reserve consisting of highly liquid earning assets. Banks maintaining greater amount of Secondary Reserves can carry lesser amount of cash as Secondary Reserves can be utilized to meet liquidity needs.

4.1.4 Primary Reserves of SBI Group and PNB

The constituents of Primary reserves as maintained by SBI Group and PNB are summarized in Table 4.1.

Table 4.1Trends in Primary Reserves of SBI Group & PNB

(Amount in Rs. crores)

Year	SBI Group			PNB		
	Cash & Balance with RBI in Current Account	Balance with other banks in Current Account	Primary reserves as %age of Total Deposit	Cash & Balance with RBI in Current Account	Balance with Other Banks in Current Account	Primary Reserves As%age of Total Deposit
1985	4,966 (93.67)	342 (6.33)	14.83	900 (99.89)	1 (0.11)	13.78
1995-96	21,398 (90.72)	2,189 (9.28)	18.40	4,350 (92.85)	335 (7.15)	17.27
2006-07	44,827 (83.27)	9,006 (16.73)	8.49	12,372 (90.46)	1,304 (9.54)	9.77
Average Rate			14.36			14.17
Trend GR Period I	15.22	12.39	0.52	14.33	58.15	-0.35
Period II	5.26	9.32	-8.50	12.93	14.06	-2.69
Period I&II	8.52	23.76	-4.54	12.19	26.61	-1.96
C.V.	49.93	105.00	34.53	95.64	90.93	21.47
T- value	10.15*	5.64*	5.35*	5.27*	12.68*	2.67*

Source : Performance Highlights of Public and Private Sector Banks, IBA Mumbai, Various Issues.**Note**: GR implies growth rate and* denotes significance at five percent level in tables.

It also relates Primary Reserves to Deposits. The growth rate for Cash and balance with RBI and Balance with other banks in current account has reduced after the reforms for both the Public Sector Banks probably due to aggressive investment activities followed by the banks as an aftermath of reforms.

(a)Cash and Balance with RBI of SBI Group and PNB

Cash and balance with RBI have constituted the major chunk

in primary reserves for both the Public Sector Banks. Initially, the share of Cash and balance with RBI was 93.67% for SBI Group and 99.89% for PNB in 1985.The share declined gradually from 90.72% and 92.85% in 1995-96 to 83.27% and 90.46% in 2006-07 for SBI Group and PNB respectively. The rise in Cash and balance with RBI and Balance with other banks in current account, in absolute terms, have been significant (at five per cent level) for both the banks.

During period I, from 1985 to 1994-95, the rise in Cash and balance with RBI in current account (as depicted by its trend growth rate) has been slightly higher for SBI Group (15.22) as compared to that of PNB, the growth rate has been lower (14.33). However, Trend Growth Rate of PNB(12.93) has been greater than that of SBI Group(5.26) during Period II, i.e. the post-reforms period(1995-96 to 2006-07).If we compare the overall trend growth rate of the two Public Sector Banks i.e.from1985 to 2006-07,then the growth rate of PNB has been greater (12.19)than that of SBI Group (8.52).The growth rate has come down after the reforms for both the Public Sector Banks probably due to aggressive lending activities followed by the banks as an aftermath of reforms.

The rise in Cash and balance with RBI in current account for has been more sporadic for PNB (95.64%) than that of SBI Group(49.93%) as shown by the Coefficient of Variation.

(b)Balance with other banks of SBI Group and PNB

Balance with other banks in current account has increased from 6.33% in 1985 to 9.28% in 1995-96 for SBI Group and from 0.11% to 7.15% for PNB during the same period. It further rose to 16.73% for SBI Group and 9.54% for PNB in 2006-07.

During period I, from 1985 to 1994-95, the rise in Balance with other banks in current account has been quite greater (as depicted by its trend growth rate) for PNB (58.15),as compared to

106

that of SBI Group (12.39). However, during Period II i.e. the post-reforms period (1995-96 to 2006-07) the trend growth rate has been higher for PNB (14.06) than that of SBI Group (9.32). If we compare the overall trend growth rates of the two Public Sector Banks i.e.from1985 to 2006-07,then the growth rate of PNB has been greater (26.61), while that of SBI Group has been lower (23.76). The rise in Balance with other banks in current account for SBI Group has been more sporadic as shown by its Coefficient of Variation (105.00%) than that for PNB (90.93%). The rise in Balance with other banks in current account, in absolute terms, has been significant for both the banks, at five per cent level of significance.

(c)Primary Reserves as Percentage of Total Deposits of SBI Group and PNB

The proportion of primary reserves in the total deposits increased from 14.83% in 1985 to 18.40% in 1995-96 for SBI Group and from13.78% to 17.27% for PNB during the same period. However, of late, the ratio declined to 8.49% for SBI Group and 9.77% for PNB in 2006-07.On an average, the proportion of primary reserves in the total deposits has been 14.36% for SBI Group and 14.17% for PNB. The decline in the proportion of primary reserves in the total deposits has been significant for SBI Group only.

During period I, from 1985 to 1994-95, the this ratio declined for PNB (-0.35), while for SBI Group, the growth rate has been higher(0.52). However, SBI Group showed greater decline(-8.50) than PNB (-2.69)during Period II i.e. the post-reforms period(1995-96 to 2006-07).If we compare the overall trend growth rates of both the selected Public Sector Banks, i.e.from1985 to 2006-07,then the rate of decline for SBI Group has been greater (-4.54) than that of PNB(-1.96).The decline in ratio of Primary Reserves to total deposits for SBI Group has been more spontaneous as shown by its Coefficient of Variation(34.53%) than that of PNB (21.47%).

Table 4.2 summarizes the constituents of Primary reserves as maintained by the two Private Sector Banks viz. ICICI Bank and CBoP along with the ratio of Primary Reserves to total Deposits.

4.1.5 Primary Reserves of ICICI Bank and CBoP

(a)Cash and Balance with RBI in Current Account of ICICI Bank and CBoP

Cash and balance with RBI in current account have increased significantly (at 5% level of significance) for both the Private Sector Banks under study.

Table 4.2: Trends in Primary Reserves of ICICI Bank & CBoP

(Amount in Rs. crores)

	ICICI Bank			CBoP		
Year	Cash & Balance with RBI in Current Account	Balance with Other Banks in Current Account	Primary reserves as %age of Total Deposit	Cash & Balance with RBI in Current Account	Balance with Other Banks in Current Account	Primary Reserves as %age of Total Deposit
1995-96	104 (86.67)	16 (13.33)	16.48	46 (57.50)	40 (42.50)	30.93
2006-07	18,707 (55.41)	15,056 (44.59)	14.65	1,07 (76.52)	331 (23.47)	9.48
Average Rate			12.68			14.28
Trend GR Period II	59.42	95.05	-1.51	23.61	32.26	-6.19
C.V.	133.68	152.86	21.83	85.43	67.89	40.63
T-value	4.88*	3.81*	0.78	4.52*	5.86*	2.72*

Source : Performance Highlights of Public and Private Sector Banks, IBA Mumbai, various issues.

During period II, from 1995-96 to 2006-07,the rise in Cash and balance with RBI in current account (as depicted by its trend growth rate) has been greater for ICICI Bank (59.42) than that of CBoP, (23.61). The share of Cash and balance with RBI in current account for ICICI Bank has decreased from 86.67% in 1995-96 to 55.41% in 2006-07, while it has increased from 57.50% to 76.52% for CBoP during the same period. The rise in Cash and balance with RBI in current account has been significant for both the Private Sector Banks under study, at five per cent level of significance. The growth has been more volatile for ICICI Bank, as indicated by its Coefficient of Variation (133.68%) than that of CBoP (85.43%).On an average, the proportion of primary reserves in total deposits has been higher for CBoP, i.e. 14.28% than that of ICICI Bank, i.e.12.68%, while the reduction in this ratio has not been significant for both the Private Sector Banks under study.

(b)Balance with other banks in current account of ICICI Bank and CBoP

The other component of Primary Reserves i.e. Balance with other banks in current account has also increased significantly at five percent level of significance, for both the Private Sector Banks under study. During period II, ICICI Bank had higher Trend Growth Rate (95.05) than that of CBoP (32.26). The rise in Balance with other banks in current account for ICICI Bank has been more sporadic as shown by its Coefficient of Variation (152.86%) than that of CBoP (67.89%). The rise in Balance with other banks in current account, in absolute terms, has been significant for both the Private Sector Banks under study, at five percent level of significance.

(c)Ratio of Primary reserves to total deposits of ICICI Bank and CBoP

Among the two Private Sector Banks, the ratio of Primary

reserves to total deposits has decreased for both the selected private sector banks. For ICICI Bank the ratio decreased from 16.48% in 1995-96 to 14.65% in 2006-07. For CBoP , this ratio reduced from 30.93% in 1995-96 to a mere 9.48% in 2006-07.

During period II, the decline in this ratio has been greater for CBoP (-6.19) than that of ICICI Bank(-1.51) i.e. from 1995-96 to 2006-07.The decline in ratio of Primary Reserves to total deposits for CBoP has been more sporadic as shown by its Coefficient of Variation (40.63%) as compared to the ratio of ICICI Bank (21.83%).

4.1.2 TRENDS IN SECONDARY RESERVES

The aggregate of highly liquid earning assets is designated as the Secondary Reserves in the banking circles. The main objective of holding the Secondary Reserves is to impart adequate liquidity to funds without adversely affecting the profitability of the bank. The assets that make up this reserve are found in the securities investment portfolio usually and in the loan accounts in some instances. Secondary Reserves act as second line of defence as they can be utilized to augment the primary reserves in times of need. Moreover, these reserves help banks to maintain a proper trade-off between liquidity and profitability.

4.2.1 Constituents of Secondary Reserves

(1)Call loans to stock broker and Commercial Banks;

(2)Short-term loans secured against self-liquidating assets or blue chips;

(3)Short-term loans to Commercial Banks;

(4)Investment in Treasury Bills;

(5)Promissory notes of short-period maturity;

(6)Balance with other banks in Demand Deposits;

()7Discounting of usance bills eligible for rediscounting from the

RBI; and

(8)Short-period Debentures of   highly credit worthy companies.

4.2.2 Trends in   Secondary Reserves of SBI Group

All the constituents of Secondary Reserves of SBI Group have recorded a significant rise (at five per cent level) as shown in Table 4.3.

Table 4.3: Trends in Secondary Reserves of SBI Group

(Amount in Rs. crores)

Year	Money at call & short notice and Balance with Banks	Bills discounted & Purchased	CC, OD & Loans Payable on demand	Govt Securities	Debentures & Bonds	Secondary Reserves as %age of total deposits
1985	1,301 (4.73)	1384 (5.03)	19,985 (7.27)	4,487 (16.32)	329 (1.19)	76.81
1995-96	11,329 (10.83)	10,043 (9.59)	49,689 (47.49)	39,385 (37.64)	4,124 (3.94)	89.307
2006-07	29,111 (6.70)	37,087 (8.54)	1,80,696 (41.59)	1,77,455 (40.84)	10,119 (2.34)	68.58
Trend GR Period I	13.70	22.87	7.45	26.06	26.41	2.62
Period II	5.13	14.18	11.16	18.23	9.72	-1.68
Period I&II	21.62	15.2	9.55	21.07	22.24	.17
C.V.	91.80	83.92	63.54	97.86	94.05	13.14
T- value	6.73*	10.36*	9.99*	10.49*	6.37*	0.12
Average rate						86.99

Source: Performance Highlights of Public and Private Sector Banks, IBA Mumbai,Various Issues.

The share of Money at call and short notice and balance with banks   increased from 4.73% in 1985 to 10.83% in 1995-96   for SBI Group, but later on declined to 6.70%   in 2006-07. The share of Bills discounted and Purchased   increased from 5.03% in 1985 to 9.59% in 1995-96, but later on declined to 8.54%   in 2006-07.

The share of Cash Credit, Overdraft & Loans Payable on demand increased from 7.27% in 1985 to 47.49% in 1995-96, but later on declined to 41.59% in 2006-07. The share of Government Securities increased from 16.32% in 1985 to 37.64% in 1995-96, and this rising trend continued, with the share increasing to 40.84% in 2006-07. The share of Debentures and bonds in Secondary Reserves Securities increased from 1.19% in 1985 to 3.94% in 1995-96, but later on, the share reduced to 2.34% in 2006-07. The ratio of Secondary Reserves as percentage of total deposits was 76.81% in 1985, which increased to 89.37% in 1995-96.However,it later decreased to 68.58% in 2006-07. The growth has been most volatile for Government Securities(97.86%),followed by Debentures and bonds(94.05%),Money at call and short notice and balance with banks(91.80%),Bills discounted and Purchased(83.92%) and Cash Credit, Overdraft & Loans payable on demand (63.54%).

4.2.3 Trends in Secondary Reserves of PNB

All the constituents of Secondary Reserves of PNB have recorded a significant rise (at 5% cent level) as depicted in Table 4.4. The share of Money at call and short notice and balance with banks decreased from 2.19% in 1985 to 1.98% in 1995-96 for PNB, but later on increased to 3.56% in 2006-07. The share of Bills discounted and Purchased increased from 7.01% in 1985 to 13.72% in 1995-96, but later on declined to 5.03% in 2006-07.

Table 4.4: Trends in Secondary Reserves of PNB

(Amount in Rs. crores)

Year	Money at call& short notice and Balance with Banks	Bills discounted& Purchased	CC, OD & Loans Payable on demand	Govt Securities	Debentures & Bonds	Secondary Reserves as %age of deposits
1985	104 (2.19)	336 (7.01)	3,023 (63.55)	1,290 (27.12)	4 (.08)	75.35
1995-96	367 (1.98)	1,379 (13.72)	8,210 (44.49)	7,538 (40.85)	1,047 (5.68)	68.366
2006-07	3,274 (3.56)	4,631 (5.03)	43,161 (46.91)	36,631 (38.81)	4,305 (4.68)	65.78
Trend GRPeriod I	15.26	17.76	11.75	18.99	81.31	0.43
Period II	15.91	12.32	16.03	17.20	14.52	-0.01
Period I&II	17.85	10.55	13.13	18.29	32.01	0.26
C.V.	99.03	63.09	84.96	94.89	93.29	7.83
T- value	6.99*	11.19*	8.68*	10.63*	11.18*	0.90
Average Rate						70.79

Source : Performance Highlights of Public Sector Banks and Private Sector Banks, IBA Mumbai,Various Issues.

The share of Cash Credit, Overdraft & Loans Payable on demand decreased from 63.55% in 1985 to 44.49% in 1995-96, but later increased to 46.91% in 2006-07. The share of Government Securities increased from 27.12% in 1985 to 40.85% in 1995-96, but later on , the share decreased to 38.81% in 2006-07. The share of Debentures and bonds in Secondary Reserves increased from 0.08% in 1985 to 5.68% in 1995-96, but later on, the share decreased to 4.68% in 2006-07.

The ratio of Secondary Reserves as percentage of total deposits was 75.35% in 1985, which decreased to 68.36% in 1995-96.It further decreased to 65.78% in 2006-07.

The growth has been most volatile Money at call and short notice and balance with banks(99.03%),followed by Government Securities(94.89%), Debentures and bonds(93.29%), Cash Credit, Overdraft & Loans payable on demand (84.96%) and Bills discounted and Purchased (63.09%).

4.2.4 Trends in Secondary Reserves of ICICI Bank

All the constituents of Secondary Reserves of ICICI Bank have recorded a significant rise (at five per cent level), except Debentures and bonds as given in Table 4.5.

Table 4.5 : Trends in Secondary Reserves of ICICI Bank

(Amount in Rs. crores)

Year	Money at call & short notice and Balance with Banks	Bills discount ed & Purchase d	CC, OD & Loans Payable on demand	Govt Securi ties	Debent ures & Bonds	Seconda ry Reserve s as %age of total deposits
1995-96	59 (34.67)	66 (7.53)	499 (57.03)	174 (19.88)	77 (8.80)	119.866
2006-07	18,414 (13.83)	11,746 (8.82)	32,864 (24.68)	67,665 (50.82)	2,463 (1.85)	57.76
Trend GR Period I	50.76	60.44	44.46	79.44	42.7	-5.44
C.V.	118.81	150.27	136.68	112.64	91.84	29.40
T- value	3.60*	4.83*	4.36*	7.84*	2.13	2.62*
Average Rate						86.45

Source : Performance Highlights of Public and Private Sector Banks, IBA Mumbai,Various Issues.
Note: (i) Figures given in parentheses   denote the percentage   share in secondary reserves.

The share of Money at call & short notice and balance with banks   decreased from 34.67% in 1995-96   to 13.83% in 2006-07 for ICICI Bank. The share of Bills discounted and Purchased increased from 7.53 in 1995-96 to 8.82% in 2006-07. The share of Cash Credit, Overdraft & Loans payable on demand   decreased from

114

57.03% in 1995-96 to 24.68% in   2006-07.

The share of Government Securities increased from 19.88% in1995-96 to 50.82% in 2006-07. The share of Debentures and bonds in Secondary Reserves, however, decreased from 8.80% in 1995-96 to 1.85% in 2006-07.

The ratio of Secondary Reserves as percentage   of total deposits   was   119.86% in1995-96, which decreased to 57.76% in 2006-07.

The growth has been most volatile for Bills discounted and Purchased (150.27%), followed by Cash Credit, Overdraft & Loans Payable on demand (136.68%), Money at call & short notice and balance with banks(118.81%), Government Securities(112.64%), Debentures and bonds(91.84%).

4.6 Trends in   Secondary Reserves of CBoP

All the constituents of Secondary Reserves of CBoP have recorded significant rise (at five per cent level), except Debentures and bonds and Bills Purchased and   Discounted, as given in Table 4.6. The share of Money at call & short notice and balance with banks decreased from 20.13% in 1995-96   to 5.56% in2006-07 for CBoP. The share of Bills discounted and purchased increased from 17.53 in 1995-96 to 33.11% in 2006-07. The share of Cash Credit, Overdraft & Loans Payable on demand   increased from 33.12% in 1995-96 to 36.80% in   2006-07. The share of Government Securities increased substantially from 16.56% in1995-96 to 54.10% in 2006-07. The share of Debentures and Bonds in secondary reserves, however, decreased drastically   from 12.66% in 1995-96 to 2.83% in 2006-07.

Table 4.6: Trends in Secondary Reserves of CBoP

(Amount in Rs. Crores)

Year	Money at call & short notice and Balance with Banks	Bills discounted & Purchased	CC, OD & Loans payable on demand	Govt. Securities	Debentures & Bonds	Secondary Reserves as %age of total deposits
1995-96	62 (20.13)	54 (17.53)	102 (33.12)	51 (16.56)	39 (12.66)	110.799
2006-07	410 (5.56)	244 (33.11)	2,712 (36.80)	3,977 (54.10)	26 (2.83)	49.57
Period II	20.26	4.66	27.98	33.16	-12.33	-6.83
C.V.	75.24	42.83	93.31	95.92	71.56	26.55
T-value	5.13*	1.06	4.71*	4.87*	1.52	11.81*
Average Rate						71.40

Source: Performance Highlights of Public and Private Sector Banks, IBA Mumbai,Various Issues.

The ratio of Secondary Reserves as percentage of total deposits was 110.79% in1995-96, which decreased significantly (at five per cent level) to 49.57% in 2006-07.

The growth has been most volatile for Government Securities(95.92%),followed by Cash Credit, Overdraft & Loans Payable on demand (93.31%),   Money at call and short notice and balance with banks(75.24%), Debentures and bonds(71.56) and Bills discounted and purchased (42.83%).

Thus, for all the four banks under study, Government securities form the major chunk of investments in Secondary Reserves. This is due to the fact that RBI regulations require banks to hold a high proportion of assets as government securities to comply with the statutory liquidity ratio (SLR) requirement. Moreover, reforms in the Government securities market viz. the transition to market-related interest rates and reduction in SLR requirement; establishment of a

Delivery versus Payment system, to reduce settlement risk, institution of the system of Primary Dealers and formation of market bodies such as Fixed Income Money Market and Derivatives Association of India(FIMMDAI)and Primary Dealers Association of India(PDAI); establishment of the Clearing Corporation of India Ltd. for providing an efficient and guaranteed settlement platform; introduction of Over the Counter Exchange(OTC) and introduction of trading of Government securities in stock exchanges, have all been responsible for the dominance of Government Securities in the investment portfolio of the four banks under study.

SBI Group and PNB have registered significant rises in all the constituents of Secondary Reserves. Debentures and bonds however , did not record a significant rise for both the selected Private Sector Banks. The trend growth rate of Debentures and bonds has reduced after the reforms for both SBI Group and PNB due to lack of development of corporate debt market. The secondary market has not developed commensurately and market liquidity remains an issue.

CBoP has been exceptional as its Bills discounted and purchased did not increase significantly for it. The ratio of Secondary Reserves as percentage of total deposits has declined for all the four banks under study, though the decline has been significant for ICICI Bank and CBoP.

The shortest planning horizon, that commercial banks face is the one associated with Reserve Position Management. As far as primary reserves are concerned, SBI Group, on an average has maintained the maximum amount as percentage of total deposit (14.36%) followed by CBoP(14.28%) PNB (14.17%), and ICICI Bank (12.68%).

However, Secondary Reserves present a different picture.

Secondary Reserves as a percentage of total deposits on an average, have been maximum for SBI Group (86.99%), followed by ICICI Bank (86.45%) CBoP (71.40%) and PNB (70.79%). PNB needs to be cautious about its Secondary Reserves. ICICI Bank is in a dubious position of having maximum Secondary Reserves and minimum Primary Reserves.

4.2 INVESTMENT MANAGEMENT

The foremost concern of a bank is to ensure its liquidity by maintaining adequate primary and secondary reserves. Investment is, thus, residual in nature. It includes gilt-edged securities and stock exchange securities as well as shares and debentures of blue-chip companies. The composition of investment account and secondary reserve account is broadly similar except that investment account includes long-term securities. Due to this fact, investments in a commercial bank include both the secondary reserve and investment account.

After meeting the liquidity requirements by keeping primary and secondary reserves and after satisfying the genuine credit needs of society, the residue left is invested by banks to acquire long-term obligations of public and private enterprises in order to improve their own earnings(Patheja,1994).

4.2.1 Importance of Investment Management in Commercial Banks in India

The economic reforms brought about deregulation, decontrol, globalization and integration of domestic financial markets to international markets, thereby increasing the complexity of risk tremendously. Apart from the traditional credit risk, banks are now faced with market risk due to fluctuations in interest rates. The multiplicity of innovative instruments for investments has made investment decisions very complex. Again, with a large part of the securities portfolio now subject to 'mark to market' valuations for compiling accounts, banks' bottom lines are vulnerable to changing interest rates and on this score as well i.e. over and above the fluctuation in the net interest margin(Rajwade,2002). The introduction of Capital Adequacy Norms required banks to maintain certain amount of capital to back their assets risks. Moreover, the Public Sector Banks have been granted permission to raise their capital from capital markets. Marketing of government securities and introduction of capital adequacy norms requiring banks to maintain certain amount of capital to back their assets risks have made security investment management all the more crucial for banks. Thus, investment management in a bank needs to be planned cautiously and judiciously.

4.2.2 Classification of Investment Portfolio of the Banks

The entire investment portfolio of the banks including (SLR securities and non-SLR securities should be classified under three categories:

(a)Available for Sale,

(b)Held for Trading,

(c)Held to Maturity.

(a)Available for Sale & Held for Trading

(i) The securities acquired by the banks with the intention to trade by taking advantage of the short-term price/interest rate movements will be classified under 'Held for Trading'.

(ii) The securities which do not fall within the above two categories will be classified under 'Available for Sale'.

(iii) The bank will have freedom to decide on the extent of holdings under 'Available for sale' and 'Held for Trading' categories. This will be decided by them after considering various aspects such as basis of intent, trading strategies, risk management capabilities, tax planning, manpower skills, capital position.

(b) 'Held for Trading': The investments classified under this category would be those from, which the bank expects to make a gain by the movement in interest rates/market rates. These securities are to be sold within 90 days.

(c)Held To Maturity: The securities acquired by the banks with the intention to hold them up to maturity will be classified under 'Held To Maturity.'

4.3.3 Investment Fluctuation Reserve (IFR)

With a view to building up of adequate reserves to guard against any possible reversal of interest rate environment in future due to unexpected developments, banks have been advised to build up IFR of a minimum of 5 per cent of the investment portfolio within 5 years is met by the securities acquired under purchase contract.

However, in the balance-sheet, the investments will continue to be disclosed as per the classifications viz.

Government Securities,

Approved securities

Shares

Debentures & bonds

Subsidiaries/JointVentures

Banks should decide the category of investment at the time of acquisition and the decision should be recorded on the investment proposals.

4.2.4 Composition of Investment Portfolio of Indian Commercial Banks

(1) Government Securities: These securities include treasury bills of Central and State Government. These securities are most preferred due to safety of principal and regularity of interest payment. The government securities are usually of short-term duration. Government securities are generally either tax-free or liberal rebate is allowed by the Government

(2)Trustee Securities: Securities of Municipalities, port trustees, improvement trustees are included in this category. These securities are less attractive as compared to Central and State Government securities but are equally safe, profitable and secured as:

(i) Semi-Government authorities or trustees own properties which are efficiently   managed by them.

(ii)   Representatives   of   Government   and   commercial organizations are also   nominated to   the executive committee of these bodies.

(iii)Legislative protection is provided to these bodies by respective State Government.

(iv)These bodies enjoy public confidence. Certain limitations are attached with   trustees securities.

(a)Some of the Electricity Boards/ Corporations are irregular in making interest payment in time.

(b)Most of these are not quoted in stock market, thereby restricting its marketability.

Income-tax is also deductible on interest (except in infrastructural bonds which is refunded after several years).

(3) Shares and Debentures of Joint Stock Companies: Shares of reputed joint stock companies provide an attractive avenue for investment.

(4) Other Investments : Apart from the discussed investments, banks have other investment alternatives also.

4.2.5 Trends in Investments of SBI Group

Government securities have been the most preferred form of Investment (as shown in Table 4.7) due to their marketability and regularity of income. Tax exemption or rebate on Government securities makes them even more lucrative for investment.

Over these years the share of investment of SBI Group has been increasing in Government Securities from 58.58% in 1985 to 70.80% in 1995-96 with a trend growth rate of 26.06 due to reforms in the Government securities market.

Table 4.7: Trends in Investments of SBI Group

(Amount in Rs. Crore)

Year	Govt. Securit ies	Other Approv ed Securiti es	Shares	Debent ures& bonds	Subsid iaries & Joint Ventur e	Others
1985	4487 (58.58)	2,631 (34.35)	14 (0.18)	29 (4.29)	53 (0.69)	146 (1.91)
1995-96	39385 (70.80)	9,735 (17.50)	492 (0.88)	4124 (7.41)	789 (1.42)	1,102 (1.98)
2006-07	177455 (83.84)	4,093 (1.93)	2,706 (1.28)	10,119 (4.78)	2,615 (1.23)	14,676 (6.93)
Trend GR Period I	26.06	13.86	35.87	26.41	17.24	31.24
Period II	18.23	-8.10	11.69	11.43	9.59	20.47
Period I&II	21.07	0	28.62	21.78	22.15	27.51
C.V.	97.86	31.40	101.04	94.05	91.23	110.28
T- value	10.49*	0.25	10.20*	7.99*	12.81*	8.88*

Source : Performance Highlights of Public Sector Banks and Private Sector Banks, IBA ,Mumbai,Various Issues.
Note: (i)Figures in parentheses denote percentage share in total investments.

The share further increased to 83.84% with a trend growth rate of 18.23 in 2006-07. Thus, there has been maximum investment has been in government securities every year. The share in investment in other approved securities has been on the decline from 34.35% in 1985 to 17.50% in 1995-96 with a trend growth rate of 13.86. During the post-reforms period, i.e. from 1995-96 to 2006-07, this share further declined to 1.93% in 2006-07 showing a negative trend growth rate of -8.10.

The share of investment in shares of joint stock companies increased from 0.18% in 1985 to 0.88% in 1995-96 with a trend

122

growth rate of 35.87.Later on, the share further rose to 1.28% in 2006-07 with a trend growth rate of 11.69 for SBI Group. The share of Debentures and Bonds increased from 4.29% in 1985 to 7.41% in 1995-96 with a trend growth rate of 26.41.Later on, the share decreased to 4.78% in 2006-07 with a trend growth rate of 11.43 for SBI Group. Investment in Subsidiaries and/or Joint Ventures increased marginally from 0.69% in 1985 to 1.42% in 1995-96(trend growth rate 17.24).However, the share later dropped to 1.23% in 2006-07 with a trend growth rate of 9.59. Other investments held by SBI Group increased from 1.91% in 1985 to 1.98% in 1995-96 with a trend growth rate of 31.24.Later on, the share of other investments further increased substantially to 6.93% in 2006-07 with a trend growth rate of 20.47. All the sources of investment have increased significantly (at five percent level) for SBI Group, except investment in other approved securities.

The variability in the growth has been maximum for Other investments as indicated by its Coefficient of Variation (110.28%),followed by shares(101.04%), Government Securities (97.86%), Debentures and bonds(94.05%).

4.2.6 Trends in Investments of PNB

The share of Government Securities in the investment portfolio has been on the rise from 55.22% in the year 1985 to 63.15% in 1995-96 with a trend growth rate of 18.99 for PNB. Later on, the share increased to 81.06% in 2006-07 with a trend growth rate of 17.20.

Table 4.8: Trends in   Investments of PNB

(Amount in Rs. Crores)

Year	Govt. Securities	Other Approved Securities	Shares	Debentures & Bonds	Subsidiaries & Joint Venture Bonds	Others
1985	1,290 (55.22)	913 (39.08)	3 (0.13)	4 (0.17)	Nil	126 (5.39)
1995-96	7,538 (63.15)	3032 (25.40)	69 (0.58)	1,047 (8.77)	80 (0.67)	170 (1.42)
2006-07	36,631 (81.06)	990 (2.19)	755 (1.67)	4,305 (9.53)	538 (1.19)	1,970 (4.36)
Trend GR Period I	18.99	15.19	39.01	81.05	27.29	17.78
Period II	17.20	-7.88	20.45	14.51	13.09	18.31
Period I&II	18.29	1.48	31.94	31.95	19.37	13.76
C.V.	94.89	33.65	115.63	93.25	74.23	136.28
T- value	10.63*	1.04	8.16*	11.18*	8.82*	3.47*

Source : Performance Highlights of Public Sector Banks and Private Sector Banks, IBA Mumbai,Various Issues.

Note: (i)Figures in parentheses denote percentage share in total investments.

On the contrary, the investments in other approved securities have been on the decline, from 39.08% in the year 1985 to   25.40% in 1995-96 with a trend growth rate of 15.19.

Again,   the   share   of other approved securities   reduced drastically to 2.19% in   2006-07 showing a negative trend growth rate of -7.88 for PNB. The investments in shares of joint stock companies   rose slightly from 0.13% in the year 1985 to 0.58% in 1995-96 with   a   trend growth rate of   39.01, but later increased substantially   to 1.67% in 2006-07 with   a   trend growth rate of 20.45.

Investments in debentures and bonds has shown a dramatic increase from 0.17% in the year 1985 to 8.77%   in 1995-96 with a trend growth rate of 81.05.These investments increased to 9.53% in

124

2006-07 with a trend growth rate of 14.51.

The investments in Subsidiaries and joint ventures have been rather constant, with mild variations during the period under study. The share in Subsidiaries and joint ventures increased from 0.67% in 1995-96 to 1.19% in 2006-07 with a trend growth rate of 13.09.

Investments in other sources increased initially, from 5.39% in the year 1985 to 1.42% in 1995-96 with a trend growth rate of 17.78.Later on, it increased to 4.36% in 2006-07 with a trend growth rate of 18.31. Thus, all the sources of investment have increased significantly at five per cent level for PNB, except investments in other approved securities.

The variability in the growth has been maximum for Other investments as indicated by its Coefficient of Variation (136.28%),followed by shares(115.63%), Government Securities (94.89%), Debentures and bonds(93.25%),Subsidiaries and joint ventures(74.23%)andthe least for Other approved securities(33.65%).

4.2.7 Trends in Investments of ICICI Bank

The investments of ICICI Bank in Government Securities have been maximum every year and their share in the investment portfolio has increased from 66.41% in 1995-96 to 74.15% in 2006-07 with a trend growth rate of 79.44.

The investments in other approved securities have been negligible and hence, trend growth rate could not be computed. The investments in shares of blue-chip companies have declined from 3.43% in 1995-96 to 2.12% in 2006-07 with a trend growth rate of 72.05.

Table 4.9: Trends in Investments of ICICI Bank

(Amount in Rs. crores)

Year	Govt Securities	Other Approved Securities	Shares	Debentures & Bonds	Subsidiaries & Joint ventures	Others
1995-96	174 (66.41)	-	9 (3.43)	77 (29.39)	-	2 (0.76)
2006-07	67,665 (74.15)		1,937 (2.12)	2,463 (2.69)	4,072 (4.46)	15,121 (16.57)
Trend GR Period I	-	-	-	-	-	-
Period II	79.44	-	72.05	42.70	48.16	104.50
Period I&II		-			-	
C.V.	112.64	137.11	96.41	91.84	138.36	130.39
T- value	7.86*	0.87	6.50*	2.13	5.86*	5.77*

Source : Performance Highlights of Public and Private Sector Banks,
IBA, Mumbai,various issues.
Note: (i)Figures in parentheses denote percentage share in total investments.

The share of Debentures & bonds has shown a drastic reduction from 29.39% in 1995-96 to 2.69% in 2006-07 with a trend growth rate of 42.70. The proportion invested in shares though decreased from 3.43% in 1995-96 to 2.12% in 2006-07.

The share of investments in subsidiaries and joint ventures was 4.46% in 2006-07. The share of investments in Other sources of investment has also increased e from 0.76% in 1995-96 to 16.57% in 2006-07.

The investments in Shares, Government securiries and Subsidiaries &Joint Ventures increased significantly at five per cent level. The variability in the growth has been maximum for Subsidiaries and joint ventures as indicated by its Coefficient of Variation(138.36%),followed by Other approved securities(137.11%),Other investments(130.39%), Government

126

Securities (112.64%),Shares(96.41%)and least for Debentures and bonds(91.84%).

4.2.8 Trends in Investments of CBoP

The investments of CBoP have been maximum in government securities like the other three banks under study as shown in Table 4.10.The share of investments in government securities has registered a steep increase from 56.67% in 1995-96 to a staggering 85.86% in 2006-07 with a trend growth rate of 33.06. On the contrary, the investments in debentures and bonds witnessed a decline from 43.33% in 1995-96 to a minimal 0.56% in 2006-07 showing a negative trend growth rate of -12.32.

Table 4.10: Trends in Investments of CBoP

(Amount in Rs. Crores)

Year	Govt. Securities	Other Approved Securities	Shares	Debenture & Bonds	Subsidiaries & Joint enventure Bonds	Others
1995-96	51 (56.67)	-	-	39 (43.33)	-	-
2006-07	3,977 (85.86)		24 (0.52)	26 (0.56)		605 (13.06)
Trend GR Period I	-	-	-	-	-	-
Period II	33.06	-	-2.11	-12.32	-	29.23
Period I&II		-	-		-	-
C.V.	93.75	-	68.02	71.51	-	129.23
T value	4.92*	-	0.25	1.52	-	5.38*

Source : Performance Highlights of Public and Private Sector Banks, IBA Mumbai, various issues.
Note: (i) Figures in parentheses denote percentage share in total investments.

The investment in shares also declined from 1.53% in 1995-96 to 0.52% in 2006-07 showing a negative trend growth rate of -2.11. Investments in other sources increased appreciably from 3.35% in

1995-96 to 13.06% in 2006-07 with a trend growth rate of 5.38.

The rise in investments in Government securities and other sources has been significant (at five per cent level) for CBoP. The bank has not made significant investments in the other approved securities and Subsidiaries & Joint Venture also have not been explored by CBoP, which need to be examined in the current globalized scenario.

The variability in the growth has been maximum for Other investments as indicated by its Coefficient of Variation (129.23%),followed by Government Securities(93.75%), Debentures and Bonds(71.51%) and the least for Shares(68.02%).

Thus, the government securities form a major chunk of the investment portfolio of all the four banks under study. As a part of the financial sector reforms, the SLR requirement of banks was gradually reduced to 25% by 1997 from its peak of 38.50% in February 1992, thus, freeing substantial reserve for investment. Moreover, the industrial sector was undergoing a phase of restructuring, reduced its demand for credit, forced banks to invest their funds in government securities. Incidentally, the period of low demand for credit coincided with the application of Capital Adequacy norms, which required banks to maintain 8% of their risk-weighted assets as capital from March 31, 1996. Consequently, investments in Government and other approved securities, which attracted zero-risk weights, became the preferred form of investments by banks.

The investments in debentures have increased significantly for both the selected Public Sector Banks, while its share has reduced substantially for their Private Sector counterparts. This is due to the lack of development of the corporate bond market. The secondary market has not developed commensurately and market liquidity remains an issue.

Investment-Asset Ratio

Investment-Asset Ratio and investment-deposit ratio are the commonly used indicators of the investment policy of banks. (Investment-Asset Ratio has been analyzed in Chapter 3, Table 3.4.) The Investment-Deposit Ratio has increased significantly (at 5% level of significance) only for SBI Group as given in Table 4.11. The Investment-Deposit ratio has reduced after the reforms for both the Public Sector Banks under study probably due to greater deposit mobilization by the banks in comparison to investment.

Table 4.11:   Investment- Deposit Ratio

Year	SBI Group	ICICI Bank	PNB	CBoP
1985	21.41	-	37.00	-
1995-96	43.31	35.99	44.01	32.37
2006-07	33.41	39.58	32.31	31.16
Trend GR Period I	7.10	-	3.07	-
Period II	0.18	2.97	-1.81	-3.58
Period I&II	2.40	-	0.55	-
C.V.	20.91	40.95	11.65	20.56
T-value	4.16*	0.79	1.54	2.63
Average	42.12	52.64	42.06	41.51

Source : Performance Highlights of Public and Private Sector Banks, IBA, Mumbai,Various Issues.

During period I, from 1985 to 1994-95, the growth in this ratio has been greater for SBI Group (7.10) than that of PNB(3.07). However, ICICI Bank has shown maximum rise as depicted in its Trend Growth Rate (2.97), followed by SBI Group(0.18). Both PNB and CBoP have suffered decline as indicated by their negative growth rate (-1.81) and (-3.58) respectively during Period II, i.e. the post-reforms period (1995-96 to 2006-07).If we compare the overall trend growth rates of both the selected Public Sector Banks i.e.from1985 to 2006-07,then the growth rate has been higher for SBI Group (2.40), than that of PNB (0.55).

The rise in shares of Investment-Deposit Ratio has been most volatile for ICICI Bank as shown by its Coefficient of Variation (40.95%),followed by SBI Group(20.91%), CBoP(20.56%), while the growth has been quite steady for PNB(11.65%).

The increase shows that on an average, the Investment-Deposit Ratio has been maximum for ICICI Bank (52.64%), followed by SBI Group (42.12%), PNB (42.06%) and minimum for CBoP (41.51%).The ratio has increased significantly only for SBI Group.

It is notable that despite the reduced regulatory requirement to invest in government and other securities approved for SLR investment, the major rise in investment operations by banks since the mid-1990s has been due to investment in government securities. It is also possible that in a declining interest rate scenario in the presence of a developing debt market, this was the most obvious strategy.

It can be concluded that all the banks have employed increasing portion of their funds in Government Securities, thereby achieving an optimum balance between profitability and liquidity. As regard investment in shares are concerned, SBI Group and PNB have increased investment in shares, while ICICI Bank has decreased investment in shares. Investment in debentures has reduced over the period for all the selected banks except for PNB due to lack of developed corporate bond market.

4.3   LIQUIDITY MANAGEMENT

Liquidity risk management lies at the heart of confidence in the banking system (Vij,2005). Liquidity, which is represented by the quality and marketability of the assets and liabilities, exposes the firm to liquidity risk(Kumar Ravi,2000). A bank's liquidity risk can arise either from a drain on deposits or from new loan demands, and the subsequent need to meet these demands by liquidating assets or borrowing funds (Cornett and Saunders,1999). Banks need to ensure that they have sufficient liquid assets to both satisfy the Reserve Bank's liquidity requirements as well as meet any unforeseen funding or large withdrawal of deposits(Lucia and Peters,1993).

The bank has three primary sources of liquidity: (1) Its cash-type assets such as Treasury bills can be sold immediately with little price risk and low transaction costs;

(2) The maximum amount of funds it can borrow on the money/purchased funds market (this internal guideline is based on the manager's assessment of the credit limit the purchased or borrowed funds market is likely to impose on the Banks);

(3) Any excess cash reserves over and above those held to meet regulatory imposed reserve requirements (Saunders,2002).

Thus, liquidity management is an inseparable part of funds management. Liquidity management relates primarily to the dependability of cash flows, both inflows and outflows, and the ability of the bank to meet maturing liabilities and customer demands for cash within the basic pricing policy framework.

4.3.1 Sources of Liquidity Risk:- Liquidity problems may arise due to any of the following reasons:

(i)   **Funding Risk:** This risk arises due to failure to replace net outflows of funds due to unanticipated withdrawal or non-renewal of wholesale deposits.

(ii)   **Time Risk:** This risk is the result of non-receipt of expected inflow of funds, eg. where borrowers fail to meet their commitments.

(iii)   **Call Risk:** It is the outcome of crystallization of contingent liabilities and inability to undertake profitable business opportunities when desired.

(iv)   **Opportunity Risk:**Requests for funds from important and valuable customers can only be profitably serviced if adequate liquidity is available.

4.3.2 General Issues in Bank Liquidity Management

The precise character of a bank's liquidity management depends, however, on its business mix and the structure of its balance-sheet, eg. whether it takes deposits from the public, provides committed loan facilities, has an active derivatives business, acts as a dealer providing (and meeting) liquidity in asset markets, or provides payment and settlement services for customers and other banks(Chaplin et al.,2002).

Banks encounter four broad categories of liquidity needs. These are the need to:

(a) Replenish the net outflow of funds either due to withdrawal or non-renewal of deposits;

(b) Compensate for non-receipt of expected inflows due to delayed repayment of loans, etc.

(c) Meet the contingent liabilities arising from invoking of letters of credit and guarantees; and

(d) Profit from new instruments and/or lending to new important clients (Subrahmanyam, 1995).

Asset Liability Management involves examination of all the assets and liabilities simultaneously on a continuous basis with a view to ensuring a proper balance between funds mobilization and their deployment with respect to their maturity, profiles, cost, yield, risk exposure etc (Satyanarayan,2004).To combat liquidity risk, it is mandatory for banks to maintain cash reserves under section 42(1) of the Reserve Bank of India Act, 1934. The Central Bank also undertakes, as the lender of last resort, to supply reserves to banks in times of genuine difficulties.

The bankers usually meet their liquidity needs from the

132

following sources:

(a)Fresh deposits/renewal of deposits,

(b)Maturity of assets/investments,

(c)Call Money Market,

(d)Discount window of RBI,

(e)Refinance facility.

4.3.3 Theories of Liquidity Management

(1) The Commercial Loan Theory: According to this theory, a commercial bank should provide short-term,   self-liquidating loans to business firms to enable them to meet their working capital requirements. The bank should refrain from loaning for long-term purposes to finance plant, equipment, permanent working capital, real estate, consumer durables and speculation. The doctrine was criticized as the character of self-liquidating loans is conditioned by the economic situation in the country. In times of depression, there is no guarantee ,even though the transaction for which the loan was provided, was genuine, that the debtor will be able to repay the debt at maturity.

(2)The Shiftability Theory: According to this theory, the problem of liquidity is not so much a problem of the maturity of loans, but one of shifting the assets to others for cash without material loss. This theory was criticized on the ground that in times of depression, even blue-chip companies lose their shiftability character.

(3)The Anticipated Income Theory: According to this theory, loan repayment schedules have to be adapted to the anticipated income or cash receipts of the borrower. Thus, continuous estimate of the future earnings of the borrowing firm has to be made for the amortization of loans.

(4)The Liabilities Management Theory: Under this approach, the bank tries to achieve the required liquidity by borrowing funds when the need arises. It involves a greater risk for the bank but also fetches higher yields due to the long-term investments. The liabilities management lays down that an individual bank may acquire reserves from several different sources by creating additional liabilities against itself, some of which are:

- Borrowings from the Central Bank;
- Raising capital funds by issuing shares and by means of retained earning.

Allocation Methods: Several approaches to allocating funds to assets have developed over the years,but the following approach is considered to be the most significant.

The Pool of Funds Approach:-

The funds available to the portfolio manager of a commercial bank are derived from numerous sources, including demand deposits, savings deposits, time deposits, and capital funds.

Fig.4(c).POOL OF FUNDS APPROACH

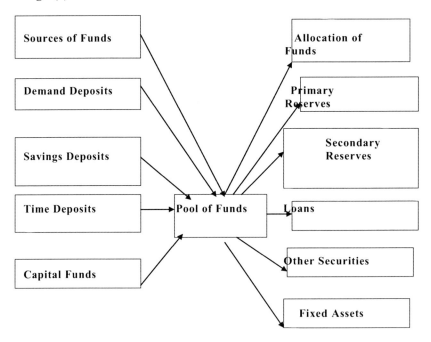

Source : Edward, W. Reed;and Edward, K. Gill.(1989) *Commercial Banking,* Fourth Edition, Prentice Hall, New Jersey,p.121.

The basic idea underlying the approach is that all funds should be pooled together and then funds should be allocated from the pool to whatever asset investment (loans, government securities cash and so on) is appropriate.

Under this approach, bank management has to identify its liquidity and profitability requirements. Allocation is undertaken according to several priorities, which are established to assist management in solving the dilemma between liquidity and profitability.

Cash is the most liquid asset and the ease with which other assets can be converted (through sale or collection) provides the standard of liquidity. Liquidity risk can be reduced by holding large amounts of assets such as cash, treasury bills but at the same time earnings from interest bearing securities have to be sacrificed. By contrast, liquid assets often have to promise additional return or liquidity premiums to compensate a Financial Institution for the relative lack of marketability and often greater default risk of the instrument (Saunders,2002).

Consequently, banks need to determine an optimal level of liquid assets which are sufficient to meet most unexpected situations while at the same time not significantly impairing the overall profit performance of the bank.

4.3.4 RBI's Guidance Note of Liquidity Risk Management

Liquidity risks originate from the mismatches in the maturity pattern of assets and liabilities. By assuring a bank's ability to meet its liabilities as they become due, liquidity management can reduce the probability of an adverse situation developing. Factors to be considered while determining liquidity of the bank's future stock of assets and liabilities include their potential marketability, the extent to which maturing assets/liability will be renewed and the normal growth in asset/liability accounts.

Banks should also evolve a system for monitoring high value deposits (other than inter-bank deposits) say Rs. 1 crore or more to track the volatile liabilities.

GAP Analysis: As a standard tool Banks should have to analyze the behavioral maturity profile of various components of on/off-balance-sheet items on the basis of assumptions and trend analysis supported by time series analysis. Apart from the above cash flows, banks should also track the impact of prepayments of loans, premature closure of deposits and exercise of options built in certain instruments which offer put/call options after specified times.

Within each time bucket there would be mismatches defending on cash inflows and outflows. While the mismatches up to one year would be relevant since these provide early warning signals of impending liquidity problems, the main focus should be on the short-term mismatches viz. 1-14 days and 15-28 days. The mismatch (negative gap) during 1-14 days and 15-28 days in normal course may not exceed 20 percent of cash outflows in each time bucket.

For a given level of Gap position, the bank can take the following positions to improve the Net Interest Income:

- Maintain a positive gap when interest rates are rising.
- Maintain a negative gap when interest rates are declining.
- Maintain a zero gap to completely hedge against any movements in the future interest rates.

A bank may face the following scenario regarding its gap profile in a particular period:

1. If the gap is zero or '1', then this implies that the rate sensitivity of assets is perfectly matched with the rate sensitivity of liabilities. Such a complete match is very rare. Nevertheless, many risk-averse banks make all efforts to achieve as small a gap as possible.

2. If the gap is positive, any increase in the interest rates would mean increase in profit and any decline in interest rates would mean decrease in profits.

3.If the gap is negative, any increase in the interest rates would mean decrease in profits, and any decline in interest rates would mean increase in profits.

4.12 Statement of Structural Liquidity as on 31st March 2000

SBI Group Outflows	1-14 days	15-28 Days	29 days and to 3 months	Over up months 3 and up 6 months	Over 3months and to 1 year	Over 6 up year and up 3 years	1Over years and toup years	5Over 5 years	Total
C as % to A	-4.48	-36.74	-14.11	-30.05	-76.75	-50.47	36.76	854.29	-10.64
D as % to A1	-4.48	-7.73	-9.11	-12.82	-30.67	-41.46	-32.80	-10.64	-10.64
ICICI Bank									
C as % to A	23.90	-5.40	-51.46	-32.45	-63.48	-13.08	3,160	4,550	-5.78
D as % to A1	23.90	12.53	-17.36	-19.88	-26.00	-21.36	-13.69	-5.78	-5.78
PNB									
C as % to A	-87.05	60.51	-20.22	10.23	-62.01	-50.97	2653.33	10466.67	-6.53
D as % to A1	-87.05	-41.69	-29.95	-21.58	-28.21	-35.02	-23.89	-6.53	-6.53
CBoP									
C as % to A	-20.25	45.92	45.37	6.83	9.09	-61.97	559.29	38.39	-7.76
D as % to A1	-20.25	-11.72	1.72	2.97	4.54	-42.38	-27.71	-7.76	-7.76

Source: Performance highlights of Public and Private Sector Banks,IBA Mumbai.(2000-01 to 2006-07)

Note:(i)C stands for Mismatch.

(ii) D for Cumulative Mismatch between Assets and Liabilities.

(iii)A stands for Assets and A1 for Cumulative Assets.

For the year ending 31st March 2000, all the four banks under study have negative gap indicating that they have been liability sensitive shown in Table 4.12. The relative Gap ratios of the four banks are as under.

SBI Group   -10.64%

ICICI Bank   -5.78%

PNB   - 7.76%

CBoP(formerly BoP)   - 6.53%

The banks can maintain a negative gap when the interest rates are declining.

Thus, among the four banks, SBI Group has been most liability sensitive (having maximum negative gap),followed   by PNB,CBoP and ICICI Bank has been least liability sensitive (having least negative gap).ICICI Bank has the maximum Interest rate sensitivity ,followed by CBoP,PNB and SBI Group.

4.13 Statement of Structural Liquidity as on 31st March 2001

SBI Group Outflows	1-14 days	15-28 Days	29 days and up to 3 months	Over 3 months and up to 6 months	Over 6 months and up to 1 year	Over 1 year and up to 3 years	Over 3 years and up to 5 years	Over 5 years	Total
C as % to A	37.46	25.97	46.65	-1.19	-21.61	-51.14	-29.33	102.20	-0.27
D as % to A1	37.46	35.8	38.39	28.78	14.38	-28.12	-28.30	-0.27	-0.27
ICICI Bank									
C as % to A	51.99	-64.52	28.70	-3.51	-54.59	-37.89	342.80	3042.25	-3.63
D as % to A1	51.99	-3.22	10.70	8.05	-5.79	-21.80	v16.31	-3.63	-3.63
PNB									
C as % to A	70.92	-31.46	-28.90	-38.99	-48.45	-58.99	194.51	2,106.44	-6.26
D as % to A1	70.92	-63.32	-51.74	-47.99	-48.13	-54.69	-45.19	-6.26	-6.26
CBoP									
C as % to A	-40.77	20.23	-32.09	-69.18	-71.76	-14.73	200.00	16,340	-9.31
D as % to A1	-40.77	-36.45	-34.26	-43.20	-48.52	-38.84	-29.79	-9.31	-9.31

Source: Performance highlights of Public and Private Sector Banks,IBA Mumbai.(2000-01 to 2006-07)

Note(i)C stands for Mismatch.

(ii) D for Cumulative Mismatch between Assets and Liabilities.

(iii)A stands for Assets and A1 for Cumulative Assets.

For the year ending 31st March 2001, again all the four banks under study have been liability sensitive as they have shown a negative gap as show in Table 4.13.

The relative Gap ratios of the four banks are as under:

SBI Group   -0.27%

ICICI Bank   -3.63%

PNB   -6.26%

CBoP   -9.31%

CBoP has been most liability sensitive,followed by PNB, ICICI Bank and SBI Group. During the year 2000-01 interest rates on deposits and advances declined resulting in the negative gap of all the four banks. A negative gap under falling interest rates leads to rise in net interest income and vice versa.

4.14 Statement of Structural Liquidity as on 31st March 2002

SBI Group Outflows	1-14 days	15-28 Days	29 days and Up to 3 months	Over 3 months and up to 6 months	Over 6 months and up to 1 year	Over 1 year and to 3 years	Over 3 years and up to 5 years	Over 5 years	Total
C as % to A	62.93	348.31	174.35	36.35	-36.39	-58.43	22.62	527.16	1.16
D as % to A1	62.93	89.2	106.78	91.9	54.92	-26.29	-25.71	1.16	1.16
ICICI Bank									
C as % to A	16.76	-3.43	-43.52	-25.49	-48.28	-26.04	138.77	421.21	9.91
D as % to A1	16.76	9.40	-22.11	23.11	-33.93	-30.66	-18.26	9.91	9.91
PNB									
C as % to A	-30.99	-21.60	29.74	0.82	104.72	-61.99	559.98	64.21	-1.90
D as % to A1	-30.99	-28.18	-9.06	-6.29	22.83	-37.28	-23.35	-1.90	-1.90
CBoP									
C as % to A	-14.83	-79.49	-59.15	-73.87	-79.41	-1.96	117.45	25,750	-12.90
D as % to A1	-14.83	-43.78	-52.74	-57.51	-62.05	-43.63	-37.82	-12.90	-12.90

Source: Performance highlights of Public and Private Sector Banks,IBA Mumbai (2000-01 to 2006-07)

Note:(i)C stands for Mismatch.

(ii) D for Cumulative Mismatch between Assets and Liabilities.

(iii)A stands for Assets and A1 for Cumulative Assets.

The statement of structural liquidity of the four banks for the year ending 31 st March 2002 shown by Table 4.14 indicates that SBI Group and ICICI Bank have been asset sensitive, while PNB and CBoP have been liability sensitive. The gap ratios are as under:-

SBI Group	1.16%
ICICI Bank	9.91%
PNB	-1.90%
CBOP	-12.90%

ICICI Bank is more asset sensitive than SBI Group while CBoP is more liability sensitive than PNB.

In case of positive gap (for SBI Group & ICICI Bank) an increase in the interest rate would mean increase in profits and any decline in interest rates would mean decrease in profits.

In case of negative gap (for PNB and CBoP) increase in the interest rates would mean a decrease in profits.   .

4.15 : Statement of Structural Liquidity as on 31st March 2003

SBIGroup Outflows	1-14 days	15-28 Days	29 days and up to 3 months	Over 3 months and up to 6 months	Over 6 months and up to 1 year	Over 1 year and upto 3 years	Over 3 years and up to 5 years	Over 5 years	Total
C as % to A	29.58	175.46	95.08	22.4	-63.43	-58.28	54.00	761.69	5.29
D as % to A1	29.58	43.66	55.49	48.9	5.21	-32.61	-24.40	5.29	5.29
ICICI Bank									
C as % to A	1.99	38.59	-39.46	-30.89	-45.20	-19.88	150.86	364.45	7.94
D as % to A1	1.99	11.63	-18.12	-21.37	-31.77	-26.11	-15.60	7.94	7.94
PNB									
C as % to A	-31.88	-35.34	-38.29	-13.34	-29.17	-63.18	234.92	2,087.87	-2.71
D as % to A1	-31.88	-32.82	-35.07	-28.35	-28.60	-51.00	-41.64	-2.71	-2.71
CBoP									
C as % to A	-59.61	-90.13	-30.61	-64.94	-58.71	-46.57	1800.00	2,658.00	-13.58
D as % to A1	-59.61	-71.46	-53.00	-55.52	-56.08	-51.36	-45.23	-13.58	-13.58

Source: Performance highlights of Public and Private Sector Banks,IBA Mumbai.(2000-01 to 2006-07)

Note:(i)C stands for Mismatch.

(ii) D for Cumulative Mismatch between Assets and Liabilities.

(iii)A stands for Assets and A1 for Cumulative Assets.

For the year ending 31st March 2003, SBI Group and ICICI Bank arefound to be asset sensitive whereas PNB and CBoP are asset sensitive whereas PNB and CBoP are liability sensitive as shown in Table 4.15. The relative Gap ratios of the four banks are as under:-

SBI Group   5.29%

ICICI Bank   7.94%

PNB   -2.71%

CBoP   -13.58%

ICICI Bank is found to be most asset sensitive whereas CBoP has been most liability sensitive. During 2002-03 there was softening of interest rates in most markets as commercial bank deposit rates continued to fall reflecting ample liquidity in the banking system.

Thus, in such a situation of decrease in interest rates, negative gap leads to increase in profits. PNB and CBoP have managed their assets and liabilities in tune with the interest rates. SBI Group and ICICI Bank have a positive gap which under falling interest rates leads to a decrease in profits. These banks should have been liability sensitive so as to reduce the positive gap and follow Liability Repricing Before Assets approach

4.16: Statement of Structural Liquidity as on 31ˢᵗ March 2004

SBI Group Outflows	1-14 days	15-28 days	29 days and up to 3 months	Over 3 months and up to 6 months	Over 6 months and up to 1 year	Over 1 years and up to 3 years	Over 3 years and up to 5 years	Over 5 years	Total
C as % to A	48.77	204.09	40.14	-32.59	-63.94	-44.7	-17.32	131.57	5.35
D as % to A1	48.77	62.43	55.49	36.31	5.56	-19.76	-19.31	5.35	5.35
ICICI Bank									
E. C as % to A	33.95	25.90	-43.75	-53.19	-17.87	-27.56	169.82	779.62	13.56
E-1 D as % to A1	33.95	31.52	-5.72	-24.55	-22.22	-24.79	-15.38	13.56	13.56
PNB									
C as % to A	18.87	74.57	16.01	32.85	-5.17	-60.93	344.6	89.82	2.03
D as % to A1	18.87	29.29	23.7	26.78	15.69	36.58	-23.16	2.03	2.03
CBoP									
C as % to A	-54.89	37.66	-16.76	15.05	25.6	-25.11	310.77	1,560	-5.85
D as % to A1	-54.89	-48.13	-38.23	-29.90	-21.28	-23.18	-18.72	-5.85	-5.85

Source: Performance highlights of Public and Private Sector Banks,IBA Mumbai.(2000-01 to 2006-07)

Note:(i)C stands for Mismatch.

(ii) D for Cumulative Mismatch between Assets and Liabilities.

(iii)A stands for Assets and A1 for Cumulative Assets.

The statement of Structural Liquidity of the selected four banks for the year ending 31st 2004, shown in Table 4.16 brings out that SBI Group, ICICI Bank and PNB are asset sensitive, whereas only CBoP is liability sensitive. The gap ratios are as under:

SBI Group	5.35%
ICICI Bank	13.56%
PNB	2.03%
CBoP	-5.85%

During the financial year 2003-04 there was general softening of interest rates (RBI Annual Report 2003-04) .The Benchmark prime lending rate (BPLR) was implemented through the operational guidelines issued by Indian Banks' Association (IBA) in Nov 2003 to improve transparency and reduce complexity in pricing of loans. Only CBoP had a negative gap, and only it capitalized the decline in interest rates to its favour by being liability sensitive.

Among the three asset sensitive banks,ICICI Bank and PNB have been the most and least Asset sensitive banks respectively.

4.17: Statement of Structural Liquidity as on 31ˢᵗ March 2005

	1-14 days	15-28 Days	29 days and up to 3 months	Over 3 months and up to 6 months	Over 6 months and up to 1 year	Over 1 year and up to 3 years	Over 3 years and up to 5 years	Over 5 years	Total
SBI Group									
C as % to A	96.96	13.69	-17.02	38.54	-78.67	-6.30	18.14	120.21	13.06
D as % to A1	96.96	85.75	49.86	47.01	-10.47	-8.56	-10.65	13.06	13.06
ICICI Bank									
C as % to A	170.24	-79.43	-27.76	-70.96	-71.93	-19.94	79.21	740.53	-22.37
D as % to A1	170.24	-10.64	-18.12	-43.92	-55.50	-45.21	-40.55	-22.37	-22.37
PNB									
C as % to A	-5.09	41.08	15.44	9.54	75.04	-65.44	330.69	102.88	6.34
D as % to A1	-5.09	4.13	8.57	8.85	23.28	-34.65	-17.11	6.34	6.34
CBoP									
C as % to A	-12.56	-20.21	0.93	-23.67	-24.66	-30.43	220.48	2,510.52	-10.04
D as % to A1	-12.56	-13.60	-8.04	-11.53	-14.97	-24.10	-19.92	-10.04	-10.04

Source: Performance highlights of Public and Private Sector Banks, IBA, Mumbai.(2000-01 to 2006-07)
Note:(i)C stands for Mismatch.
 (ii) D for Cumulative Mismatch between Assets and Liabilities.
 (iii)A stands for Assets and A1 for Cumulative Assets.

The statement of structural liquidity presented in Table 4.17 depicts that of the selected four banks for the year ending 31st 2005, SBI Group and PNB have been asset sensitive while ICICI Bank and CBoP have been liability sensitive. The relative gap ratios are indicated as below:

SBI Group 13.06%

 PNB   6.34%

CBoP   -10.04% and

ICICI Bank -22.37%.

During the financial year 2004-05, the interest rates were rising. If the gap is positive, any increase in the interest rates would mean increase in profits and any fall in interest rates would mean decrease in profits.

Thus, SBI Group and PNB have maintained a positive gap keeping in view the interest rate scenario. Both the private sector banks have not responded favourably to the rising interest rates and have been liability sensitive. They should have followed Assets Repricing Before Liability Approach .While the deposits rates of banks have declined from 13 per cent in 1995-96 to about 5 per cent in 2004-05 the average lending rates declined from about 17 per cent to about 10 per cent during the same period (RBI,2004-05). However, the effective lending rates did not fall commensurately with the fall in nominal interest rates.

4.18: Statement of Structural Liquidity as on 31st March 2006

SBI Group Outflows	1-14 days	15-28 Days	29 days and up to 3 months	Over 3 months and to 6 months	Over 6 months and up to 1 year	Over 1 year and up to 3 years	Over 3 years and up to 5 years	Over 5 years	Total
C as % to A	-7.74	-20.24	4.85	-28.31	-64.13	13.17	-23.25	90.33	3.09
D as % to A1	-7.74	-9.97	-5.77	-10.74	-25.15	-10.05	-12.62	3.09	3.09
ICICI Bank									
C as % to A	1.35	-33.29	-47.20	-39.04	-46.21	21.31	40.71	768.70	4.16
D as % to A1	1.35	-9.37	-29.74	-32.62	-37.17	-19.67	-15.04	4.16	4.16
PNB									
C as % to A	-49.80	-43.45	-10.48	28.12	247.81	224.39	270.82	53.48	-7.48
D as % to A1	-49.80	-48.39	-36.64	-23.18	10.76	46.23	70.56	-7.48	-7.48
CBoP									
C as % to A	-16.71	-42.50	-33.82	-9.53	-12.45	22.33	-45.93	4995	0.43
D as % to A1	-16.71	-24.49	-28.46	-23.14	-19.89	-3.84	-9.86	0.43	0.43

Source: Performance highlights of Public and Private Sector Banks, IBA Mumbai.(2000-01 to2006-07).
Note:(i)C stands for Mismatch.
(ii) D for Cumulative Mismatch between Assets and Liabilities.
(iii)A stands for Assets and A1 for Cumulative Assets.

The statement of structural liquidity for the year ending 31st March 2006 shown by Table 4.18 depicts the relative Gap ratios of the four banks under study as:

SBI Group	3.09%
ICICI Bank	4.16%
PNB	-7.48%
CBoP	0.43%

During the financial year 2005-06. the interest rates on savings deposits and NRI deposits were prescribed by the RBI. It was felt that deregulation would facilitate better asset liability management for banks and competitive pricing to benefit the holders of savings accounts. The lending rates regulated by RBI were the concessional rates (below BPLR of the respective banks) for certain sectors such as exports and small loans up to Rs2 lakh under the differential rate of interest (DRI) scheme.

Thus, there was a fall in deposit rates and lowering of cost of funds over the period (RBI,2005-06) Thus, in a falling interest scenario, PNB has shown a most favourable negative gap. The remaining three banks have been asset sensitive showing a positive gap. CBoP and ICICI Bank with the values of 0.43% and 4.16% have shown the minimum and maximum positive gap respectively.

4.19: Statement of Structural Liquidity as on 31st March 2007

SBI Group Outflows	1-14 days	15-28 Days	Over 29 days and up to 3 months	Over 3 months and up to 6 months	Over 6 months and up to 1 year	Over 1 year and up to 3 years	Over 3 years and up to 5 years	Over 5 years	Total
C as % to A	3.62	-2.34	-27.58	-31.89	-60.37	22.37	-30.01	91.52	1.90
D as % to A1	3.62	2.78	-8.75	-14.15	-26.82	-8.29	-12.59	1.90	1.90
ICICI Bank									
C as % to A	-17.20	11.90	-48.31	-46.11	-37.73	0.62	51.15	564.50	-0.56
D as % to A1	-17.20	-8.46	-29.31	-35.16	-36.11	-24.32	-18.41	-0.56	-0.56
PNB									
C as % to A	109.70	29.00	13.30	15.70	33.80	169.00	424.00	-52.70	2.15
D as % to A1	109.70	87.50	-39.28	32.50	32.80	65.10	93.70	2.15	2.15
CBoP									
C as % to A	-47.16	-43.49	-46.72	-25.86	34.31	20.39	392.92	9,104	-1.06
D as % to A1	-47.16	-46.05	-46.36	-41.50	-39.29	-19.19	-13.44	-1.06	-1.06

Source: Performance highlights of Public and Private Sector Banks, IBA Mumbai. (2000 -01 to2006-07)

Note: (i)C stands for Mismatch.

(ii) D for Cumulative Mismatch between Assets and Liabilities.

(iii)A stands for Assets and A1 for Cumulative Assets.

Table 4.19 presents the relative gap ratios of the four banks under study for the year ending 31st March 2007.These are as under :

SBI Group   1.90%,

ICICI Bank -0.56%

PNB   2.15%

CBoP   -1.06%

There was hardening of interest rates both on the liability and assets sides. Hence, at times of rising interest rates, it is profitable to have more assets and positive gap. Both the Public Sector Banks viz. SBI Group and PNB have shown a positive gap, it has been negative in the case of ICICI Bank and CBoP. The two Private Sector Banks should have been asset-sensitive to benefit from the rising interest rate scenario.

4.4 Liquidity Measurement-Stock Approach

Liquidity ratios provide the primary means of judging a bank's liquidity position. Liquidity may be regarded as either a stock or flow concept. Under the stock approach assets which can be converted into cash are considered. When viewing liquidity from a flow approach, the ability to convert liquid assets along with the ability of the economic unit to borrow and to generate cash from operations is considered. An accurate forecast of cash needs and the expected level of liquid assets and cash receipts over a given time period is required to obtain a realistic appraisal of bank's liquidity position would require The stock concept is commonly used to measure liquidity. A number of ratios have been evaluated.

4.4.1 Loan to Deposit Ratio: This ratio indicates the degree of already used available resources by the bank to accommodate the credit needs of the customers. The portion of deposits invested in loans rises with the decline in liquidity.

Table 4.20: Trends in Loan/Deposits Ratio

Year	SBIGroup	ICICI Bank	PNB	CBoP
1985	N.A.	-	N.A.	-
1995-96	14.04	11.64	11.39	-
2006-07	41.78	65.62	34.89	5.82
Trend GR Period I	-	-	2.26	-
Period II	10.13	34.73	10.66	13.91
Period I&II	-		-	
C.V.	80.84	97.68	76.61	52.23
T- value	8.55*	2.85*	12.41*	4.30*
Average Rate	14.78	46.25	14.01	29.80

Source: Performance Highlights of Public and Private Sector Banks, IBA, Mumbai, various issues. N.A. stands for not available.

Bank-wise analysis provides that this ratio has increased over the period under study, and the increase is significant for all the banks under study at five percent level of significance.

During period I, from 1985 to 1994-95, the trend growth rate for this ratio could not be computed due to non-availability of data. ICICI Bank has shown maximum growth in Loan-Deposit ratio as depicted by the trend growth rate (34.73),followed by CBoP(13.91), PNB(10.66), while for SBI Group, the growth rate has been the least(10.13) during Period II i.e. the post-reforms period(1995-96 to 2006-07).

After the merger, the ratio has been well above the Prudential Limit of 65% only for ICICI Bank. The rise in Loan-Deposit ratio has been most erratic for ICICI Bank as shown by its Coefficient of Variation (97.68%),followed by SBI Group(80.84%), PNB(76.61%) and CBoP(52.23%).On an average, the loan to deposits ratio has been highest for ICICI Bank (46.25%),followed by CBoP(29.80%), SBI Group(14.78%) and the least for PNB(14.01%). ICICI Bank needs to be more cautious and selective in framing its lending policies, while PNB and CBoP can afford a more liberal approach towards granting loans.

4.4.2 Purchased Funds to Total Assets Ratio: Here, Purchased funds include the entire inter-bank and other money market borrowings, including certificate of Deposits and Institutional deposits.   Bank-wise analysis shows that this ratio has been rising for all the banks highlighted in Table 4.21.

Table 4.21: Trends in Purchased Funds/Total Assets

Year	SBI Group	ICICI Bank	PNB	CBoP
1985	49.50	-	45.29	-
1995-96	41.66	56.90	54.16	40.47
2006-07	50.89	67.18	47.56	60.83
Trend GR Period I	-2.65	-	1.02	-
Period II	1.91	0.47	-1.18	-0.25
Period I&II	0.36	-	-0.54	-
C.V.	10.18	8.40	7.34	14.24
T-value	1.00	0.52	2.56*	0.34
Average Rate	47.57	67.41	50.80	58.23

Source: Performance Highlights of Public and Private Sector Banks, IBA, Mumbai, Various Issues.

For SBI Group, this ratio   declined   from 49.50% in 1985 to 41.66% in 1995-96 ,while for PNB, it increased   from 45.29%   to 54.16% during the same period. Later on, the ratio increased to 50.89% for SBI Group, while it decreased to 47.56% in 2006-07 for PNB.

For ICICI Bank, this ratio increased from 56.90% in 1995-96 to 67.18% in 2006-07. Similarly, CBoP also showed an increase in this ratio from 40.47% to 60.83% during the same period.   The rise in this ratio has been significant (at 5% level of significance) for PNB only.

During period I, from 1985 to 1994-95,the rise in Purchased Funds to Total Assets ratio has been greater for PNB (1.02) than that

155

of SBI Group, (-2.65). SBI Group has shown the maximum rise as depicted in its Trend Growth Rate (1.91), followed by ICICI Bank(0.47), CBoP(-0.25) and PNB(-1.18) during Period II i.e. the post-reforms period(1995-96 to 2006-07). If we compare the overall trend growth rates of both the selected Public Sector Banks i.e. from 1985 to 2006-07, then the growth rate has been higher for SBI Group i.e. (0.36) than that of PNB(-0.54).

The rise in Purchased Assets/Total Assets has been most volatile for CBoP as shown by its Coefficient of Variation(14.24%),followed by SBI Group(10.18%),ICICI Bank(8.40%), while the growth has been most steady for PNB(7.34%). An increase in this ratio implies greater dependence on external sources of funds and vice versa.

On an average, this ratio has been the highest for ICICI Bank (67.41%),followed by CBoP(58.23%),PNB(50.80%) and least for SBI Group (47.57%). ICICI Bank has been relying heavily on purchased funds and PNB is following a conservative policy in this regard.

4.4.3 Liquid Assets to Total Assets Ratio: Cash in hand, Balances with RBI, money at call and short notice are included under the category of cash and near cash assets(Liquid Assets). The Prudential limit for this ratio has been fixed at 5%.This ratio has increased significantly for all the four banks at 5% level of significance. This ratio has declined for both the Private Sector Banks, viz. ICICI Bank and CBoP by approximately 8% from 1995-96 to 2006-07as shown in Table 4.22. Initially, ICICI Bank, being a new bank, maintained liquid resources cautiously while PNB has reduced the liquid assets gradually over the period under study.

Table 4.22 : Trends in   Liquid Assets/ Total Assets

Year	SBIGroup	ICICIBank	PNB	CBoP
1985	7.79	-	12.77	-
1995-96	17.53	14.07	14.98	14.62
2006-07	6.41	6.40	8.83	6.26
Trend GR Period I	3.30	-	-2.13	-
Period II	-10.18	-15.12	-3.84	-5.55
Period I&II	-2.44	-	-3.26	-
C.V.	32.11	65.01	27.53	35.36
T-value	2.09*	4.00*	4.47*	2.95*
Average ratio	13.36	13.01	12.30	8.44

Source: Performance Highlights of Public Sector Banks and Private Sector Banks, IBA, Mumbai, various issues.

During period I, from 1985 to 1994-95, the rise in this ratio has been greater for SBI Group(3.30) while for PNB, the growth rate has reduced(-2.13). During Period II i.e. the post-reforms period(1995-96 to 2006-07) all the four banks under study have experienced decline in this ratio, the maximum decline being for ICICI Bank(-15.12),SBI Group(-10.18),CBoP(-5.55) and PNB(-3.84). If we compare the overall trend growth rates of both the selected Public Sector Banks, i.e. from 1985 to 2006-07,then the growth rates have decreased   for both SBI Group(-2.44)and PNB (-3.26) after the reforms due to greater credit expansion by the banks.

The rise in Liquid Assets /Total Assets ratio has been most volatile for ICICI Bank as shown by its Coefficient of Variation (65.01%),followed   by CBoP(35.36%),SBI Group(32.11%), while the growth has been most steady for PNB, its Coefficient of Variation being 27.53% only.

On an average also, this ratio is maximum for SBI Group (13.36), followed   by   ICICI Bank(13.01),PNB(12.30) and minimum for CBoP

(8.44). Both the Public Sector Banks have moderate liquidity compared to the Private Sector Banks. The optimal level of liquidity has to be attained by every bank by reconciling the objective of profitability as liquidity is inversely related to profitability.

4.4.4 Current Ratio = Current Assets /Current Liabilities

Current Assets consist of Cash and near Cash assets and Government Securities. Current Liabilities comprise of Bills Payable, Branch adjustment, interest accrued and other provisions. This ratio is commonly used measure to gauge the liquidity of bank.

Table 4.23:   Trends in   Current Ratio

Year	SBI Group	ICICI Bank	PNB	CBoP
1985	1.19	-	4.57	-
1995-96	1.96	5.21	6.33	2.00
2006-07	3.01	2.34	5.01	3.97
Average Rate	2.36	4.94	5.39	4.67
Trend GR Period I	3.95	-	-0.02	-
Period II	5.32	-12.19	-1.41	1.07
Period I&II	5.54	-	-0.22	-
C.V.	37.45	64.50	13.49	30.19
T-value	9.27*	2.57*	0.56	0.17

Source: Performance Highlights of Public and Private Sector Banks, IBA, Mumbai, Various Issues.

Current ratio has increased for all the banks over the period of study except ICICI Bank which registered a decrease in this ratio from 5.21% in 1995-96 to 2.34% in 2006-07, indicating substantial fall in liquidity as shown in Table 4.23 .The ratio increased from 1.19% in 1985 to 1.96% in 1995-96 for SBI Group and from 4.57% to 6.33% for PNB during the stated period. However, the ratio reduced to 5.01% for PNB, while it increased to 3.01% for SBI Group in 2006-07.CBoP also improved this ratio from 2.00% in 1995-96 to 3.97% in 2006-07.

The rise in current ratio has been significant at 5% level of significance for SBI Group and ICICI Bank only.

During period I, from 1985 to 1994-95, this ratio has recorded growth rate (3.95) for SBI Group while for PNB its negative value of -0.02 has shown a decline. During Period II, i.e. the post-reforms period(1995-96 to 2006-07) PNB and ICICI Bank have experienced decline in this ratio, the decline being greater for ICICI Bank(-12.19) than that of PNB(-1.41). The trend growth rates of SBI Group and CBoP have been 5.32 and 1.07 respectively. If we compare the overall trend growth rates of both the selected Public Sector Banks i.e. from1985 to 2006-07,then the growth rate has improved for SBI Group(5.54) while it has decreased of PNB (-0.22). The rise in Current Ratio has been most volatile for ICICI Bank as shown by its Coefficient of Variation (64.50%), followed by SBI Group (37.45%), CBoP (30.19%), while the growth has been most steady for PNB(13.49%).On an average, this ratio has been highest for PNB(5.39),followed by ICICI Bank(4.94%), CBoP(4.67%) and least for SBI Group (2.36%). A higher current ratio provides greater liquidity and safety to a bank but an excessively high ratio implies blocking of lendable resources which can impede profitability. An optimum ratio needs to be achieved to ensure liquidity coupled with profitability.

4.6 CONCLUSIONS

Reserve Position Management

As far as primary reserves are concerned, SBI Group, CBoP and PNB, on an average have maintained similar amount in the form of primary reserves as a proportion of total deposits while ICICI Bank has the least primary reserves in relation to deposits. The position in the case of Secondary Reserves is different. Secondary Reserves as a percentage of total deposits have decreased for all the four banks under study. Secondary Reserves as a percentage of total deposits, on an average, have been maximum for SBI Group, followed by ICICI Bank, CBoP and PNB.

Investment Management

The Investment Portfolio of the selected four banks has shown that the government securities form a major chunk of the investment portfolio for all the four banks under study. PNB and SBI Group have a wide portfolio of investments ranging from government and approved securities to Subsidiaries & Joint ventures. The share of investments in Debentures and bonds has reduced for all the banks under study due to lack of development of corporate debt market .The secondary market has not developed commensurately and market liquidity remains an issue. Both the Private Sector Banks have been reluctant to invest in approved securities probably due to their lesser marketability. All the banks have increased investment in shares and subsidiaries and joint ventures over the years, except CBoP, as it has never invested in subsidiaries and joint ventures.

Liquidity Management

Various liquidity ratios have been calculated to ascertain the liqiudity position of the four banks viz. Liquid Assets/Total Assets ratio, which declined for all the banks under study, the decline being the most for ICICI Bank, followed by SBI Group, CBoP and PNB. However, Liquid Assets/Total Assets ratio has been well above the Prudential Limit of 5% for all the four banks. Current Ratio has declined for both ICICI Bank and PNB and increased for SBI Group and CBoP over the period under study. Purchased Funds/Total Assets ratio has reduced for PNB and CBoP, while it has increased for ICICI

Bank and SBI Group. Loan/Deposits ratio has increased for all the banks. Loan/Deposits ratio has been above the Prudential Limit of 65%only for ICICI Bank, that too in the later years of the study . As per RBI Guidelines, banks are preparing Gap Statements to find out the extent of asset liability mismatch and take remedial measures. From the year 2000 to 2007, the gap statements indicate that SBI Group and ICICI Bank have maintained their assets and liabilities according to the interest rate scenario. PNB and CBoP have had adverse gap for a couple of years.

On an average, banks have become cautious with regard to their asset liability mismatch and are making efforts to reduce the magnitude of gap to avoid financial crisis.

Thus, in all the areas of asset management, ICICI Bank and SBI Group have more or less similar position and are giving each other tough competition. PNB has been conservative and consistent towards lending funds, over the years. CBoP needs to explore new horizons to become a force to reckon with though its liquidity position has improved remarkably after the merger.

REFERENCES

Bakshi, Swapan.(2005),"Financial Intermediation: An Overview of Risks," in S.B. Verma (ed.) *Risk Management*, Deep & Deep Publications Pvt. Ltd., New Delhi.

Bakshi, Swapan(2005),"Risk Management in Banks for Improved Corporate Governance," *The Management Accountant*, Vol. 40, No.11, November.

Banerjee, Amalesh.(2002),"Macro-Economic Aspect of Financial Reform," in Amalesh Banerjee and S.K. Singh (eds.), *Banking and Financial Sector Reforms in India*, Deep & Deep Publications Pvt. Ltd., New Delhi.

Barsky, P. Noah;and Catanach, H. Anthony.(2005)," Evaluating Business Risk in the Commercial Lending Decision," *Commercial Lending Review*, Vol. 20, No. 3, May -June,p.3.

Bhasin, Niti.(2006),*Banking Developments in India-1947 to 2007, Growth Reforms and Outlook*, New Century Publications, New Delhi.

Chaplin, Graeme.; Emblow, Alison.;and Michael, Ian.(2002)," Banking System Liquidity-Development & Issues," in,K. Seetapathi(ed.), *Risk Management in Banks,* ICFAI Banking Series, ICFAI Press, Hyderabad, p.29.

Chawla, O.P.(1998),"Asset Liability Management," *The Financial Express,* 7th February,p.7.

Cornett, & Saunders. (1999) *Fundamentals of Financial Institutions Management*, Irwin Mc Graw Hill International Edition, Finance Series.

162

De, Lucia, R.D.;and Peters, J. (1993)*Commercial Bank Management-Functions and Objectives*, Serendip Publications. Third Edition.

Dharmarajan,S.(2004)"Asset Liability Management Model for managing Liquidity and Interest Rate Risk in Cooperative Banks," *Vinimaya*, Vol.XXV, No.1, April-June, pp.31-33.

Dhanasekaran, Bai Kasture.(2002)," Banking Sector Reforms in India An Assessments," in Amalesh Banerjee and S.K Singh (eds.), *Banking and Financial Sector Reforms in India*, Deep & Deep Publications Pvt. Ltd., New Delhi, p.100.

Hingorani, N.L.(1983)," Major Issues in Lending Policy," in Sampat P Singh. (ed.) *Bank Lending-Some Controversial Issues*," NIBM, Pune, pp.94-95.

Hudson, Robert; Colley, Alan; and Largan, Mark.(2000),*Capital Markets & Financial Management in Banking*, Glen Lake Publishing Co. Ltd, Fitzroy Dearborn Publishers, Chicago & London.

Indian Financial System and Commercial Banking, *The Indian Institute of Banking,* Macmillan Publishers.

Joshi, C. Vasant; and Joshi, C. Vinay.(2000),*Managing Indian Banks-The Challenges Ahead*, Response Books Pvt. Ltd., New Delhi.

Khurana, S.K.(2000), *Asset Liability Management*, Skylark Publications, New Delhi.

Kumar, Ravi T.(2000)*Asset Liability Management,* Vision Books Pvt. Ltd., New Delhi.

Mehta, Sangita.(1998)," Defusing time bombs ticking in the books," *Business Standard*, September 24, p.10.

Management Policies for Commercial Banks (1980),Prentice Hall Englewoods, New Jersey,3rd edition.

Nag, Anirban.(1998)"RBI asks banks to set up system for Asset-Liability Management," *The Financial Express*, September 16, p.1.

Nandwana, B.M.(2002),"Asset Liability Management in Banks,'' in Mohana P. Rao and T.K. Jain (eds.), *Management of Banking and Financial Institutions*, Deep&Deep Publications Pvt. Ltd., New Delhi.

Passah, P.M.(2002)" Banking and Financial Sector Reforms in India Rationale Progress, Efficacy and future Agenda,'' in Amalesh Banerjee and S.K. Singh (eds.), *Banking and Financial Sector Reforms in India*, in Deep & Deep Publications Pvt. Ltd., New Delhi.

Patheja, Anju.(1994) *Financial Management of Commercial Banks*," South Asia Publications, New Delhi.

Prasad, Narendra.(2002),'' *Banking and Financial Sector Reforms in India*," in Amalesh Banerjee and S.K. Singh (eds.), *Banking and Financial Sector Reforms in India*, Deep & Deep Publications Pvt. Ltd.,New Delhi.

Raghavan, R.S.(2005),"Risk Management-An Overview," in S.B. Verma (ed.), Risk Management, Deep & Deep Publications Pvt Ltd, New Delhi, p.4.

Rajwade, A.V.(2002),"Issues in Asset-Liability Management-I" Economic & Political Weekly, Vol. XXXVII, No.5, Feb 2, p.378.

RBI(2005),Instructions for Banks & Banking Operations,Taxmann Publications, Sixth Edition.

Reed, W. Edward.; and Gill, K. Edward.(1989) Commercial Banking, Prentice Hall, New Jersey, Fourth Edition .

Satyanarayan, B.(2004)," An Overview of Risk Management in Indian Banking," in M.P. Srivastava & S.R. Singh (eds.), Indian Banking in the New Millennium, Anmol Publications Pvt. Ltd., New Delhi, p.311.

Saunders, Anthony.(2002)Financial Institutions Management-A Modern Perspective, Third Edition, Irwin Mc-Graw Hill Series in Finance, International Edition, Singapore.

Sehgal, Madhu;and Kher, Rajni.(2002),"Asset Liability Management in the Indian Banks,"in P. Mohana Rao and T.K.Jain (eds.), Management of Banking and Financial Institutions, Deep & Deep Publications Pvt. Ltd, New Delhi, p.92.

Sen, Gupta A.K. (1994)," Study of Credit Policy and Decision systems in Banks, "Project Report, April, NIBM , Pune, p.6.

Srivastava, R.M.;and Nigam, Divya.(2005),"Management of Loans in Commercial Banks," in Management of Indian Financial Institutions, Himalaya Publishers, Mumbai.

Subrahmanyam, Ganti.(1995),"Asset Liability Management, for Banks in a Deregulated Environment "Prajnan,Vol. XXIII, No.1, pp.11-27.

Suneja, H.R.(1992), Management of Bank Credit, Himalaya Publishing House, Mumbai.

Vij, Madhu.(2005)," Asset Liability Management," in S.K. Tuteja (ed.), Management Mosaic, Excel Books, New Delhi,pp.333-367.

CHAPTER-5
LIABILITIES MANAGEMENT

Liabilities Management, as it was called initially, originated in USA and Canada in the seventies. Its purpose was to find or finance holdings of remunerative assets efficiently and profitably as possible (Kamath, 1996).

Bank management in India has long been liability based and the success of each bank was evaluated based on its ability to mobilize deposits, till the late 1980s (Bhat, 1999). The deregulation of domestic interest rates, volatility in the domestic debt and foreign exchange markets and introduction of new financial instruments has posed a question of efficient liquidity and interest rate risk management within banks(Mehta,1998). Assets of varying maturities are funded by liabilities of varying maturities, which leads to a mismatch, causing risk. This risk is compounded by the fact that the earnings from these assets and liabilities are affected by market determined interest rate (Bhusunurmath, 1998). Today, banks are exposed to new products, both fund-based and non-fund based, thus effective asset liability match is a must or else it could be in big trouble.

According to the Basel study paper, measuring and managing liquidity are the most important activities of commercial banks, whereby banks can ensure that they have the ability to meet their liabilities as they come due. Thus, liquidity needs to be maintained to avoid the effect of asset-liability mismatch as liquidity shortfall in a single institution can have repercussion across the whole banking sector.

Often liabilities are accepted in advance of commitments, such liabilities being deployed subsequently in the acquisition of remunerative assets. At the time of maturity, mismatches occur which can be dangerous for banks.

The importance of these mismatches can be understood by the observation of RBI Governor in Sept. 1995: "Banks are advised to use utmost caution in offering interest rates on various maturities of term deposits and then should ensure that they do not get locked into excessively long deposit maturities and in this connection should undertake a review to ensure against overall asset-liability mismatches"(Kamath, 1996).

The RBI is trying to ensure that the short-term liability should not be used to meet long-term assets. Banks fund their long-term assets through call money market borrowings and when liquidity becomes tight as a result of the Cash Reserve Ratio (CRR) imposition, they have to pay extremely high rates of interest (Sharma and Kulkarni, 2006).

With the advent of new private banks and the proposed reduction in the holdings of the Central Government in the nationalized banks, the depositors will commence watching the maturity patterns of assets and liabilities and also the extent of mismatch and they may decide to withdraw funds if any persistent large mismatch is noticed. Thus, the importance of management of liabilities has been felt.

The liability management involves:

(a) Choosing the sources of financing to be used, that is, choosing between deposit financing and non-deposit financing;

(b) Determining the amount of funds needed; and

(c) Obtaining funds at lowest possible cost with the least risk exposure (Patheja, 1994).

Liability management requires consideration of the extra risk as well as the difference between the cost of obtaining funds and the return that can be earned when the funds are invested in loans or securities (Reed and Gill, 1989). Thus, the relationship between asset management and liability management is a critical determinant of a bank's profitability.

5.1 ASPECTS OF LIABILITIES MANAGEMENT

According to Kane, liability management covers two distinct phenomena i.e. LM-1 defined as the process of supplementing asset management with very short-term borrowing (also known as Reserve-Position Liability Management) and LM-2 (called Loan-Position Liability Management) refers to the process of closely managing all liabilities whatever their maturity (Patheja,1994).

Reserve-Position Liability Management (LM-1): It is a technique used to systematically supply a bank with liquidity by issuing new short-term liabilities. The purpose is to procure funds as needed to augment the liquidity stored in the balance-sheet. The main investment of LM-1 is one-day borrowings from inter-bank call money market. Thus, when a bank temporarily loses reserves because of deposits withdrawals or net additions to earning assets, it bids for funds in call money market, in the opposite case of temporary excess reserves, it lends funds in call money market. In this way, LM-1 saves the banking system from volatility.

Loan-Position Liability Management (LM-2): It involves mainly the expansion of a bank's loan portfolio through the use of discriminatory interest rate competition with respect to non-traditional liabilities. Certificate of Deposit (CD) is a good example of LM-2 instrument. The cost and the maturity of the instrument used for borrowing funds play a vital role in liability management. The bank should be on the one hand, able to raise funds at a low cost and on the other, ensure that the maturity profile of the instrument does not lead to or enhance the liquidity risk and the interest rate risk (Kumar, 2000).

The Liabilities Management Theory: The liabilities management theory emerged in the 1960s.The theory lays that it is unnecessary to observe traditional standard in regard to self-liquidating loans and liquidity reserves, for reserve money can be borrowed or "bought" in the money market whenever a bank experiences a reserve deficiency.

5.2 INSTRUMENTS OF LIABILITIES MANAGEMENT

(1) Reserve-Position Liability Management: Call and notice money is a major instrument of adjusting bank liabilities to meet loan demands and liquidity needs. The key feature of this instrument is its very short maturity-one to fourteen days. Call money is used to meet deficits in reserve compliance requirements and other liquidity needs. The effective cost of call money funds is higher than the actual interest rate as the banks have to maintain CRR/SLR on the call money borrowings.

(2) Inter-bank Participation: RBI introduced the Inter-bank participation certificates (PCs) to provide additional instrument for meeting short-term liquidity needs within the banking system. However, the scope of this source of liquidity is limited particularly when other banks too are sailing in the same boat and facing liquidity crisis. The PCs scheme was replaced by two types of Inter-bank participants (IBPs), one on risk-sharing basis and the other without it. The IBPs with risk sharing could be issued for 91 to 180 days and the rate of interest on them was fixed by participating banks subject to a minimum of 14 per cent per annum. The IBPs without risk were treated as part of the net demand and time liabilities of the borrowing banks and were subject to CRR and SLR requirements.

(3)   Certificates of Deposits: An active primary and secondary market trading in CDs until recently has given the instrument immense prominence in the practice of liability management by the public as well as the private sector banks in India. CDs provide an effective instrument of short-term debt. Their maturity varies from three months to one year and can be issued to raise wholesale deposits to match demands for wholesale credit.

(4)   Borrowings from Other Commercial Banks: Another way by which a commercial bank can create additional liabilities to acquire services is by borrowings from other banks. Commercial banks with deficient legal reserves borrow from other banks with excess reserves. The rates on bank loans are very sensitive to changing forces of supply and demand in the money market and are linked competitively to other rates. Such loans are generally given on a one-day, unsecured advances basis.

A bank raises funds through   various sources such as:

- Capital
- Reserves & Surplus
- Deposits
- Borrowings
- Other Liabilities & Provisions.

Different liabilities exist within each category and have been discussed in the following paragraphs.

5.3   CAPITAL

All banks need capital to cover and extend fixed assets and business investments, to enable trading to continue and increase, to maintain the confidence of depositors and to ensure viability in the face of loss arising from inevitable business and political fluctuation and uncertainty, particularly in an inflationary climate(Desai,2006).If better-capitalized banks can raise funds at relatively low rates and these are offered on attractive terms to better rated safe clients, better-capitalized banks could earn higher profits(Datar and Banerjee,2007). The capital of the nationalized banks, which is fully contributed by the government, will also include the contributions made by the government for participating in the World Bank projects.

For banks incorporated outside India, but having branches in India also, the capital will consist of the start-up capital as prescribed by RBI. New banks will be incorporated under the Indian Companies Act, 1956 and will have a capital requirement of Rs. 100 crore for incorporation. Banks will have to show in their capital account the various classes of capital, viz. authorized, issued, subscribed, called-up. The capital account will, however, be represented by the paid-up capital which will be arrived at after deducting the calls-in-arrears and adding up the paid-up value of forfeited shares to the called-up capital.

5.3.1 Functions of Bank Capital

- **Protective Function:** Capital provides a cushion to absorb possible losses so that depositors may be fully protected at all times. It should provide a margin of safety that preferably would allow a bank to continue operations without loss of momentum and, at least, would buy time for it in which it may re-establish its operational momentum (Srivastava and Nigam, 2005).

- **Operational Functions**: The secondary function of the capital funds is to provide for the operations of banking operations, i.e. acquisition of fixed assets such as building, furniture etc. For expansion and diversification activities the requirement of capital is greater.

- **Regulatory Functions**: Apart from providing operational needs and protection, the capital of bank also performs regulatory functions. These functions arise only because of the public special interest in the successful operations of banking firms and laws and regulations that enable public agencies to exercise some control over these operations.

5.3.2 Concept of Capital Adequacy in a Commercial Bank

Banking is based on trust which needs to be maintained at all costs. In the Indian milieu, the capital adequacy of banks becomes all the more important due to the presence of nationalized banks and the social character of bank management. The classical definition of Capital Adequacy is as under: "Capital is adequate either when it reduces the chances of future insolvency of an institution to some pre-determined level or alternatively, when the premium paid by the bank to an insurer is 'fair', that is, when it fully covers the risk borne by the insurer. Such risks, in turn, depend upon the risk in the portfolio selected by the bank, on its capital and on terms of the insurance with respect to when insolvency will be determined and what loss will be paid."(Sen, 1992)

Thus, the entire edifice of the conceptual framework of capital adequacy consists of conceptualizing two broad aspects:

- Meaning of the word "bank capital"

- Assessing the risks involved in the banking operations.

Historical Development

Prior to the reforms, there was a continuous deterioration in the risk-reward ratio in the core lending business of the banks, both nationally and internationally. A need was, therefore, felt to have a mechanism for a stringent and standardized supervision of banks for proper regulation of their business practices (Kumar, 2003).

This resulted in the formation of Basel Committee on Banking Supervision (BCBS), a Committee of central banks and bank supervisors/regulators from major industrialized countries. The regulatory/supervisory standards viz. Capital Accord (1988) and Core Principles for Effective Banking Supervision (1997) were evolved in the expectation that supervisors across the world would follow more closely these standards. These were subsequently endorsed by the Group of Ten countries, viz. G-10 countries representing the developed world. A minimum target of Risk-Asset-Ratio of 8 per cent was agreed to be achieved by the end of 1992.

This harmonization approach of the norms for soundness and adequacy of bank capital has two dimensions as under:

- Uniform definition of capital for both Tier-I & Tier-II.
- Uniform classification of assets according to the risk associated with them (both for in and off-balance-sheet items)

Definition of Capital: Core Capital or Tier-I Capital mainly comprised of equity and disclosed reserves. This should constitute at least 50 percent of the total capital base. Supplementary capital or Tier-II capital comprised of unpublished reserves, revaluation reserves, general provision and hybrid capital instruments which are close to equity but have some features of debts. This part of capital can maximum be equal to the Tier-I capital.

Subsequently, Narasimham Committee recommended that all Indian banks should achieve capital adequacy of 8% by March 1996, which was later increased to 9% by March 2000. RBI proposed to raise CAR to 10% by March 2002.

The classification of assets according to the risk weightage to be allotted has been a problem in Indian banks. Apart from the problem of classification, the major impediments encountered are two-fold-firstly, lack of proper information as to the various categories as stated and secondly, very little discretion available to the national supervisory authorities for classification (Sen, 1992).Thus, to remove the above lacunae, the new Basel Capital Accord, known as Basel-II was released in April 2003. The object of the New Capital Accord is to have an improved Capital Adequacy Framework to foster a strong emphasis on risk management. The focus has been on strengthening the regulatory capital framework for large and internationally active banks through minimum capital requirement which is more sensitive to the risk profile and risk management (Jain, 2004). Basel-II suggested capital adequacy not only for credit risk and market risk but for operational risk also as shown in Figure 5(a).

Fig.5 (a): CAPITAL FRAMEWORK UNDER BASEL-II NORMS

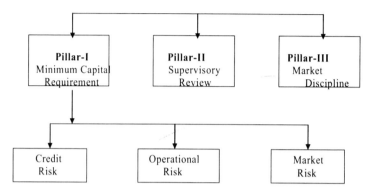

Capital Requirement under Basel-II Accord:

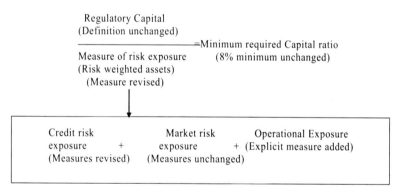

Source: Jain Parasmal (2004) "Basel II-Accord Issues & suggestions," *IBA Bulletin*, Vol. XXVI, No. 6, pp.4-7.

Capital fund, according to it, will comprise of:

Tier-I: Shareholders' equity treated as profits,

Tier-II: Supplementary capital,

Tier-III: Subordinated debt with minimum maturity of 2 years.

5.3.3   Scope of Application: The impact of the chosen Basel II approaches on capital requirements for individual banks and across the banking system should achieve the following objectives:

- Provide banks with a fully operational version of the rules;
- Evaluate the impact of the rules on capital ratios, concentrating on those components which contribute to significant changes;
- Allow banks to assess how the changes resetting from the new rules fit into their overall risk profile; and
- Enable banks to discuss issues as they arise through a continuous dialogue with their supervisors to ensure that the rules are interpreted accurately and consistently (Vidyarthi and Gupta, 2007).

A discernible feature observed in the trends of Capital Adequacy Ratio has been the decline in Capital Adequacy Ratio of Private Sector Banks in the initial years, i.e. from 1995-96 to the later years of the study.

Table 5.1 depicts the trends in Capital Adequacy of the four Banks under study from 1995-96 to 2006-07. Initially, the minimum Capital Adequacy Ratio (CAR) was fixed at 8% to be achieved by all banks by March 1996. All the four Banks achieved this ratio comfortably except PNB, which barely achieved the ratio. Both the Private Sector Banks under study had CAR far in excess of the stipulated ratio; with ICICI Bank having CAR of 17.52% and CBoP(formerly Bank of Punjab) having CAR of 35.03% in 1995-96. This ratio was further raised to 9% by RBI to be achieved by March 2000. RBI further raised the CAR to 10% by March 2002. The growth in Capital Adequacy Ratio has been significant (at 5% level of significance) only for PNB, while the decline has been significant for CBoP.

Table 5.1: Trends in Capital Adequacy

Year	SBI Group	ICICI Bank	PNB	CBoP
1995-96	11.60	17.52	8.23	35.03
2006-07	12.20	11.69	12.30	11.05
Trend GR Period II	4.20	-2.50	4.26	-6.72
C.V.	27.27	21.62	17.16	46.79
T-value	1.06	1.64	5.30*	2.83*
Average Rate	11.33	13.00	11.03	14.78

Source: Performance Highlights of Public and Private Sector Banks IBA,Mumbai, Various Issues.
Note: (i) GR stands for growth rate in all the tables.
(ii) *denotes significance at five percent level in all the tables.
(iii)C.V. stands for Coefficient of Variation in all the tables.

The concept of Capital Adequacy was introduced in 1995; hence, trend growth rate of Period II only has been computed. During Period II, i.e. the post-reforms period(1995-96 to 2006-07) both the Public Sector banks recorded increase in this ratio, the trend growth rate being slightly higher for PNB(4.26) than SBI Group(4.20).However, both the Private Sector Banks registered decrease in this ratio, the decline being greater for CBoP (-6.72) than ICICI Bank(-2.50).

The trend in Capital Adequacy Ratio has been most volatile for CBoP as shown by its Coefficient of Variation (46.79%) ,followed by SBI Group(27.27%),ICICI Bank(21.62%),while the growth has been quite steady for PNB(17.16%).On an average, the Capital Adequacy Ratio has been the highest for CBoP(14.78%),followed by ICICI Bank(13.00%),SBI Group(11.33%) and PNB(11.03%).

178

The capital adequacy acts as a cushion for a bank to meet unforeseen losses. It was recognized that to continue to infuse capital on an on-going basis through budgetary sources of the Government would not be possible and these banks were allowed to raise money from the capital market. Initially, foreign direct investment was allowed up to 49%, which was raised to 74% in 2003-04 to augment the capital base of banks.

5.4 RESERVES & SURPLUS

After the capital, the next vital item on the liabilities side of the balance-sheet of a bank is Reserves & Surplus. This consists of many reserves viz. Statutory Reserve, Capital Reserve, Revaluation Reserve, Share Premium, Revenue and other reserves, Investment Fluctuation Reserve, Contingency Reserves, General Reserve, Redemption Reserve and Balance in Profit and Loss Account. Reserves & Surplus complement the Capital of a bank and aid in meeting financial commitments of a commercial bank.

The Reserves & Surplus have increased   significantly (at five per cent level) for all the four banks during the period under study as shown in Table 5.2.

During period I, from 1985 to 1994-95, the rise in this ratio has been greater for PNB (34.41), while for SBI Group, the growth rate has been lower(26.93). During Period II, i.e. the post-reforms period (1995-96 to 2006-07) reserves & surplus have risen for all the four banks under study, the maximum rise being for ICICI Bank(107.01), followed by CBoP (52.58), PNB (26.31) and SBI Group(17.76)

Table 5.2: Trends in Reserves & Surplus

(Amount in Rs. crores)

Year	SBI Group	ICICI Bank	PNB	CBoP
1985	548	-	58	-
1995-96	6,122	7	798	3
2006-07	41,905	23,414	10,120	1,215
Trend GR Period I	26.93	-	34.41	-
Period II	17.76	107.01	26.31	52.58
Period I&II	24.90	-	28.55	-
C.V.	105.53	127.58	131.56	167.19
T-value	11.11*	6.21*	7.13*	3.33*

Source: Performance Highlights of Public and Private Sector Banks,
Various Issues, IBA,Mumbai.

If we compare the overall trend growth rates of the two Public Sector Banks, i.e. from1985 to 2006-07, then the growth rates have decreased for both SBI Group(24.90)and PNB (28.55) from period I.

The rise in reserves & surplus has been most volatile for CBoP as shown by its Coefficient of Variation (167.19%),followed by PNB(131.56%),ICICI Bank(127.58%), while the growth has been most steady for SBI Group (105.53%).

5.5 DEPOSITS

In the commercial banking system, the level of deposits depends primarily on the amount of credit extended by banks in the form of loans and investments. Deposits are the vital sources of funds for commercial banks which are used in rendering credit services to their customers. Various innovative schemes have been introduced for the depositors to evince their interest for saving their funds in banks. Compound rates of interest, loan facilities to deposits, safety and liquidity of funds, allowing old age benefit, incentive of percentage on interest, children education and marriage, the benefit of life insurance cover, trial of luck, easy transfer of funds and so on are some of the important attractions offered to the depositors.

Types of Deposits: Indian banks accept mainly two kinds of deposits: demand deposits and term deposits.

(1) Term Deposits: These are also known as fixed deposits. Such deposits can be for different maturity periods on which depends the rate of interest.

(2)Demand deposits: These are further sub-divided as current deposits and savings deposits.

- **Current Deposits**: Current accounts are chequable accounts and there are no restrictions on the amount or number of withdrawals from these accounts.

- **Savings Deposits**: Savings deposits earn interest. Although cheques can be drawn on savings accounts, yet the number of withdrawals and the maximum amount that might at any time, be withdrawn from an account without previous notice are restricted.

5.5.1 Trends in Fixed Deposits from Public: In modern banks, deposits take the form of numerous deposits schemes with bewildering rates of interest for a variety of maturities to meet diverse needs of the public and to attract different classes of savers, apart from traditional fixed deposits, savings bank and current accounts, although these form the bread and butter of any bank's balance-sheet (Suneja, 1992).

The deposits from public are of three types; fixed, current and savings. Deposits are the most important sources of a bank's liquidity. Moreover, the success of a bank depends largely on its ability to attract deposits.

Table 5.3: Trends in Fixed Deposits from Public

(Amount in Rs. crore)

Year	SBI Group	ICICI Bank	PNB	CBoP
1985	17552 (51.79)	-	2919 (47.77)	-
1995-96	69119 (56.96)	442 (68.32)	15264 (57.49)	187 (67.51)
2006-07	356301 (57.97)	165717 (76.91)	74495 (54.10)	8621 (65.78)
Trend GR Period I	16.30	-	17.33	-
Period II	16.22	70.59	15.54	27.43
Period I& II	17.14	-	15.33	-
C.V.	88.87	132.37	86.56	97.69
T- value	12.86*	5.55*	10.89*	4.12*

Source:Performance Highlights of Public and Private Sector Banks, Various Issues,IBA, Mumbai.

Note:(i)Figures given in parentheses denote the percentage share in total deposits from Public in the relevant tables.

For this purpose, the commercial banks have to adopt every mode of presentation from advertisement to even door to door canvassing to attract deposits from any section of society (Abrol, 1987).

The major chunk of deposits of all the four banks under study is constituted by fixed deposits. Fixed deposits have increased significantly for all the four banks under study (at five percent level).

Bank-wise analysis shown in Table 5.3 reveals that the share of Fixed deposits in the total deposits of SBI Group increased from 51.79% in 1985 to 56.96% in 1995-96. During the later years of reforms, the share increased to 57.97% in 2006-07. The share of Fixed deposits in the total deposits of PNB increased from 47.77% in 1985 to 57.49% in 1995-96. During the later years of reforms, the share was 54.10% in 2006-07. As far as the two Private Sector Banks are concerned, again the major share in the total deposits has been held by fixed deposits. The share of Fixed deposits in the total deposits was 68.32% in 1995-96 for ICICI Bank, which increased to76.91% in 2006-07, while the share decreased from 67.51% to 65.78% in 2006-07 for CBoP during the same period.

During period I, from 1985 to 1994-95, the rise in fixed deposits has been greater for PNB (17.33) than that of SBI Group, the growth rate has been lower (16.30).During Period II, i.e. the post-reforms period (1995-96 to 2006-07) fixed deposits have risen for all the four banks under study, the maximum rise being for ICICI Bank (70.59), followed by CBoP (27.43), SBI Group (16.22) and PNB (15.54). If we compare the overall trend growth rates of the two Public Sector Banks i.e.from1985 to 2006-07,then the growth rate has been higher for SBI Group(17.14) than that of PNB (15.33). The rise in Fixed deposits has been most volatile for ICICI Bank as shown by its Coefficient of Variation (132.37%), followed by CBoP (97.69%), SBI Group(88.87%), while the growth has been quite steady for PNB (86.56%)during the period under study.

5.5.2 Trends in Savings Deposits from Public: The rate of interest on savings deposits is less than that of fixed deposits. Savings bank deposits are basically meant to promote thrift by providing facilities for savings at attractive terms. The savings bank accounts in the commercial banks offer liberal withdrawal facilities, apart from accepting standing instructions in regard to payment of bills and making remittances.

Table 5.4: Trends in Savings Deposits from Public

(Amount in Rs. crores)

Year	SBI Group	ICICI Bank	PNB	CBoP
1985	9136 (26.96)	-	1969 (32.22)	-
1995-96	28464 (23.46)	19 (2.94)	8273 (31.16)	37 (13.36)
2006-07	172082 (28.00)	28839 (13.38)	48089 (34.91)	2501 (19.08)
Trend GR Period I	11.47	-	15.33	-
Period II	18.16	95.68	17.53	41.55
Period I & II	15.72		16.58	-
C.V.	94.85	143.95	93.96	105.04
T- value	9.39*	5.08*	10.14*	6.60*

Source: Performance Highlights of Public and Private Sector Banks, Various Issues, IBA, Mumbai.

Savings deposits have been at the core of the banks' customer acquisition efforts and have recorded significant rise for all the four banks under study. After the initiation of reforms, the rise has been greater for the two Public Sector Banks than during the pre-reforms period.

Bank-wise analysis given in   table 5.4 reveals that the share of Savings deposits in the total deposits of SBI Group decreased from 26.96% in 1985 to   23.46% in 1995-96. A major rationalization of deposits rates was effected in April 1987 when the maximum rate was reduced by one percentage point to ten per cent applicable for deposits of two years' maturity (Rangarajan,1990). The share   of Savings deposits in the total deposits of PNB decreased from 32.22% in 1985 to 31.16% in 1995-96. However, the share increased to 28.00% for SBI Group and 34.91% for PNB in 2006-07.

As far as the two Private Sector Banks are concerned, the share of Savings deposits increased from 2.94% in 1995-96 to 13.38% in 2006-07 for ICICI Bank and from 13.36% to 19.08% for CBoP, during the same period. The Savings deposits have increased significantly (at 5% level of significance) for all the four banks under study.

During period I, from 1985 to 1994-95, the rise in Savings deposits has been greater for PNB (15.33) than that of SBI Group (11.47). During Period II, i.e. the post-reforms period (1995-96 to 2006-07) Savings deposits have risen for all the four banks under study, the maximum rise being for ICICI Bank (95.68),followed by CBoP(41.55), SBI Group(18.16)and PNB(17.53). If we compare the overall trend growth rates of the two Public Sector Banks i.e.from1985 to 2006-07,then the growth rate has been higher for PNB(16.58) than that of SBI Group (15.72).

The rise in Savings deposits has been most volatile for ICICI Bank as shown by its Coefficient of Variation (143.95%),followed by CBoP (105.04%),SBI Group(94.85%), while the growth has been most steady for PNB(93.96%)during the period under study.

5.5.3 Trends in Current Deposits from Public

The next major component of deposits is the Current Deposit. The banks do not pay interest on current deposits rather realize incidental charges for servicing such accounts. The Current deposits have also increased significantly (at 5% level of significance) for all the four banks under study as shown in Table 5.5.

The share of current deposits in the total deposits was 21.24% in 1985 for SBI Group, which decreased to 19.59% in 1995-96. During

the later years of the reforms, the share reduced   to 14.04% in 2006-
07 for SBI Group.

Table 5.5: Trends in Current Deposits from Public

(Amount in Rs. crores)

Year	SBI Group	ICICI Bank	PNB	CBoP
1985	7198 (21.24)	-	1223 (20.01)	-
1995-96	23769 (19.59)	186 (28.75)	3013 (11.35)	53 (19.13)
2006-07	86298 (14.04)	20911 (9.70)	15135 (10.99)	1983 (15.13)
Trend GR Period I	14.79	-	12.11	-
Period II	11.70	56.26	17.13	31.21
Period I& II	12.24	-	12.16	-
C.V.	70.29	123.43	81.15	96.42
T- value	13.49*	6.06*	8.96*	5.11*

Source: Performance Highlights of Public and Private Sector Banks,
Various Issues, IBA, Mumbai.

The share   of Current deposits in the total deposits of   PNB
decreased from   20.01%   in 1985 to   11.35%   in 1995-96.It further
reduced   to   10.99% in 2006-07.

As far as the two Private Sector Banks are concerned, the share of
Current deposits reduced from 28.75% in 1995-96 to 9.70% in 2006-07
for ICICI Bank and from 19.13%   to 15.13% for CBoP during the same
period.

During period I, from 1985 to 1994-95, the rise in Current
deposits has been greater for SBI Group (14.79) than that of PNB
(12.11). During   period II, i.e. the post-reforms period (1995-96 to
2006-07) Current deposits   have risen for all the four banks under study
, the maximum rise being for ICICI Bank(56.26),followed   by
CBoP(31.21),   PNB(17.13) and SBI Group(11.70). If we compare the
overall   trend growth rates of the two Public Sector Banks i.e.from1985

to 2006-07,then the growth rates have been almost similar for both SBI Group (12.24)and PNB(12.16).

The rise in Current deposits has been most volatile for ICICI Bank as shown by its Coefficient of Variation (123.43%),followed by CBoP(96.42%),PNB(81.15%), while the growth has been most steady for SBI Group (70.29%),during the period under study.

A discernible feature of the various types of deposits from the public has been the rising dominance of fixed deposits and declining share of current deposits in the total deposits of all the four banks under study. The main reason for this has been the liberalization of withdrawal rules for savings banks' deposits and deregulation of interest rates on deposits. Only the rates on the savings deposits are regulated by RBI. Savings deposits, which reflect the strength of the retail liability franchise, are the focus of the banks' customer acquisition efforts.

5.5.4 Trends in Fixed Deposits from Banks: The Fixed deposits from banks have also increased significantly (at 5% level of significance) for all the four banks under study. Tables 5.6 and 5.7 depict the trends in fixed and current deposits respectively accepted from banks by the selected four banks under review.The share of Fixed deposits in the total deposits from banks of SBI Group increased from 32.22% in 1985 to 41.43% in 1995-96.However, in the later years of the reforms, the share decreased 29.03% in 2006-07.

Table 5.6: Trends in Fixed Deposits from Banks

(Amount in Rs. crores)

Year	SBI Group	ICICI Bank	PNB	CBoP
1985	611 (32.22)	-	152 (75.25)	-
1995-96	2832 (41.43)	82 (98.80)	470 (82.02)	1 (100.00)
2006-07	5457 (29.03)	14579 (96.91)	810 (37.83)	1692 (96.25)
Trend GR Period I	13.21	-	11.18	-
Period II	8.10	59.37	2.49	64.02
PeriodI&II	10.81	-	9.78	-
C.V.	69.95	104.72	61.06	122.00
T- value	6.15*	7.40*	5.39*	4.38*

Source: Performance Highlights of Public and Private Sector Banks,
Various Issues, IBA, Mumbai.
Note:(i) Figures in parentheses denote the percentage share in total deposits from banks.

The share   of Fixed deposits in the total deposits from banks of PNB   increased from   75.25%   in 1985 to   82.02%   in 1995-96.However, the share gradually reduced to 37.83% in 2006-07.

As far as the two Private Sector Banks are concerned, again the major share in the total deposits has been held by fixed deposits from banks. The share of Fixed deposits in the total deposits decreased from 98.80% in 1995-96 for ICICI Bank to 96.91% in 2006-07 and from100% to 96.25% for CBoP during the same period.

During period I, from 1985 to 1994-95, the rise in Fixed deposits has been greater for SBI Group, i.e. 13.21 while for PNB, the growth rate has been 11.18.   During Period II, i.e. the post-reforms period (1995-96 to 2006-07) Fixed deposits   have risen for all the four banks under study, the maximum rise being for   CBoP (64.02) followed by ICICI Bank (59.37), SBI Group (8.10) and PNB (2.49). If we compare the overall   trend growth rates of the two Public Sector Banks i.e. from

188

1985 to 2006-07, then the growth rate has been a little higher for SBI Group (10.81) than that of PNB(9.78).It has been found that after the initiation of reforms, the Fixed Deposits from banks have decreased for the two Public Sector Banks under study.

The rise in Fixed Deposits from banks has been most volatile for CBoP(122.00%), followed by ICICI Bank(104.72%),SBI Group (69.95%), while the growth has been most steady for PNB, its Coefficient of Variation being only 61.06%.

5.5.5 Trends in Current Deposits from Banks

The Current deposits from banks have also increased significantly (at 5% level of significance) for all the four banks under study. After the initiation of reforms, the Current Deposits from banks have increased for the two Public Sector Banks.

Table5.7: Trends in Current Deposits from Banks

(Amount in Rs. crores)

Year	SBI Group	ICICI Bank	PNB	CBoP
1985	1285 (67.77)	-	50 (24.75)	-
1995-96	4004 (58.57)	1 (1.20)	103 (17.98)	-
2006-07	13337 (70.96)	465 (3.09)	1331 (62.17)	66 (3.75)
Trend GR Period I	9.38	-	0.63	-
Period II	9.49	71.79	28.84	53.09
Period I & II	10.44	-	14.87	-
C.V.	61.69	118.37	171.28	117.80
T-value	14.38*	5.71*	3.87*	6.53*

Source: Performance Highlights of Public and Private Sector Banks, Various Issues, IBA, Mumbai.

Note: (i)Figures given in parentheses denote the percentage share in total deposits from banks.

The share of Current deposits in the total deposits from banks of SBI Group initially decreased from 67.77% in 1985 to 58.57% in

189

1995-96.During the later years of the reforms, the share increased to 70.96% in 2006-07. The share of Current deposits in the total deposits from banks of PNB decreased from 24.75% in 1985 to 17.98% in 1995-96, while it increased phenomenally to 62.17% in 2006-07 for PNB.

The share of Current deposits in the total deposits increased from 1.20% in 1995-96 for ICICI Bank to 3.09% in 2006-07 and from a scratch to 3.75% for CBoP during the same period.

During period I, from 1985 to 1994-95,the rise in Current deposits from banks has been greater for SBI Group(9.38), while for PNB, the growth rate has been (0.63). During Period II, i.e. the post-reforms period (1995-96 to 2006-07) Current deposits from banks have risen for all the four banks under study, the maximum rise being for ICICI Bank(71.79), followed by CBoP (53.09), PNB (28.84) and SBI Group(9.49). If we compare the overall trend growth rates of the two Public Sector Banks, i.e. from 1985 to 2006-07,then the growth rate has been greater for PNB (14.87) than that of SBI Group (10.44).

The rise in Current Deposits from banks has been most volatile for PNB as indicated by its Coefficient of Variation i.e.171.28%, followed by ICICI Bank(118.37%),CBoP (117.80%), while the growth has been most steady for SBI Group, its Coefficient of Variation being only 61.69%.

It is clear that the share of fixed deposits from banks has reduced while that of current deposits has increased over the period under study. The decline may be probably due to the decline in interest rates on fixed deposits offered by banks.

One notable feature of the trends in inter-bank deposits has been the increasing dominance of current deposits in the total deposits from banks for SBI Group and PNB in the later years of the study, during which current deposits have held the major share. This is mainly due to the large branch network of these banks and spread of banking habit to mobilize current deposits in a big way.

Both the Private Sector Banks under study have mainly focused on fixed deposits. Only in the later years of the study importance was given to current deposits as depicted by their rising share in total deposits of the banks. ICICI Bank still focuses on fixed deposits as the share of current deposits go a long way in acquiring and retaining customers, thus providing a competitive edge in the banking arena.

5.6 BORROWINGS

Borrowed Funds: These sources of funds are of a non-depository nature and are useful when a bank temporarily needs more funds than are being deposited and experiences paucity of funds. The borrowings can be from the following sources:

5.6.1 Borrowings from the RBI: The Reserve Bank of India is traditionally the 'lender of the last resort.' RBI provides liquidity to the banks when all other sources of funds have been exhausted. The RBI usually provides such liquidity to scheduled commercial banks by way of credit refinance, export credit refinance, standby refinance against pledge of Government securities in times of mismatch between sources and uses of funds and discretionary refinance to tide over temporary financial stringencies during the busy season. The assistance from RBI helps in procuring loanable resources. RBI fixes the refinance limits according to its terms and conditions. RBI is also authorized to make loans and advances to the scheduled banks repayable on demand or on the expiry of fixed period not exceeding 90 days against certain security e.g. gold, silver, bill of exchange and promissory notes (as are eligible for purchase and discount by RBI).

RBI introduced with effect from 1st Nov. 1970 a scheme of Rediscounting bills of exchange under section 17(2)(a) of the RBI Act. The scheme covered genuine trade bills, i.e. those that evidenced sale and/or dispatch of goods only. However, of late RBI has not been extending rediscounting facility under the scheme to banks and no bills have been rediscounted by the banks since 1991.

The Committee for Banking Sector Reforms, 1998 recommended that the RBI's support to the market should be through a Liquidity Adjustment Facility (LAF) operated by way of repo and reverse repo providing a reasonable corridor to market players (Machiraju, 2002). Consequently, RBI introduced Interim Liquidity Adjustment Facility (ILAF) through lending against collateral of Government Securities at various interest rates. The General Refinance Facility was replaced by Collateralized Lending Facility (CLF) from 21.4.1999.

Methods of Borrowings from RBI

- Rediscounting Purchase of eligible bills.
- Loans & advances against certain securities

Advances to banks by RBI against approved securities under section 17 (4a) of the Reserve Bank of India Act, 1934, viz.

(i) Stocks, funds, securities (other than immovable property) in which a trustee is authorized to invest trust money.

(ii) Gold or silver documents of title to the same.

(iii) Such bills of exchange and promissory notes as are eligible for purchase/discount by RBI or those guaranteed as to the repayment of the principal of interest by a State Government.

(iv)   Promissory note of any scheduled bank or state cooperative bank supported by documents of title to goods.

The securities lodged for obtaining demand loans should be proportionate to the limits sanctioned to it, subject a margin of 5% in the case of Government securities maturing within 10 years and a margin of 10% in the case of those maturing after 10 years. Same margins as in above item in the case of advances against other trustee securities, where market quotations were available.

Trends in Borrowings from RBI

The Borrowings from RBI have not increased significantly (at 5% level of significance) for any of the four banks under study. Table 5.8 highlights that the share of borrowings from RBI in 1995-96 was 30.66% for SBI Group. The share of borrowing from RBI for PNB was 68.23% in 1995-96.

Table 5.8: Trends in   Borrowings from RBI

(Amount in Rs. crores)

Year	SBI Group	ICICI Bank	PNB	CBoP
1985	N.A.	-	N.A.	-
1995-96	4510 (30.66)	71 (33.65)	900 (68.23)	20 (100)
2006-07	2455 (5.08)	0	600 (30.79)	13 (1.4)
C.V.	125.02	142.93	177.71	139.09
T- value	0.55	0.93	0.85	1.06

Source: Performance Highlights of Public and Private Sector Banks, Various Issues,
        IBA, Mumbai.
Note:(i)N.A. stands for not available.
        (ii)Figures given in parentheses denote the percentage share in total borrowings.

The share of borrowings from RBI has followed a very erratic pattern for all the four banks under study. The share of borrowings from RBI was 5.08% for SBI Group and 30.79% for PNB in 2006-07.

The share of borrowings from RBI was 33.65% for ICICI Bank in 1995-96 which declined drastically to nil in 2006-07.The share of borrowings from RBI for CBoP was 100% in 1995-96, which declined to only 1.40% in 2006-07. The borrowings from RBI have decreased for all the banks under study. The trend growth rates could not be calculated for the borrowings from RBI due to lack of adequate data.

The rise in borrowings from RBI has been most volatile for PNB as indicated by its Coefficient of Variation (177.71%),followed by ICICI Bank(142.93%),CBoP(139.09%), while the growth has been quite steady for SBI Group(125.02%).

5.6.2 Borrowings from Other Banks: In order to transact business, banks in India, quite frequently, open their current accounts with other banks in India and abroad at places where they are not represented and make overdraft arrangements with them on secured or unsecured basis. Inter-bank liabilities consist of demand and time liabilities and borrowings from banks. Inter-bank indebtedness arising out of transfer of deposits from one person to another is offset in the clearing house and any remaining balances are covered by the transfer of banker's deposits with the central bank. The settlement of inter-bank indebtedness does not affect the level of aggregate deposits of the banking system. The core of inter-bank borrowing is the call money market where funds are borrowed and lent by banks to each other for one day and short notice for a period up to 14 days. The securities lodged to secure the borrowings represent a part of investment of the borrowing bank.

Trends in Borrowings from banks

The Borrowings from other banks have increased significantly (at 5% level of significance) for SBI Group and ICICI Bank only as shown in Table 5.9.

For SBI Group, its share in the total borrowings was 0.20% in 1995-96, which increased to 3.58% in 2006-07. The share of borrowings from banks was 3.79% in 1995-96 for PNB, which reduced to 1.13% in 2006-07.

Table 5.9: Trends in Borrowings from other banks

(Amount in Rs. crores)

Year	SBI Group	ICICI Bank	PNB	CBoP
1985	N.A.	-	N.A.	-
1995-96	30 (0.20)	105 (49.76)	50 (3.79)	-
2006-07	1731 (3.58)	4267 (8.32)	22 (1.13)	548 (58.86)
Trend GR Period I	-	-	-	-
Period II	37.13	59.56	20.60	-
Period I & II	-	-	-	-
C.V.	167.98	105.76	130.30	189.69
T- value	3.60*	6.30*	0.58	1.31

Source: Performance Highlights of Public and Private Sector Banks,
Various Issues, IBA, Mumbai.
Note:(i) N.A. stands for not available.
(ii)Figures in parentheses denote the share in total borrowings.

The share of borrowings from banks was 49.76% in 1995-96 for ICICI Bank, which reduced to 8.32% in 2006-07. CBoP experienced a rise in the share of borrowings from banks, from nil in 1995-96 to 58.86% in 2006-07.

For the period I, from 1985 to 1994-95, the trend growth rate could not be computed due to non-availability of data. During Period

II, i.e. the post-reforms period (1995-96 to 2006-07) borrowings from other banks have risen for all the four banks under study, the maximum rise being for ICICI Bank(59.56), followed by SBI Group(37.13)and PNB(20.60).The trend growth rate of CBoP could not be calculated due to inadequate data.

The rise in Borrowings from other banks has been most volatile for CBoP as indicated by its Coefficient of Variation (189.69%),followed by SBI Group,(167.98%),PNB(130.30%), while the growth has been quite steady for ICICI Bank(105.76%).

5.6.3 Borrowings from Institutions and Agencies: Apart from borrowings from RBI, banks supplement their sources by resource to refinancing and/or bill rediscounting facilities from many financial institutions: Industrial Development Bank of India (IDBI) and Small Industries Development Bank of India (SIDBI), National Bank for Agricultural and Rural Development (NABARD), Export-Import Bank of India (EXIM Bank), National Housing Bank (NHB) and Discount and Finance House of India (DFHI).

Table 5.10 depicts the trends in borrowings from Institutions and Agencies of the selected four banks. The data for the total borrowings of SBI Group and PNB from 1985 to 1990-91, are available and the data for the various types of borrowings from 1991-92 onwards is available. The total borrowings have increased from 1985 to 1990-91 for both the selected Public Sector Banks.

Trends in Borrowings from Institutions and Agencies

The Borrowings from institutions and agencies have increased significantly (at 5% level of significance) only for SBI Group. For SBI Group, its share in the total borrowings was 8.76% in 1995-96,which increased to 16.39% in 2006-07.The share of borrowings from Institutions and agencies was 26.76% in 1995-96 for PNB, which reduced to 16.06% in 2006-07. The share of borrowings from Institutions and agencies was 15.17% in 1995-96 for ICICI Bank, which increased to 17.85% in 2006-07. Similarly, CBoP also registered a rise in the share borrowings from of institutions and agencies from a scratch in 1995-96 to 23.63% in 2006-07.

Table 5.10: Trends in Borrowings from Institutions &Agencies

(Amount in Rs. crore)

Year	SBI Group	ICICI Bank	PNB	CBoP
1985	N.A.	-	N.A.	-
1995-96	1289 (8.76)	32 (15.17)	353 (26.76)	-
2006-07	7922 (16.39)	9151 (17.85)	313 (16.06)	220 (23.63)
Trend GR Period I				
Period II	14.89	114.06	2.70	43.83
Period I & II	-	-	-	-
C.V.	84.96	123.70	65.03	206.20
T- value	2.98*	2.04	1.44	2.09

Source: Performance Highlights of Public and Private Sector Banks, Various Issues, IBA, Mumbai.
Note:(i) N.A. stands for not available.
(ii)Figures given in parentheses denote the percentage share in total borrowings.

During Period II, i.e. the post-reforms period (1995-96 to 2006-07) borrowings from institutions and agencies have risen for all the four banks under study, the maximum rise being for ICICI Bank(114.06),followed by CBoP (43.83), SBI Group(14.89) and PNB(2.70). The rise in Borrowings from institutions and agencies has been most volatile for CBoP as indicated by its Coefficient of Variation (206.20%),followed by ICICI Bank(123.70%),SBI Group (84.96%), while the growth has been most steady for PNB (65.03%).

5.6.4 Borrowings from outside India: The growth in borrowings from outside India has been significant (at five per cent level) for all the banks except CBoP as depicted in Table 5.11. During period I, from 1985 to 1994-95, the trend growth rate could not be computed due to non-availability of data.

Table 5.11: Trends in Borrowings from outside India

(Amount in Rs. crores)

Year	SBI Group	ICICI Bank	PNB	CBoP
1985	N.A.	-	N.A.	-
1995-96	8883 (60.38)	3 (1.42)	16 (1.21)	0
2006-07	36215 (74.94)	37838 (73.82)	1014 (52.03)	150 (16.11)
Trend GR Period I	-	-	-	-
Period II	14.60		67.84	
Period I& II	-	-	-	-
C.V.	73.53	148.78	154.55	201.54
T- value	4.20*	4.75*	3.44*	2.86*

Source: Performance Highlights of Public and Private Sector Banks, Various Issues, IBA, Mumbai.

Note:(i) N.A. stands for not available.

(ii)Figures given in parentheses denote the percentage share in total borrowings.

During Period II, i.e. the post-reforms period (1995-96 to 2006-07) borrowings from outside India have risen for all the four banks under study, the rise being greater for PNB (67.84) than that of SBI Group (14.60). The trend growth rate could not be computed for the two Private Sector Banks due to inconsistency of data.

The rise in Borrowings from outside India has been most volatile for CBoP as indicated by its Coefficient of Variation (201.54%), followed by PNB (154.55%),ICICI Bank (148.78%), while the growth has been most steady for SBI Group (73.53%).

All the four banks have stopped relying on RBI for funds in the later years of the study; hence no significant relation could be established over the period under study. CBoP has relied mostly on other banks and institutions & agencies for borrowings as compared to other sources, however the rise in the latter source has also not been significant at five percent level of significance for the bank. The major components of borrowings for ICICI Bank have been borrowing from other banks and from outside India. For CBoP also, the vital components of borrowings are from other banks and from institutions and agencies.

5.7 OTHER LIABILITIES AND PROVISIONS

This category of liabilities includes:

(i)   Bills Payable

(ii)   Inter-Office adjustments

(iii)   Interest accrued

(iv)   Others (including provisions).

5.7.1 Trends in Bills Payable

The Bills Payable have increased significantly (at 5% level of significance) for all the four banks under study as shown in Table 5.12.

The data of Bills payable and total of other liabilities and provisions is only available from 1985 to 1990-91. Henceforth, the data for all the constituents under this liability are available. For SBI Group, the share of Bills Payable in the total other liabilities and provisions was 51.71% in 1985,which decreased to 24.43% in 1995-96.The share of Bills Payable in other liabilities and provisions was 39.53% in 1985 for PNB, which increased to 42.72% in 1995-96.However,in the later years of reforms, the share of Bills Payable

199

increased to 30.69% in 2006-07 for SBI Group. PNB experienced a decline in the share of Bills Payable, which was 9.33% in 2006-07.

The share of Bills Payable in other Liabilities and provisions was 43.55% in 1995-96 for ICICI Bank, which reduced to 11.07% in 2006-07.

Table 5.12 : Trends in Bills Payable

(Amount in Rs. crores)

Year	SBI Group	ICICI Bank	PNB	CBoP
1985	650 (51.71)	-	34 (39.53)	-
1995-96	8972 (24.43)	27 (43.55)	804 (42.72)	12 (20.00)
2006-07	24876 (30.69)	4234 (11.07)	950 (9.33)	440 (34.05)
Trend GR Period I	31.58	-	39.4	-
Period II	7.84	59.50	6.18	29.49
Period I& II	15.56	-	16.65	
C.V.	68.69	119.10	71.08	105.05
T- value	14.89*	6.89*	10.06*	4.39*

Source: Performance Highlights of Public and Private Sector Banks, Various Issues, IBA, Mumbai.

Note:(i) N.A. stands for not available.

(ii)Figures given in parentheses denote the percentage share in total other liabilities &provisions.

However, in the case of CBoP the share of Bills Payable in other Liabilities and provisions increased from 20.00% in 1995-96 to 34.05% in 2006-07.

During period I, from 1985 to 1994-95, PNB registered a trend growth rate of 39.40, which was higher than SBI Group's growth rate of 31.58. During Period II, i.e. the post-reforms period (1995-96 to 2006-07) bills payable have risen for all the four banks under study, the maximum rise being for ICICI Bank (59.50) followed by CBoP (29.49), SBI Group(7.84) and PNB(6.18). If we compare the overall trend growth rates of the two Public Sector Banks, i.e. from 1985 to 2006-07, then the growth rate has been a little greater for PNB (16.65) than that of SBI Group(15.56). The rise in bills payable has been most volatile for ICICI Bank as indicated by its Coefficient of Variation (119.10%),followed by CBoP (105.05%),PNB (71.08%), while the growth has been most steady for SBI Group(68.69%).

5.7.2 Trends in Inter-office Adjustments

Inter-Office adjustments have recorded significant growth (at five percent level) for both SBI Group and PNB, as shown in Table 5.13. For SBI Group, the share of Inter-Office adjustments in the total other Liabilities and provisions was 2.20% in 1995-96,which decreased to a mere 1.75% in 2006-07.The share of Inter-office adjustments in other Liabilities and provisions was 3.40% in 1995-96 for PNB, which increased to 12.77% in 2006-07. Similarly, CBoP also had Inter-Office adjustments in 1995-96 (the share being as high as 35%), which reduced to nil in 2006-07.

The Trend Growth rate could not be computed for Period I due to non-availability of data from 1985 to 1990-91. Similarly, the trend growth rates for ICICI and CBoP could not be computed due to inadequate data. The growth in Inter-Office adjustments has been higher for SBI Group (29.30) than that of PNB (11.94) during Period II.

Table 5.13: Trends in Inter-office adjustments

(Amount in Rs.crore)

Year	SBI Group	ICICI Bank	PNB	CBoP
1985	N.A.	-	N.A.	-
1995-96	806 (2.20)	0	64 (3.40)	21 (35.00)
2006-07	1423 (1.75)	0	1300 (12.77)	0
Trend GR Period I	-	-		-
Period II	29.30	-	11.94	-
Period I & II	-	-		-
C.V.	131.18	181.78	124.17	218.73
T-value	2.27*	2.20	2.63*	0.81

Source: Performance Highlights of Public and Private Sector Banks,
   Various Issues, IBA, Mumbai.
Note: (i) N.A. stands for not available.
   (ii)Figures given in parentheses denote the percentage share in total other
   liabilities &provisions.

The Coefficient of Variation has been the most for CBoP (218.73%) indicating maximum variation, followed by ICICI Bank(181.78%),and SBI Group(131.18%), while it has been the least for PNB (124.17) indicating a stable growth.

5.7.3 Interest Accrued

Both the Public Sector Banks were able to reduce the liability due to Interest accrued towards the later years of study. The interest accrued has increased significantly (at 5% level of significance) for ICICI Bank and CBoP only. The share of interest accrued in the total other Liabilities and provisions was 24.60% in 1995-96,which decreased to 7.36% in 2006-07 for SBI Group. The share of interest accrued in other Liabilities and provisions was 3.40% in 1995-96 for PNB, which decreased to 2.41% in 2006-07.

Table 5.14: Trends in Interest Accrued

(Amount in Rs. crores)

Year	SBI Group	ICICI Bank	PNB	CBoP
1985	N.A.	-	N.A.	-
1995-96	9033 (24.60)	4 (6.45)	64 (3.40)	2 (3.33)
2006-07	5968 (7.36)	2041 (5.34)	245 (2.41)	118 (9.13)
Trend GR Period I	-	-	-	-
Period II	-2.49	89.85	5.08	21.18
PeriodI& II	-	-	-	-
C.V.	55.34	106.66	40.97	86.44
T value	1.53	4.28*	0.53	2.99*

Source: Performance Highlights of Public and Private Sector Banks,
Various Issues, IBA, Mumbai.
Note:(i) N.A. stands for not available.
(ii)Figures given in parentheses denote the percentage share in total other
liabilities &provisions.

The share of Interest accrued in other Liabilities and
provisions was 6.45% in 1995-96 for ICICI Bank, which reduced
slightly to 5.34% in 2006-07. However, CBoP registered a rise in the
share of interest accrued in other Liabilities and provisions
borrowings from banks, from 3.33% in 1995-96 to 9.13% in 2006-07.
During period I, from 1985 to 1994-95, the trend growth rate could not
be computed as the data was not available from 1985 to 1990-91.During
Period II, i.e. the post-reforms period (1995-96 to 2006-07) interest
accrued has risen for all the four banks under study, the maximum rise
being for ICICI Bank (89.85) followed by CBoP(21.18) and
PNB(5.08).The growth rate of Interest accrued reduced (-2.49) only
for SBI Group.

The rise in Interest accrued has been most volatile for ICICI
Bank as indicated by its Coefficient of Variation (106.66%),followed

by CBoP (86.44%),and SBI Group (55.34%), while the growth has been most steady for PNB (40.97%).

5.7.4 Trends in Provisions and Others

Provisions and others have increased significantly (at 5% level of significance) for all the four banks under study due to the introduction of Asset Classification and Provisioning Norms. For all the banks under study, Provisions have constituted the major share in Other liabilities and Provisions as a result of the introduction of Asset Classification and Provisioning Norms as depicted in Table 5.15.

The share of Provisions and others in the total other Liabilities and provisions was 48.77% in 1995-96, which increased appreciably to 60.19% in 2006-07 for SBI Group. The share Provisions and others in other Liabilities and provisions was 50.48% in 1995-96 for PNB, which also increased substantially to 75.49% in 2006-07.

Table 5.15: Trends in Provisions and Others

(Amount in Rs. crores)

Year	SBI Group	ICICI Bank	PNB	CBoP
1985	N.A.	-	N.A.	-
1995-96	17908 (48.77)	31 (50.00)	950 (50.48)	25 (41.67)
2006-07	48788 (60.19)	31954 (83.58)	7683 (75.49)	734 (56.81)
Trend GR Period I	-	-	-	-
Period II	7.67	100.04	24.17	36.60
Period I & II	-	-	-	-
C.V.	46.52	113.76	91.92	111.07
T- value	5.24*	7.27*	7.38*	5.25*

Source: Performance Highlights of Public and Private Sector Banks, Various Issues, IBA, Mumbai.

Note:(i) N.A. stands for not available.

(ii)Figures given in parentheses denote the percentage share in total other liabilities &provisions.

The share of Provisions and others in other Liabilities and provisions was 50.00% in 1995-96 for ICICI Bank, which increased to 83.58% in 2006-07. CBoP also registered a rise in the share of Provisions and others in other Liabilities and provisions, from 41.67% in 1995-96 to 56.81% in 2006-07. During period I, from 1985 to 1994-95, the trend growth rate could not be computed as the data was not available for the period 1985 to 1990-91.During Period II, i.e. the post-reforms period (1995-96 to 2006-07) Provisions and other liabilities have risen for all the four banks under study, the maximum rise being for ICICI Bank (100.04) followed by CBoP (36.60), PNB (24.17) and SBI Group (7.67).

The rise in Other Liabilities has been most volatile for ICICI Bank as indicated by its Coefficient of Variation (113.76%),followed closely by CBoP (111.07%), and PNB (91.92%), while the growth has been most steady for SBI Group(46.52%).

5.8 CONCLUSIONS

Liabilities management has become a vital area of concern for banks today as assets have to be managed in tandem with liability for commercial banks. On the basis of the study undertaken with regard to the liabilities of the four selected banks, the following observations have been made:

- Capital is the most important constituent of the liabilities of a bank; hence its adequacy needs to be attained by the banks at all costs. Over the period under review from 1995-96 to 2006-07, the capital adequacy ratio has increased significantly only for PNB, while it has declined substantially for the two private sector banks, viz. ICICI Bank and CBoP. This is a matter of grave concern for the two banks and needs to be looked into for assuring the confidence of the investors especially for CBoP. Moreover, with the introduction of Basel-II norms, the operational risk has also come into focus along with credit risk and market risk, for which more capital has to be provided.

- Reserves and surplus complement the capital of a bank and have risen significantly for all the four banks under study.

- Deposits form the major sources of funds for banks. Deposits from public provide the funds for lending to banks. All the types of deposits from public, viz. Fixed, Savings and Current deposits have increased significantly for all the four banks under study during the period under review. Deposits from banks; fixed and current have also grown significantly for all the four banks under study. Customer service demands improvement especially in the public sector banks to increase deposits. The deposits insurance cover needs to be enhanced from the present limit of one lakh. The private sector banks need to tap rural areas for deposits. To this end, they need to open up branches in such areas. Moreover,with the introduction of liberalized economy, Foreign Direct Investment (FDI) has paved the way for generating funds.

- All the four banks under study have over the years, stopped approaching the RBI for borrowings due to the availability of cheaper sources of funds. Borrowings from other banks have increased significantly for SBI Group and ICICI Bank. Borrowings from institutions and agencies have grown significantly only for SBI Group while it has decreased for PNB. Borrowings from abroad have increased significantly for all the four banks. ICICI Bank and CBoP should access foreign capital as now FDI has been allowed up to 74%. Both the private sector banks are relying broadly on institutions and agencies for funds. They should borrow from other banks also as too much dependence on a single source may cause problems for these banks in the long run. However, the two Public Sector Banks are borrowing from all three sources, viz. from banks, institutions and agencies and from outside India.

- Among the other liabilities and provisions of banks, bills payable have increased significantly for all the four banks under study. The rise in liability due to inter-office adjustments has increased significantly for both the selected Public Sector Banks. Interest accrued has increased significantly for ICICI Bank and CBoP, while other liabilities (including provisions) have grown significantly for all the four banks under study. Bills seem to be most popular among banks to even out short-term liquidity within the perimeter of the banking system. Provisions have risen for all the four banks due to the introduction of asset classification and provisioning norms adopted by all the banks as a result of the economic reforms.

With the interest rate deregulation generating intense competition for funds banks have started focusing on the mix of liabilities and their costs. Thus, there has been a conscious shift towards, "Liability Management" to gain control over the liabilities and interest rate on deposits is the key. By altering the interest rates on deposits and other sources of funds, banks can manage funds better. Banks have realized that profitability is a function of risk management which encompasses the entire structure of a bank's business, the relationship between assets and liabilities and the returns generated from them in the milieu of risks.

On the liability side, there has not been much compositional change since the initiation of forms, as deposits continue to account for the major share of the total liabilities.

This is also due to the fact that after the reduction in cash reserve ratio and statutory reserve ratio, banks are concentrating on deposits mobilization with greater vigour as banks have more lendable resources at their disposal. Deposits are thus, the key to bank's profitability as they provide credit for lending which enables the banks to attain profits.

REFERENCES

Abrol, Prem Nath(1987),*Commercial Banking,* Anupma Publishers, Distributors, New Delhi.

Bhat, Prasanna(1999), "A System for Asset-Liability Management" *Hindustan Business Line*, August 19, p. 14.

Bhusunurmath, Mythili(1998), "Teaching Old Dogs New Tricks" *The Economic Times*, 21 September,p. 9.

Datar,M.K; and Banerjee, Saumya Sankar(2007), "Simultaneity Between Bank Profitability and Regulatory Capital, " *Prajnan*, NIBM,April-June,p. 36.

Desai, Vasant(2006),*Banks and Institutional Management,* Himalaya Publishing House, Mumbai.

Jain, Parasmal(2004); "Basel-II Accord Issues and Suggestions, " *IBA Bulletin* Vol. XXVI, No.6 pp.4-7.

Kamath,M.V.(1996), "Asset Liability Management, "*Canbank QuarterlyReview*,October-March,Vol.I,No.4&Vol.VII,No.1, p.10.

Kumar, Ranjana(2003), " Move Towards Risk Based Supervision of Banks -The Role of the Central Banks and the Market Player, " *Vinimaya*, Vol. XXIV, No.6, p. 5.

Kumar, Ravi T.(2000), *Asset Liability Management*, ICFAI Vision series Finance, Vision Books. New Delhi.

Machiraju, H.R.(2002), *Indian Financial System,* Vikas Publishing House Pvt. Ltd., New Delhi.

Mehta, Sangita (1998), "Defusing Time Bombs Ticking in the Books", *The Business Standard*, Sept. 24, p. 10.

Patheja, Anju(1994), *Financial Management of Commercial Banks,* South Asia Publications, New Delhi.

Rangarajan, C. (1990), "Optimum Utilization of Resources under the Constraints of Credit Policy", in Amiya Sen Kumar, Malay Gupta, Swapan Chakrabarti (eds.) *Banking in the 1990s*, Himalaya Publishing House, Bombay, p.341.

RBI(2005),*Instructions for Banks and Banking Operations,* Authorized Publication of RBI, Taxmann Publications, Sixth Edition.

Reed, W. Edward;and Gill, K. Edward(1989),*Commercial Banking*, Prentice Hall. New Jersey, Fourth Edition.

Sen, A.K.(1992), "Capital Adequacy in Banks-Challenges & Strategies"*Indian Management*, Vol. 31,No. 3,June,pp.30-33.

Sharma, Kapil;and Kulkarni, P.R.(2006),"Asset Liability Management Approach in Indian Banks: A Review & Suggestion," *The Journal of Accounting and Finance*, Vol. 20, No.2, Apr- Sept, pp.8-10.

Srivastava, R.M;and Nigam, Divya(2005), *Management of Financial Institutions*, Himalaya Publishing House, Mumbai.

Suneja, H.R.(1992), *Management of Bank Credit*, Himalaya Publishing House, Bombay.

Vidyarthi, V.P;and Gupta, K.R Satendra(2007), "Capital Accord and Three Pillars of Basel-II, "in Mohan Prasad Srivastava, Pradeep `Kumar Pandey and V.P. Vidyarthi (eds.) *Banking Reforms and Globalisation*, APH Publishing Corpn, New Delhi p. 79.

CHAPTER-6
TRENDS IN PROFITABILITY

The banking sector has been under transition ever since India attained her independence (Qamar, 2003). Up to 1969, banking sector was in the hands of private operators and banks had been pursuing their commercial motive of augmenting their earnings. However, in the post-nationalization era, banks lost their commercial character and social banking concept pushed profit motive to the background. Proliferation of non-remunerative small loaning under Government sponsored schemes, excessive statutory pre-emption, political interference and providing services at a price that had hardly purified costs made matters worse for Indian commercial banks (Srivastava and Nigam, 2005).

The reforms sought to improve the banks' profitability by lowering pre-emption (through reductions in the cash reserve and statutory liquidity ratios) and to strengthen the banking system through the institution of eight per cent capital adequacy norms; in addition to income recognition, asset classification and provisioning requirement in line with international best practices. The profits are needed by the banks for a number of reasons such as: banks are basically commercial organizations, to sustain themselves, RBI desires to maintain certain level of capital fund in relation to their risk weighted assets, i.e. eight per cent up to March 1999, for making provisions against the loan assets, in view of the modified rules relating to Income Recognition and for making huge investment of capital nature for mechanization and computerization (Prasad, 2006).

Today, the bank-management of India is facing a two-faceted challenge-to improve their profitability on the one hand and to serve the public in new ways and means with greater efficiency and effectiveness on the other (Amandeep, 1993).

6.1 FACTORS AFFECTING PROFITABILITY OF BANKS

The various factors which promote the profitability performance of the Indian banks are listed below:

1. **Branch Network: The** growth of Indian banking sector prior to nationalization was not satisfactory keeping in view the socio-economic requirements of the country (Raut and Das, 1996). Hence, after nationalization, massive branch expansion was carried out. More particularly, with the advent of the social control measures, and the subsequent nationalization of major commercial banks, the Public Sector Banks started opening their branches in rural areas, relatively less developed regions of the country on a massive scale. If we analyze the trends in branch expansion of the four banks under review (refer Tables 3.6 to 3.9, Chapter 3), it is observed that both the Public Sector Banks, viz. SBI group and PNB have the highest proportion of rural and semi-urban branches in each year of the study, while both the Private Sector Banks are solely motivated by profits and thus are reluctant in entering the rural areas which lack infrastructure. The rural branches take longer time to break-even and thus are avoided by private sector banks, which cater to the urban elite only.

2. **Priority Sector Lending:** After the nationalization of the major Public Sector Banks, priority sectors have been allotted 40 per cent of the total bank credit. The commercial banks in general and the Public Sector Banks in particular have achieved the target in many years in quantitative terms. But in qualitative terms, there is an apprehension that the advances to priority sector resulted in

212

problems of interest income loss due to highly subsidized lending rate, additional manpower requirement for supervision of small loans, mounting over-dues, poor recovery and raising volume of non-performing assets which adversely affect the profits and profitability of Public Sector Banks (Anbumani and Niranjana, 2002). (Refer Chapter 3, Table 3.10).

3. Deposit Mobilization: Mobilization of deposits from the hitherto untapped sources, particularly from the under-banked and un-banked areas, has been one of the prime objectives of nationalization of banks. The larger the amount of deposits a bank holds the greater leverage it has.

4. Credit Policies: The credit policies of the RBI affect the profitability of banks considerably. Prior to the reforms substantial portion of the lendable resources were blocked in maintaining the statutory pre-emption in the form of CRR and SLR apart from providing for priority sector credit. Thus, banks had little funds for granting loans and advances and profitability suffered adversely. In order to prevent further erosion in profitability, reforms were initiated. Restrictions on interest rate fixation and directed credit programmes were lifted. Statutory pre-emption in the form of CRR and SLR were reduced gradually thereby making more funds available for lending.

5. Competition: The reforms were initiated to usher in competition among banks and to enhance the efficiency of banks. In order to increase the efficiency and quality of service of the nationalized banks, the Narasimham Committee recommended that the banking industry be made more competitive by removing restrictions on entry and expansion of foreign banks.

6. Composition of Assets: Assets of a bank consist of long-term assets such as investments, loans and advances and current assets such as cash, marketable securities and money at call and short notice. Higher the liquidity of an asset, lesser will be its revenue. Thus, returns on long-term assets will be higher than those from short-term assets. Hence, the proportion of liquid assets in total assets is a vital factor in the analysis of profitability.

7. Market Share: Market share of a bank in the banking industry influences the quantum of profits. With the ushering in of the reforms, a number of private sector banks have emerged as dynamic components of the Indian banking system, reducing not only the market share of Public Sector Banks but also those of Foreign Banks.

8. Spread and Burden: Profit of a bank is determined and influenced mainly by spread and burden. The magnitude of spread (the difference between the interest earned and interest paid by the banks) depends upon:

(i) **Interest earned** (being affected by the total earning assets, their composition and yield); and

(ii) **interest paid** (being affected by the total interest paying liabilities, their composition and interest rates) which get influenced mainly by government and Reserve Bank of India's policies and to some extent by composition and cooperation among the Banks, and the quality of asset and liability management decision(Amandeep,1993). The second determinant of profit is burden, which is represented by the excess of non-interest expenditure over non-interest income of the banks. The magnitude of burden depends upon **Non-interest income** being affected by

214

range, volume and service charges, which in turn, get influenced by competition among banks, discretionary powers given to the managers and cost of services and **Non-interest expenses.** These linkages of Spread and Burden are depicted in Fig.6(a).

Fig.6(a): Spread and Burden-Their Backward Linkages

Variable to be influenced	I	II	III	IV
		Interest earned	(a) Total earning assets (b) Composition of earning assets (c) Yield on each type of asset	(a) Government & RBI policies (b) Competition & co-operation among banks (c) Quality of asset management decisions
	SPREAD	Interest Paid	(a) Total interest-paying liabilities (b) Composition of interest paying liabilities (c) Interest rate on each component	(a) Govt & RBI policies (b) Competition & cooperation among banks (c) Quality of liability management decision
PROFIT		Non-interest income	(a) Range and volume of services (b) Service Charges	(a)Competition among banks (b)Discretionary powers to managers (c)Cost of services
	BURDEN	Manpower Expenses	(a)Number, seniority and composition of employees (b)Salary structure	(a)Recruitment, promotion and placement policies (b)Wage agreements & policies
		Other Expenses	(a)Nature and volume of business (b)Systems and procedures	(a)Quality of expenditure decision (b)Budgeting & cost control

Source: Varde, Varsha S and Singh Sampat (1983),*Profitability of Commercial Banks*, NIBM, Pune, p7.

Non-interest expenses comprising of Manpower expenses being affected by salary structure, number, seniority and composition of employees, and in turn get influenced by the quality of expenditure decisions, budgeting and cost control techniques (Varde and Singh, 1983).

9. Revenue Diversification Initiatives: One of the hallmarks of the modern banking institutions is that they have tended to become one-stop shop for financial products and services. Intense competition for business with increasing volatility in market is putting immense pressure on the management of banks to maintain spread, profitability and long-term viability. Commission and fee-income have the added advantage of not requiring allocation of capital. The Private Sector Banks have cashed on the fee-based sources of income primarily by providing consumer-centric services with the aid of technology adoption and upgradation. The Public Sector Banks have also introduced core banking solutions and are trying to tap the fee-based sources of income.

10. High Level of NPAs: The reform period has witnessed remarkable improvements in the assets quality of banks. The higher proportion of NPAs in priority sector advances as a result of the directed and pre-approved nature of loans sanctioned under sponsored programmes, the absence of any security, lack of effective follow-up due to large number of accounts, legal recovery measures being considered not cost-effective, vitiation of the repayment culture consequent to loan waivers schemes, etc.(Singh,2002).

11. Rising Establishment Expenses: Establishment expenditure is dependent upon number of employees and scale of their enrolments. Public Sector Banks introduced Voluntary Retirement Scheme (VRS) in

216

2000-01 to downsize and rationalize the staff cost. Outgo on account of provisions for provident fund and pension liability of the Public Sector Banks increased significantly in the post-VRS period, especially during 2002-03 and 2003-04(RBI, 2004-05). The Private Sector Banks being more techno-savvy, have comparatively lower proportion of wage bills in Non-interest expenditure as compared to the Public Sector Banks. However, the share of Private Sector Banks in the other operating expenses is higher than their Public Sector counterparts (as depicted in Table 6.12) as they are in the stage of branch expansion and are spending for full-fledged internet banking.

12. Interest Rate Changes: The interest rate risk is the risk of decline in earnings due to the changes in interest rates. Majority of the items of a bank's balance-sheet are affected by the rate of interest. The earnings move in tandem with the interest rates. The declining interest rate regime has put the banks in a tight situation. The essentials of interest rate risk management as follows:

(1)   A structured framework for the banks to manage interest rate volatility, failing which banks may become vulnerable to asset liability mismatch.

(2)   Banks must have an adequate and timely interest rate risk reporting system, which includes ALM risk data warehouse and reporting aspects.

(3)   Banks must make a clear distinction between their trading activity and balance-sheet exposure.

(4)   Banks can limit their exposure to changes in interest rates by restricting their quantum of mismatch between the re-pricing of assets in comparison to liabilities (Sinha, 2006).

Fig.6(b):Performance Focus of Asset-Liability Management: Net Interest Margin

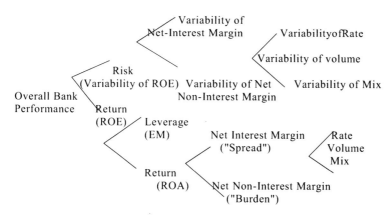

- ROE stands for Return on Equity
- EM stands for Equity Multiplier
- ROA stands for Return on Assets

Source: Sinkey, Jr. F. Joseph (1992), *Commercial Banks' Financial Management in the Financial Services Industry*, Macmillan Publishing Co, New York, p.364.

Thus, profitability is the result of the interplay of various factors. It is an index of operational efficiency of banks and is vital for their sustenance and growth. Declining trends in profits have become a major issue of concern for all. To ensure the survival and growth of the banking sector, it becomes highly imperative to identify various factors which have been responsible for the decline in profitability so that remedial action can be taken and with the deregulation of interest rate structure, the banks have been exposed to interest rate risks. The Net Interest Margin has come under severe pressure. Asset-Liability

Management envisages the process of managing Net Interest Margin within the overall risk.

The key objective of ALM is that of sustaining profitability in such a manner as to augment capital resources (Sehgal and Kher, 2002). ALM is a profit planning tool which manages interest rate volatility (Subramanian, 2002).

Trend analysis is done to evaluate the profitability of the selected banks. In order to analyze the trends in the context of profitability of the banks, some indicators have been selected:

1. Income
2. Expenditure
3. Spread
4. Burden
5. Net profit

6.2 TRENDS IN INTEREST INCOMES OF BANKS

The constituents of a bank's income are interest and discount and other income. The component-wise analysis reveals the relative significance of each component in the total income. Other income consists of commission, exchange brokerage and other receipts.

After the advent of the reforms, the pace of growth of interest income has reduced for both the selected Public Sector Banks due to competition posed by their Private Sector counterparts.

For all the four banks under study, interest on advances and discount received forms a major chunk of the total income as depicted in Table 6.1.

The share of interest income in the total income was initially 88.17% in 1985, which decreased to 83.22% in 1995-96 for SBI Group. The share of interest income in the total income was initially 94.01%

in 1985, which decreased to 89.52% in 1995-96 for PNB. Later on, the share increased to 87.84% for SBI Group and 91.72% for PNB in 2006-07.

Table 6.1: Trends in Income of Banks

(Amount in Rs. crores)

Year	SBI Group		ICICI Bank		PNB		CBoP	
	I.I.	N.I.I.	I.I.	N.I.I.	I.I.	N.I.I.	I.I.	N.I.I.
1985	2,892 (88.17)	388 (11.83)			565 (94.01)	36 (5.99)		
1995-95	17,114 (83.22)	3,450 (16.78)	116 (82.27)	25 (17.73)	3,118 (89.52)	365 (10.48)	28 (84.85)	5 (15.15)
2006-07	56,339 (87.84)	7,799 (12.16)	22,994 (79.50)	5,929 (20.50)	11,537 (91.72)	1,042 (8.28)	1,268 (75.79)	405 (24.21)
Average Share	85.91	14.09	79.16	20.84	89.42	10.58	79.47	20.53
Trend GR Period I	20.45	23.92	-	-	19.33	25.64	-	-
Period II	11.04	11.61	65.63	71.60	11.98	13.02	28.49	33.16
Period I&II	14.91	17.15			14.89	20.02	28.49	
C.V.	73.31	82.25	124.21	118.77	76.26	92.97	91.33	105.17
T-value	19.84*	12.40*	6.00*	6.88*	16.19*	9.21*	4.63*	4.25*

Source: Performance Highlights of Private and Public Sector Banks, IBA Mumbai, Various Issues, various years.

Note: (i)* denotes significance at 5%level in all the tables.
  (ii)GR stands for growth rate in all the tables.
  (iii)Figures in parentheses indicate the percentage share of each component of income to the total income of banks.
  (iv)N.I.I. stands for Non-Interest Income.
  (v)I.I. stands for Interest Income.
  (vi)T.I. stands for Total Income.

The share of interest income reduced from 82.27% in 1995-96 to 79.50% in 2006-07 for ICICI Bank, and from 84.85% in 1995-96 to 75.79% in 2006-07.

During period I, from 1985 to 1994-95, the trend growth rate for Interest income of SBI Group (20.45) has been slightly greater than that of PNB (19.33). During Period II, i.e. the post-reforms period

220

(1995-96 to 2006-07) interest income has   risen for all the four banks under study, the maximum rise being for ICICI Bank (65.63) followed by CBoP (28.49), PNB (11.98) and SBI Group (11.04).

If we compare the overall   trend growth rates of interest income for the two Public Sector Banks, i.e. from 1985 to 2006-07, then the growth rate has been slightly greater for SBI Group (14.91) than that of PNB(14.89). The rise in interest income has been most spontaneous for ICICI Bank as indicated by its Coefficient of Variation (124.21%) followed by CBoP (91.33%), PNB (76.26%) while the growth has been quite steady for SBI Group(73.31%). Thus, on an average, PNB has the maximum contribution of interest income to the total income,(89.42%) followed by SBI Group(85.91%), CBoP (79.47%) and ICICI Bank(79.16%).Thus, for all the four selected banks, interest income has increased significantly(at five per cent level of significance).

Income from commission, exchange and brokerage is another component of the total income. A glance at Table 6.1 provides   that the share of non-interest income in the total income has increased for all the four banks under study. The   share of non-interest income in the total income was initially 11.83% in 1985, which increased to 16.78% in 1995-96 for SBI Group. The   share of non-interest income in the total income was initially 5.99% in 1985, which increased to 10.48% in 1995-96 for PNB. In the later years of the study, the non-interest income as percentage of total income for SBI Group and PNB declined to 12.16% and 8.28% respectively   in 2006-07.

For ICICI Bank, the share of non-interest income   increased from 17.73% in 1995-96   to   20.50% in 2006-07. CBoP also   experienced rise from 15.15% in 1995-96   to   24.21% in 2006-07. Other income or Non-Interest income has also increased significantly in absolute terms, (at five per cent level of significance) for all the four banks under study.

During period I, from 1985 to 1994-95, the trend growth rate of non-interest income for PNB (25.64) has been greater than that of SBI Group (23.92). During Period II, i.e. the post-reforms period (1995-96 to 2006-07) Non-Interest income has risen for all the four banks under study, the maximum rise being for ICICI Bank (71.60) followed by CBoP(33.16), PNB(13.02)and SBI Group(11.61). If we compare the overall trend growth rates of the two Public Sector Banks, i.e. from 1985 to 2006-07, then the growth rate has been higher for PNB (20.02) than that of SBI Group(17.15). However, on an average, share of Non-interest income is highest for ICICI Bank (20.84%) followed by CBoP (20.53%), SBI Group (14.09%) and PNB (10.58%).

The rise in Non-interest income has been most spontaneous for ICICI Bank as indicated by its Coefficient of Variation (118.77%),followed by CBoP (105.17%),PNB (92.97%), while the growth has been quite steady for SBI Group (82.25%).

6.2.1 Interest Income

The main constituents a of banks' interest income are interest and discount, income from investment and interest on balance with RBI and other inter-bank balances. Interest and discount income has increased significantly (at 1% level of significance) for all the four banks under study.

6.2.2 Trends in Interest and Discount Income

Prior to the reforms, data for income from interest and discount is only available for both SBI Group & PNB, which has been reflected in Table 6.2. After the advent of the reforms, the pace of growth of

Interest and discount income   has improved for the two Public Sector
Banks due to deregulation of interest rates and credit expansion.

The share of income from interest and discount has decreased
from 100%   in 1985 for both SBI Group   and   PNB to 53.60% and
48.68% in 1995-96 respectively.

The share, however, increased to 64.16% for SBI Group and 66.26% for
PNB in 2006-07. ICICI Bank also recorded an increase in the share of
income from interest and discount from 60.34% in 1995-96   to
70.00% in 2006-07.

Table6.2: Trends in Income from Interest and Discount

(Amount in Rs. crore)

Year	SBI Group (%Share)		ICICI Bank (%Share)		PNB (%Share)		CBoP (%Share)	
1985	2,892	100.00	-		565	100.00	-	
1995-96	9,173	53.60	70	60.34	1,518	48.68	12	41.38
2006-07	36,147	64.16	16,096	70.00	7,644	66.26	984	77.60
Trend GR Period I	9.96		-		7.72		-	
Period II	10.57		69.61		13.59		34.07	
Period I&II	9.96				11.02			
C.V.	67.26		131.25		75.42		118.47	
T-value	8.41*		5.70*		8.45*		3.91*	
Average share		49.69		58.22		51.51		54.10

Source: Performance Highlights of Public and Private Sector Banks, IBA,
Mumbai, Various Issues.

The rise in the share of income from interest and discount has
been the most for CBoP, from 41.38% in 1995-96 to 77.60% in
2006-07.

During period I, from 1985 to 1994-95, the trend   growth rate
for interest and discount income   of SBI Group (9.96) has been greater
than that of PNB   (7.72). During Period II, i.e. the post-reforms period
(1995-96 to 2006-07) interest and discount income has increased for all

223

the four banks under study, the maximum rise being for ICICI Bank (69.61) followed by CBoP (34.07), PNB (13.59) and SBI Group (10.57). If we compare the overall trend growth rates of the two Public Sector Banks, i.e. from 1985 to 2006-07, then the growth rate has been greater for PNB (11.02) than that of SBI Group(9.96).

The rise in interest and discount income has been most spontaneous for ICICI Bank as indicated by its Coefficient of Variation (131.25%) ,followed by CBoP(118.47%),PNB (75.42%), while the growth has been quite steady for SBI Group(67.26%).

6.2.3 Income from investment

The income from investment has recorded significant increase in absolute terms (at 5% level of significance) for all the four banks under study as depicted in Table 6.3. The increase in investment income is attributed to the rising investment by both types of banks, especially in Government securities. Banks are required to invest statutorily minimum 25% of their net and demand liabilities in Government and other approved securities as per Banking Regulation Act, 1949.

However, the share of interest income from investment in total income decreased from 38.16% in 1985 to 29.31% for SBI Group and from 45.67% in 1995-96 to 31.12% in 2006-07 for PNB.

Prior to the reforms, this rate was as high as 38.50% in February, 1992, which gradually declined to 25 per cent by October 1997(RBI, 2005-06). This decline in SLR is a result of the deregulation of the interest rates. In the declining interest rate scenario, such investments became particularly attractive due to their high yields and non-risky nature, thereby augmenting the share of income from investment in total income.

224

Table 6.3: Trends in Interest on Investment of Banks

(Amount in Rs. crore)

Year	SBI Group (% share)		ICICI Bank (% share)		PNB (% share)		CBoP (% share)	
1985	nil	-	-		nil	-	-	
1995-96	6,530	38.16	40	34.48	1,424	45.67	7	24.14
2006-07	16,512	29.31	5988	26.04	3,589	31.12	243	19.16
Trend GR Period I	-		-		-		-	
Period II	11.35		61.77		10.48		23.10	
Period I&II	-				-			
C.V.	55.74		112.74		50.70		52.24	
T-value	10.70*		6.45*		20.71*		5.34*	
Average Share		39.73		34.25		43.02		39.50

Source: Performance Highlights of Public and Private Sector Banks,IBA,Mumbai, Various Issues.

However, for the two Private Sector Banks, the scenario has been different, with both the banks experiencing a decline in share of income from investment, from 34.48% in 1995-96 to 26.04% in 2006-07 for ICICI Bank   and from 24.14% to 19.16% for CBoP during the same period.   Income on investment has increased significantly for all the four banks under study.

During period I, from 1985 to 1994-95, the trend   growth rate for income from investment of SBI Group   and   PNB could not be computed as Interest and discount was the only source of Interest income from 1985 to 1990-91. During Period II, i.e. the post-reforms period (1995-96 to 2006-07) income on investment   has increased for all the four banks under study, the maximum rise being for ICICI Bank (61.77) followed by CBoP(23.10), SBI Group(11.35) and PNB(10.48).

The rise in income on investment has been most spontaneous for ICICI Bank as indicated by its Coefficient of Variation (112.74%), followed by SBI Group (55.74%),CBoP (52.24%), while the growth has been quite stable for PNB (50.70%).

6.2.4 Interest on Cash Balances which are kept with RBI and Other Inter-bank Funds:

Interest on cash balances which are kept with RBI and other inter-bank funds have increased significantly (at 5% level of significance) for all the banks under study except for PNB as presented in Table6.4.

The share in interest income on balance with RBI &other inter-bank funds has reduced from 6.25% in 1995-96 to 4.64% in 2006-07 for SBI Group. Similarly, the share has reduced from 5.61% to 2.22% for PNB during the same period.

Table6.4: Trends in Interest on Balance with RBI & Other Inter-bank Funds (Amount in Rs. crores)

Year	SBI Group (%share)		ICICI Bank (% share)		PNB (% share)		CBoP (% share)	
1985	nil	-			nil	-		
1995-96	1,070	6.25	6	5.17	175	5.61	10	34.48
2006-07	3,106	4.64	808	3.51	256	2.22	39	3.07
Trend GR Period I	-		-		-		-	
Period II	12.15		50.21		0.96		23.21	
Period I&II	-				-			
C.V.	49.69		114.41		17.68		80.61	
T-value	4.50*		4.44*		0.51		4.98*	
Average share		6.79		6.51		4.34		6.32

Source: Performance Highlights of Public and Private Sector Banks, IBA,Mumbai, Various Issues.

During period I, from 1985 to 1994-95, the trend growth rate for interest on cash balances with RBI and other inter-bank funds of SBI Group and PNB could not be computed as Interest and discount was the only source of Interest income from 1985 to 1990-91. During Period

226

II, i.e. the post-reforms period (1995-96 to 2006-07) interest on cash balances with RBI and other inter-bank funds has increased for all the four banks under study, the maximum rise being for ICICI Bank (50.21) followed by CBoP (23.21), SBI Group(12.15) and PNB(0.96). The rise in interest on cash balances with RBI and other inter-bank funds has been most spontaneous for ICICI Bank as indicated by its Coefficient of Variation(114.41%),followed by CBoP (80.61%), SBI Group (49.69%), while the growth has been quite stable for PNB(17.68%).

6.2.5 Income from Other Sources of Interest

Other sources of interest income have risen significantly (at five per cent level of significance) for all the banks except PNB, as presented in Table 6.5. The share of income from other sources has declined from 1.99% in 1995-96 to 1.02% in 2006-07 for SBI Group, while it increased from 0.03% in 1995-96 to 0.41% in 2006-07 for PNB.ICICI Bank did not have any income from this source in, however, its share was 0.44% in 2006-07.The share of income from other sources was 0.16% in 2006-07for CBoP.

During period I, from 1985 to 1994-95, the trend growth rate of SBI Group and PNB could not be computed as interest and discount was the only source of interest income from 1985 to1990-91. During Period II, i.e. the post-reforms period (1995-96 to 2006-07) other sources of interest income have increased for all the four banks under study, the maximum rise being for ICICI Bank (70.44) followed by PNB(26.30),SBI Group(5.77) and CBoP suffered a decline as depicted by its trend growth rate (-50.00).

Table 6.5: Trends in Other Interest Incomes

(Amount in Rs. crores)

Year	SBI Group (%share)		ICICI Bank (%share)		PNB (%share)		CBoP (%share)	
1985	nil	-	-		nil	-	-	
1995-96	340	1.99	-	0.00	1	0.03	-	-
2006-07	573	1.02	101	0.44	47	0.41	2	0.16
Trend GR Period I	-		-			-	-	
Period II	5.77		70.44		26.30		-50.00	
Period I&II	-		-			-	-	-
C.V.	66.63		126.28			115.45	248.63	
T-value	3.09*		3.06*		2.10		2.30*	
Average Share		3.77		1.10		1.09		0.32

Source: Performance Highlights of Public and Private Sector Banks, IBA, Mumbai, Various Issues.

The rise in other sources of interest income has been most spontaneous for CBoP as indicated by its Coefficient of Variation (248.63%),followed by ICICI Bank (126.28%), PNB (115.45%), while the growth has been most stable for SBI Group(66.63%). Statistically, for SBI Group, all the four sources of interest income have increased significantly (at 5% level of significance) over the period under review. For PNB, interest/discount and income from investment have grown significantly at five per cent level of significance.

For both the Private Sector Banks, viz. ICICI Bank and CBoP, interest and discount income forms an important chunk of total income. Both the banks started granting loans and advances extensively and are earning substantial interest on them, thus, giving their public sector counterparts tough competition. Due to deregulation, the lending rates of commercial banks have been gradually deregulated. Keeping in view the international practice on lending rates as also for providing further operational flexibility to commercial banks in deciding their lending rates, a system of benchmark Prime Lending Rate (PLR) has been adopted since 2004 wherein banks enjoy the flexibility in pricing loans and advances based on market benchmarks(RBI,2004-05).

6.3 TRENDS IN OTHER   INCOMES OF BANKS

With increasing competition due to deregulation of interest rates and entry of private sector banks, fee-based incomes are the only hope for them to augment their total incomes. 'Other incomes' refer to all non-interest earnings of banks, viz. income from commission, exchange and brokerage, sale of investment, sale of land, building, exchange transactions, income derived from dividend, leasing business etc.

However, the three heads, viz. commission, exchange and brokerage; exchange transactions; and sale of investment account for over 85 percent of other income of banks (Uppal and Kaur, 2007). Hence, the income from these significant heads is only taken up for analysis.

6.3.1 Trends in Income from Commission, Exchange and Brokerage

The income from commission, exchange and brokerage forms the major chunk of non-interest   income for all the four banks under study as depicted in Table 6.6. The main reason for the stupendous growth of 'other incomes' has been their ability to augment earnings in the wake of declining interest spreads in a deregulated scenario. Moreover, fee-incomes which form the major component of 'other incomes' do not require capital, thus putting lesser strain on banks' financial resources. Thus, the key to profitability lies in exploiting the non- interest sources of incomes by banks.

The share of fee-income for SBI Group was 98.45%   in 1985,which decreased to 66.64% in 1995-96.PNB also registered a decline from 88.89% in 1985 to   56.98% in 1995-96.Both the Private

Sector Banks, viz. ICICI Bank and CBoP also improved their share of fee-income from 36.00% and 60.00% to 73.05% and 88.15% respectively in 1995-96 and 2006-07. However, the share of fee-income increased to 93.09% for PNB and 85.41% for SBI Group in 2006-07. During period I, from 1985 to 1994-95, the trend growth rate for income from commission, exchange and brokerage of SBI Group (18.51) has been slightly greater than that of PNB (18.12). During Period II, i.e. the post-reforms period (1995-96 to 2006-07) income from commission, exchange and brokerage has increased for all the four banks under study, the maximum rise being for ICICI Bank (81.68) followed by CBoP (48.21), PNB (13.64) and SBI Group (8.34).

Table 6.6: Trends in Income from Commission, Exchange and Brokerage

(Amount in Rs. crore)

Year	SBI Group	ICICI Bank	PNB	CBoP
1985	382	-	32	-
	(98.45)		(88.89)	
1995-96	2299	9	208	3
	(66.64)	(36.00)	(56.98)	(60.00)
2006-07	6661	4331	970	357
	(85.41)	(73.05)	(93.09)	(88.15)
Trend GR Period I	18.51	-	18.12	-
Period II	8.34	81.68	13.64	48.21
Period I& II	14.39	-	16.35	-
C.V.	66.11	145.88	86.21	183.37
T-value	28.14*	5.05*	11.85*	3.11*

Source: Performance Highlights of Private and Public Sector Banks, IBA Mumbai,
Various years.
Note: (i) Figures in parentheses denote the share in total other income.

If we compare the overall trend growth rates of the two Public Sector Banks i.e. from 1985 to 2006-07, then the growth rate has been greater for PNB (16.35) than that of SBI Group(14.39). After the advent of the reforms, the pace of growth of income from commission, exchange and brokerage has reduced for the two Public Sector Banks due to competition generated by the Private Sector Banks.

The rise in income from commission, exchange and brokerage has been most spontaneous for CBoP as indicated by its Coefficient of Variation (183.37%),followed by ICICI Bank (145.88%),PNB (86.21%), while the growth has been quite steady for SBI Group(66.11%).

6.3.2 Trends in Income from sale of investment

Income from sale of investment appears as another significant source under 'other income' of banks, is presented in Table 6.7.

Table 6.7: Trends in Income from Sale of Investment

(Amount in Rs. crore)

Year	SBI Group	ICICI Bank	PNB	CBoP
1985	N.A.	-	N.A.	-
1995-96	-	-	-	-
2006-07	831 (10.65)	1115 (18.80)	#	7 (1.73)
C.V.	100.67	117.87	85.84	174.60
T- value	1.31	5.18*	0.62	0.60

Source: Performance Highlights of Private Sector and Public Sector Banks, IBA Mumbai, various years.

Note :(i)N.A. stands for not available.
(ii)# indicates loss in 2006-07 for PNB.

The data for this income was not available for all the four banks in 1995-96.However, ICICI Bank had the highest share(18.80%) in 2006-07, ,followed by SBI Group,(10.65%) and CBoP,(1.73%).PNB suffered losses on account of this source.

Income from sale of investment has increased significantly (at 5% level of significance) only for ICICI Bank. The trend growth rates for all the four banks could not be calculated for all the four banks under study due to non-availability of data from 1985 to 1990-91 for the two public sector banks.

The rise in this income has been most spontaneous for CBoP as indicated by its Coefficient of Variation (174.60%),followed by ICICI Bank (117.87%),SBI Group (100.67%), while the growth has been quite steady for PNB(85.84%).

6.3.3 Income from exchange transactions

Share of income from exchange transactions, also known as foreign exchange (forex) income in 'other income' declined for all banks under study as shown in Table 6.8.

Table 6.8: Trends in Income from Exchange Transactions

(Amount in Rs. crores)

Year	SBI Group	ICICI Bank	PNB	CBoP
1985	N.A.	-	N.A.	-
1995-96	1104 (32.00)	8 (32.00)	78 (21.36)	1 (20.00)
2006-07	568 (7.28)	644 (10.86)	177 (16.99)	48 (11.85)
Trend GR Period I	-	-	-	-
Period II	-0.86	47.19	7.95	24.00
Period I& II	-	-	-	-
C.V.	33.78	143.24	51.04	100.84
T- value	0.97	4.55*	7.65*	3.59*

Source: Performance Highlights of Private and Public Sector Banks, Various Issues,IBA Mumbai, various years.

The share of exchange transactions for SBI Group was 32.00% in 1995-96 for SBI Group, which slipped to 7.28% in 2006-07.However, for PNB,ICICI Bank and CBoP, this share declined from 21.36%, 32.00% and 20.00% to 16.99%, 10.86% and 11.85% respectively during the same period.

During period I, (from 1985 to 1994-95), the trend growth rate of SBI Group and PNB could not be computed due to non-availability of data for the period 1985 to 1990-91 for both the selected Public Sector Banks. During Period II, i.e. the post-reforms period (1995-96 to

2006-07) income from exchange transactions has risen for all the banks under study except SBI Group, which showed a decline. ICICI Bank registered the maximum growth (47.19), followed by CBoP (24.00) and PNB(7.95).SBI Group a suffered as decline indicated by its trend growth rate (-0.86).

The rise in income from exchange transactions has been most spontaneous for ICICI Bank as indicated by its Coefficient of Variation(143.24%),followed by CBoP (100.84%), PNB (51.04%), while the reduction has been most steady for SBI Group(33.78%).

The rise in income from exchange transactions has been significant for CBoP, while for SBI Group, fee-income contributed the most. However, PNB recorded a significant rise in both fee-income and forex income.

6.4 TRENDS IN INTEREST EXPENDED (COMPONENT-WISE)

Interest paid on deposits and borrowings (from RBI and banks) form the major chunk of the total expenses incurred by banks. Table 6.9 presents the trend of the components of interest expended.

6.4.1 Trends in Interest expended on deposits and borrowings

The interest expended on deposits was 100% each for both the Public Sector Banks in 1985 and it was the only interest expenditure of these banks. The share of this expense was 83.14% and 91.91% for SBI Group and PNB respectively in 1995-96, which increased to 84.58% and 93.27% for both the banks respectively in 2006-07. However, ICICI Bank registered rise from 64.70% in 1995-96 to 71.21% in 2006-07.

For ICICI Bank, interest on deposits and borrowings has increased throughout the period under review. The share of interest on deposits and borrowings in the total interest expenses for CBoP was very high, i.e.100.00% in 1995-96.

Table 6.9: Trends in Interest expended on deposits

(Amount in Rs.crore)

Year	SBI Group	ICICI Bank	PNB	CBoP
1985	2105 (100.00)	-	418 (100.00)	-
1995-96	9037 (83.14)	55 (64.70)	1920 (91.91)	7 (100.00)
2006-07	28639 (84.58)	11648 (71.21)	5617 (93.27)	653 (93.55)
Trend GR Period I	15.66	-	16.56	-
Period II	9.99	58.80	9.62	29.42
Period I& II	13.35	58.80	13.51	-
C.V.	68.77	136.82	60.77	78.17
T- value	16.91*	4.58*	11.78*	4.61*

Source: Performance Highlights of Private and Public Sector Banks, IBA Mumbai,
Various Issues.

Note: (i) Figures in parentheses denote the share in total interest expended.

Due to an expansion over-drive, this share declined to 93.55% in 2006-07 for CBoP. Interest on deposits and borrowings has increased significantly (at 5% level of significance) for all the banks under study.

During period I, from 1985 to 1994-95, the trend growth rate of interest on deposits and borrowings for PNB (16.56) has been greater than that of SBI Group (15.66). During Period II i.e. the post-reforms period (1995-96 to 2006-07) interest on deposits and borrowings has risen for all the four banks under study, the maximum rise being for ICICI Bank (58.80) followed by CBoP(29.42), SBI Group(9.99) and PNB(9.62). If we compare the overall trend growth rates of the two Public Sector Banks, i.e. from 1985 to 2006-07, then the growth rate has been slightly greater for PNB (13.51) than that of SBI Group(13.35). The rise in interest on deposits and borrowings has been most spontaneous for ICICI Bank as indicated by its Coefficient of Variation (136.82%),followed by CBoP (78.17%),SBI Group (68.77%) and least for PNB(60.77%).

6.4.2 Interest on RBI/ Inter Bank-Borrowings: ICICI Bank and CBoP registered a significant rise in this source of interest expenditure at five percent level of significance throughout the period under study. The expenditure due to Interest on RBI/ Inter Bank borrowings declined from 8.09% in 1995-96 to 6.99% in 2006-07 for SBI Group and from 2.87% to 1.03% for PNB during the same period as highlighted in Table 6.10. ICICI Bank also experienced reduction from 10.57% in 1995-96 to 7.95% in 2006-07. The share of this interest expenditure was 4.87% in 2006-07 for CBoP.

This reduction was due to the introduction of Liquidity Adjustment Facility by RBI to support the market players, by way of repo and reverse repo based on the recommendations of the Second Narasimham Committee (RBI, 2005-06).

During period I, from 1985 to 1994-95, the trend growth rate could not be computed as the interest expended on deposits was the only interest expenditure for both the Public Sector Banks in 1985.

During Period II, i.e. the post-reforms period (1995-96 to 2006-07) interest on RBI /Inter Bank borrowings has risen for all the four banks under study, the maximum rise being for ICICI Bank (64.92) followed by CBoP(30.32), PNB(12.74) and SBI Group(4.42).

6. 10: Trends in Interest expended on RBI/Inter-Bank funds

(Amount in Rs. crores)

Year	SBI Group	ICICI Bank	PNB	CBoP
1985	nil	-	nil	-
1995-96	879 (8.09)	9 (10.57)	60 (2.87)	-
2006-07	2366 (6.99)	1300 (7.95)	62 (1.03)	34 (4.87)
Trend GR Period I	-	-	-	-
Period II	4.42	64.92	12.74	30.32
Period I& II	-	-	-	-
C.V.	74.57	165.62	64.73	96.58
T- value	0.78	3.86*	0.97	2.66*

Source: Performance Highlights of Private and Public Sector Banks, IBA Mumbai, Various Issues.

Note: (i) Figures in parentheses denote the share in total interest expended.

The rise in interest on RBI /Inter-Bank borrowings   has been most erratic   for ICICI Bank as indicated by its Coefficient of Variation (165.62%),followed   by CBoP   (96.58%), SBI Group   (74.57%),while the growth has been most steady for PNB (64.73%).

6.4.3 Other interest expenditures

Table 6.11 depicts that other interest payments increased significantly for all the four banks under study at 5% level of significance. The share of expenditure due to other interest payments was almost constant for SBI Group i.e. 8.78% in 1995-96 and 8.43% in 2006-07.Similarly,for PNB,   the share was 5.22% in 1995-96,which increased   a little to 5.69% in 2006-07 for PNB. ICICI Bank, however, experienced a reduction from 24.70% in 1995-96 to 20.85% in 2006-07. CBoP   had the least share of other interest expenditure i.e.1.57% in 2006-07.

During period I, from 1985 to 1994-95, the trend   growth rate could not be computed as   the Interest expended on deposits was the only interest expenditure for both the Public Sector Banks during the period 1985 to 1990-91.

Table 6.11: Trends in Interest expended on Other Borrowings

(Amount in Rs. crore)

Year	SBI Group	ICICI Bank	PNB	CBoP
1985	nil	-	nil	-
1995-96	954 (8.78)	21 (24.70)	109 (5.22)	-
2006-07	2854 (8.43)	3410 (20.85)	343 (5.69)	11 (1.57)
Trend GR Period I	-	-	-	-
Period II	9.29	86.19	10.74	39.86
Period I& II	-	-	-	-
C.V.	65.52	125.34	48.84	108.61
T- value	3.47*	3.74*	8.31*	6.92*

Source: Performance Highlights of Private and Public Sector Banks, IBA Mumbai, various years.

During Period II, i.e. the post-reforms period (1995-96 to 2006-07) Other interest payments have risen for all the four banks under study, the maximum rise being for ICICI Bank (86.19) followed by CBoP (39.86),   PNB(10.74) and SBI Group(9.29).

The rise in other interest payments has been most variable   for ICICI Bank as indicated by its Coefficient of Variation(125.34%),followed   by CBoP   (108.61%),SBI Group (65.52%), while the growth has been most steady for PNB(48.84%).

Thus, on the deposits side, a bank is free to offer any rate and only savings rate is administered by RBI. As part of the reforms, interest rate on deposits beyond fifteen days has been freed and banks can now charge differential rates on deposits of similar maturity.

6.5 TRENDS IN TOTAL EXPENDITURE (COMPONENT-WISE)

Expenditure of a commercial bank consists of both interest and non-interest expenditure. The non-interest expenses consist of manpower expenses being effected by salary structures, number, seniority and composition of employees, and in turn get influenced by wage agreement, recruitment, promotions and placement policies and other expenses being effected by nature and volume of business and systems and procedures and which themselves get influenced by the quality of expenditure decisions, budgeting and cost control technique followed by the banks (Varde and Singh, 1983). Prior to the economic reforms the interest paid on deposits was regulated by the RBI and banks had practically little control over it. Moreover, the establishment expenses are also fixed in the short period.

Table 6.12: Trends in Expenditure (Component-wise)

(Amount in Rs. crore)

Year	SBI Group			ICICI Bank			PNB			CBoP		
Year	IE	EE	OE	IE	EE	OE	IE	EE	OE	IE	EE	OE
1985	2,105 (64.89)	814 (25.09)	325 (10.02)	-	-	-	418 (70.97)	118 (20.03)	53 (9.00)	-	-	-
1995-96	10,870 (65.29)	4,319 (25.93)	1,463 (8.78)	85 (75.89)	4 (3.57)	23 (20.54)	2,089 (67.41)	756 (24.39)	254 (8.20)	7 (36.84)	2 (10.53)	10 (52.63)
2006-07	33,859 (67.93)	10,470 (21.00)	5,517 (11.07)	16,358 (70.97)	1,617 (7.02)	5,073 (22.01)	6,023 (64.42)	2,352 (25.16)	974 (10.42)	699 (49.75)	221 (15.73)	485 (34.52)
Average share	68.13	22.38	9.49	74.45	5.28	20.28	68.61	22.01	9.38	60.63	6.76	32.61
Trend GR Period I	18.43	16.25	16.30	-	-	-	17.81	18.51	16.10	-	-	-
Period II	9.79	9.15	13.13	65.75	79.27	72.42	8.83	12.59	12.81	30.32	43.30	34.24
Period I&II	13.69	13.33	13.64	-	-	-	12.85	15.3	13.86	30.32		
C.V.	68.67	68.41	76.73	121.84	134.61	127.51	65.21	79.11	79.13	78.26	172.09	105.45
T-value	18.97*	20.43*	12.63*	5.89*	5.75*	6.38*	22.26*	14.13*	10.35*	4.77*	3.26*	4.93*

Source: Performance Highlights of Private Sector and Public Sector Banks, IBA Mumbai, various years.

Note: (i) I.E. stands for interest expenses.
(ii) E.E. stands for establishment expenses.
(iii) O.E. stands for other operating expenses.
(iv) Figures in parentheses denote the share in total expenditure.

239

In the recent years, the management of the banks have attempted to reduce their organizational structure, by departmentalization and by introduction of data processing equipments and cost improvement techniques (Amandeep, 1993).

6.5.1 Trends in Interest Expenses

The trends in various types of expenditure, viz. interest expenses, establishment expenses, and operating expenses are depicted in Table 6.12. The Public Sector Banks were earlier in a state of monopoly, but with the entry of Private Sector Banks, had to face competition. After the advent of the reforms, there has been reduction in the expenditure related to interest expenses for the two Public Sector Banks due to deregulation of interest rates.

Interest paid on deposits and borrowings forms one of the major components of the expenses incurred by all the four banks. Generally this expenditure is incurred in mobilizing various types of deposits recurring deposits, viz. time deposits, saving deposits demand deposits, cumulative deposits etc. The share of interest expenses in the total expenses increased from 64.89% for SBI Group in 1985 to 65.29% in 1995-96. The share of interest expenses of PNB decreased   from 70.97% in 1985 to 67.41% in 1995-96. The share of interest expenses later on increased to 67.93% for SBI Group, while it reduced to 64.42% for PNB in 2006-07, as the interest rates were deregulated and determined by market forces ushering in competition. Among the Private Sector Banks, the share of interest expenses reduced for ICICI Bank from 75.89% in 1995-96 to 70.97% in 2006-07. The share was 36.84% in 1995-96 for CBoP, which increased to   49.75% in 2006-07. ICICI Bank, due its large branch network and urban orientation has been giving all the banks tough competition and hence, has mobilized larger deposits resulting into more interest payment. After the second phase of reforms, the Public Sector Banks have woken up to competition, thus challenging the Private Sector Banks. CBoP initially had lesser deposits and incurred huge expenditure on technology adoption due to which its other operating expenses reached an all-time high share of 52.63% in the total expenses in 1995-96. Interest expenses form the major chunk of total expenses for all the four banks, the average share being 68.13% for SBI Group, 68.61% for PNB, 74.45% for ICICI Bank and 60.63% for CBoP.

Interest expenses have increased significantly in absolute terms (at 5% level of significance) for all the banks under study.

During period I, from 1985 to 1994-95, the trend growth rate of SBI Group (18.43) has been marginally greater than that of PNB (17.81). During Period II, i.e. the post-reforms period (1995-96 to 2006-07) interest expenses have risen for all the four banks under study, the maximum rise being for ICICI Bank (65.75) followed by CBoP (30.32), SBI Group(9.79) and PNB(8.83). If we compare the overall trend growth rates of the two Public Sector Banks, i.e. from 1985 to 2006-07, then the growth rate has been slightly greater for SBI Group (13.69) than that of PNB(12.85). The pattern of growth of Interest Expenses has been most volatile for ICICI Bank as depicted by its Coefficient of Variation (121.84%), followed by CBoP (78.26%), SBI Group (68.67%)and least for PNB (65.21%).On an average, the share of interest expenses has been the highest for ICICI Bank(74.45%), followed by PNB(68.61%), SBI Group(68.13%) and the least for CBoP (60.63%).

6.5.2 Trends in Establishment Expenses

The next major item of expenditure consists of establishment expenses (salaries, allowances, provident fund, bonus etc). After the advent of reforms, there has been reduction in the expenditure related to Establishment Expenses for the two Public Sector Banks due to introduction of Voluntary Retirement Scheme in 2000-01.

For SBI Group, the share increased slightly from 25.09% in 1985 to 25.93% in 1995-96. Later on, its share declined to 21.00%in 2006-07.Similarly, for PNB the share of establishment expenses increased from 20.03% in 1985 to 24.39% in 1995-96. Later on, the share increased to 25.16% in 2006-07.

For ICICI Bank, the share of establishment expenses has almost doubled from 3.57% in 1995-96 to 7.02% in 2006-07. Similarly the share of establishment expenses in the total expenses of CBoP experienced a rise from 10.53% in 1995-96 to 15.73% in 2006-07 due to the effect of merger.

On an average, the establishment expenses of the selected public sector banks have been quite high, on an average, (22.38% for SBI Group and 22.01% for PNB) due to the large expenditures incurred under Voluntary Retirement Scheme. However, both the selected private sector banks, viz. ICICI Bank and CBoP had lesser share of Establishment expenses, i.e. 5.28% and 6.76% respectively.

Establishment expenses have increased significantly (at 5% level of significance) for all the banks under study. During period I, from 1985 to 1994-95, the trend growth rate of PNB (18.51) has been greater than that of SBI Group (16.25). During Period II, i.e. the post-reforms period (1995-96 to 2006-07) establishment expenses have risen for all the four banks under study, the maximum rise being for ICICI Bank (79.27) followed by CBoP (43.30), SBI Group (12.59) and PNB (9.15). If we compare the overall trend growth rates of both the

242

selected public sector banks, i.e. from 1985 to 2006-07, then the growth rate has been mildly greater for PNB (15.30) than that of SBI Group(13.33). After the advent of the reforms, there has been reduction in the expenditure related to interest expenses for both the public sector banks due to deregulation of interest rates.

The pattern of growth of interest expenses has been most volatile for CBoP (172.09%), followed by ICICI Bank (134.61%), PNB (79.11%) and least for SBI Group(68.41%).

6.5.3 Trends in Other Expenses

The next component of expenditure is the other expenses consisting of current and non-current expenses like stationery, advertisement, directors' fees, rent, taxes depreciation and repair. These expenses have been quite high for the Private Sector Banks due to installation and upgradation of information technology. Other expenses have also increased significantly (at 5% level of significance) for all the banks under study.

The share of other expenses in the total expenses reduced from 10.02% for SBI Group in 1985 to 8.78% in 1995-96. Later on, the share increased to 11.07% in 2006-07.The share of other expenses reduced from 9.00% in 1985 to 8.20% in 1995-96.However, it increased to 10.42% in 2006-07.

Among the Private Sector Banks, the share of other expenses increased from 20.54% in 1995-96 to 22.01% in 2006-07 for ICICI Bank. The share of other expenses has been the highest for CBoP among all the four selected banks, though it reduced from 52.63% in 1995-96 to 34.52% in 2006-07.On an average, the share of other expenses has been maximum for CBoP (32.61%), followed by ICICI Bank (20.28%), SBI Group (9.49%) and PNB (9.38%).

During period I, from 1985 to 1994-95, the trend growth rate of SBI Group (16.30) has been marginally greater than that of PNB(16.10). During Period II, i.e. the post-reforms period (1995-96 to 2006-07) other expenses have risen for all the four banks under study, the maximum rise being for ICICI Bank (72.42), followed by CBoP(34.24), SBI Group (13.13) and PNB (12.81). If we compare the overall trend growth rates of the two public sector banks i.e. from 1985 to 2006-07, then the growth rate has been greater for PNB(13.86) than that of SBI Group (13.64).

The pattern of growth of other expenses has been most volatile for ICICI Bank as depicted by the Coefficient of Variation (127.51%),followed by CBoP (105.45%),PNB (79.13%), while it has been smooth for SBI Group(76.73%).

Statistically, the growth in all the types of expenditure viz. interest expenditure, establishment expenses and other expenses have been significant for each of the four selected banks at five percent level of significance during the period under study.

6.6   SPREAD   RATIOS

The difference between interest earned and interest paid constitutes the 'spread'. Spread along with non-interest income earned as commission, service charges etc. form the revenue pool, out of which manpower and other expenses are met (Padmavathi and Hemachandrika, 2006). Hence, it is the amount of this spread and its components i.e. interest earned and interest paid in relation to the average working funds which is significant for the banks to analyze their profitability. RBI has issued Guidelines for banks to disclose certain ratios viz. Interest Income, Non Interest Income, hence all the spread and burden ratios are calculated in terms of Average working funds to enable comparison of all ratios.

Average Working Funds= Fortnightly Average of Total Assets.

The three spread ratios employed are:

(a) Interest Earned as Percentage of Average Working Funds

Interest earnings relate to funds based income earned from the traditional banking business i.e. of lending funds. The ratio of interest earned as percentage of Average Working Funds indicates the rate of income a bank earns on its total assets. Table 6.13 presents the ratio of interests earned to Average Working Funds of the four banks under review.

For SBI Group and PNB, this ratio has increased from 7.59% and 8.23% in 1985 to 9.16% and 9.90% in 1995-96 respectively due to deregulation.

A system of Benchmark Prime Lending Rate (PLR) has been adopted by Indian banks since 2004 to afford flexibility to banks in pricing loans and advances based on market benchmarks.

Table 6.13: Trends in Interest Earned/Average Working Funds

Year	SBI Group	ICICI Bank	PNB	CBoP
1985	7.59	-	8.23	-
1995-96	9.16	10.02	9.90	5.99
2006-07	7.25	8.04	7.69	8.78
Average	8.49	8.98	9.01	8.81
Trend GR Period I	1.77	-	1.82	-
Period II	-3.17	-3.05	-3.39	0.03
Period I&II	1.28	-	-0.25	-
C.V.	13.22	15.80	11.87	18.14
T-value	0.13	3.09*	0.53	0.15

Source: Performance Highlights of Private and Public Sector Banks,IBA Mumbai, various years.

Thus, with falling interest rates, the lending rates are also declining, thereby reducing the interest earnings of banks. Interest earned as percentage of average working funds has shown significant reduction (at 5% level of significance) for ICICI Bank only.

For the Private Sector Banks, this ratio reduced for ICICI Bank from 10.02% in 1995-96 to 8.04% in 2006-07, while it rose from 5.99% to 8.78% for CBoP during the same period. This ratio reduced for all the banks, expect CBoP due to the gradual deregulation of the lending rates of commercial banks.

During period I, from 1985 to 1994-95, the trend growth rate of interest earned as percentage of average working funds has been greater for PNB(1.82) than that of SBI Group (1.77). During Period II, i.e. the post-reforms period (1995-96 to 2006-07) however, the trend growth rate has fallen for all the banks under study except CBoP. The maximum reduction in this ratio has been experienced by PNB (-3.39), followed by SBI Group i.e. (-3.17) and ICICI Bank (-3.05).Only CBoP has recorded a rise of (0.03) in this ratio. The reduction has been due to lesser generation of income from traditional sources of income in the wake of deregulation of interest.

The pattern of growth of interest earned as percentage of average working funds has been most volatile for CBoP as depicted by its Coefficient of Variation (18.14%),followed by ICICI Bank (15.80%), SBI Group (13.22%),while it has been quite smooth for PNB (11.87%).

On an average, however the ratio of interest earned as percentage of average working funds has been maximum for PNB (9.01%), followed by ICICI Bank (8.98%), CBoP(8.81%) and SBI Group (8.49%).

(b) Interest paid as Percentage of Average Working Funds

Interest expenditure consists of funds based expenditure incurred to earn interest income. The major constituents of interest expenditure consist of interest paid on deposits, borrowings, and balances from RBI and inter-bank borrowings. Table 6.14 shows the ratio of interest expenses as percentage of average working funds of the banks under study. For SBI Group the ratio increased marginally from 5.53% in 1985 to 5.82% in 1995-96. Later on, this ratio decreased to 4.35% in 2006-07.

Table 6.14: Trends in Interest Paid/Average Working Funds

Year	SBI Group	ICICI Bank	PNB	CBoP
1985	5.53	-	6.07	-
1995-96	5.82	7.34	6.63	1.5
2006-07	4.35	6.11	4.12	4.84
Average Rate	5.71	7.08	6.03	5.85
Trend GR Period I	0.35	-	0.77	-
Period II	-3.69	-4.39	-6.42	0.28
Period I&II	-1.53	-4.39	-2.26	0.28
C.V.	13.65	32.32	19.26	33.35
T-value	4.07*	1.76	3.98*	0.52

Source: Performance Highlights of Private and Public Sector Banks,
IBA Mumbai,Balance-sheets of banks , various years.

PNB also experienced a minor increase in the ratio from 6.07% in 1985 to 6.63% in 1995-96.However, in the later years of the study, the ratio declined gradually to 4.12% in 2006-07.For ICICI Bank, the interest paid as Percentage of Average Working Funds also reduced from 7.34% in 1995-96 to 6.11% in 2006-07. However, the ratio increased from 1.50% in 1995-96 to 4.84% in 2006-07 for CBoP. The reduction in interest paid has been due to decline in the deposit rates of banks from 13 per cent in 1995-96 to about 5 per cent in 2004-05(RBI, 2004-05).

Interest paid as percentage of average working funds has increased significantly (at 5% level of significance) for SBI Group and PNB only.

During period I, from 1985 to 1994-95, the trend growth rate of interest paid as percentage of average working funds has been greater for PNB (0.77) than that of SBI Group (0.35). During Period II, i.e. the post-reforms period (1995-96 to 2006-07) however, the trend growth rate has fallen for all the banks under study except CBoP .The maximum reduction in this ratio has been experienced by PNB(-6.42), followed by ICICI Bank(-4.39), SBI Group(-3.69),while CBoP recorded trend growth rate of 0.28.

The pattern of growth of interest paid as percentage of average working funds has been most volatile for CBoP as depicted by the Coefficient of Variation (33.35%),followed closely by ICICI Bank (32.32%),PNB (19.26%), while it has been the most smooth for SBI Group (13.65%).

On an average, this ratio has been maximum for ICICI Bank (7.08%), followed by PNB (6.03%), CBoP (5.85%) and SBI Group (5.71%). Since the mid-1990s, consistent with soft interest rate policies, both interest income & interest expenditure of banks as proportions of total assets have declined (Mohan, 2005).

(c)Spread as Percentage of Average Working Funds

The ratio of spread as percentage of average working funds is an important indicator of profitability. After the initiation of reforms, income from the conventional sources of banking business is on the decline reflecting greater diversification of banks into non-fund based business in the wake of deregulation of interest rates. This ratio can also be calculated by taking the difference between interest earned and interest paid as proportion of average working funds. Table 6.15 depicts the trends in this ratio for the four selected banks.

Table 6.15: Trends in   Spread / Average Working Funds

Year	SBI Group	ICICI Bank	PNB	CBoP
1985	2.06	-	2.16	-
1995-96	3.34	2.67	3.27	4.49
2006-07	2.90	1.93	3.57	3.94
Average Rate	2.78	1.89	2.97	2.95
Trend GR Period I	6.12	-	5.42	-
Period II	-0.12	-2.23	0.93	1.82
Period I&II	2.14	-	3.05	-
C.V.	19.88	30.01	21.03	27.26
T-value	3.39*	1.09	7.27*	0.65

Source: Performance Highlights of Private and Public Sector
Banks,IBA Mumbai,various years.

The increase in the ratio has been from 2.06% and 2.16% to 3.34% and 3.27% for SBI Group and PNB respectively during the period 1985 to 1995-96.

For ICICI Bank, this ratio reduced from 2.67% in 1995-96 to 1.93% in 2006-07.CBoP also suffered a decline from 4.49% to 3.94% during the same period.   Spread earned as percentage of average working funds has shown a significant rise for both the Public Sector Banks, i.e. SBI Group and PNB at 5% level of significance.

During period I, from 1985 to 1994-95, the trend   growth rate   of spread as percentage of average working funds   has been   greater for SBI Group (6.12) than that   of PNB (5.42). During Period II, i.e. the post-reforms period (1995-96 to 2006-07) however, the trend growth rate   has fallen for ICICI Bank (-2.23) and SBI Group (-0.12), the decline being more for the former. The growth rate has been greater for

CBoP (1.82) than that of PNB (0.93). The overall growth rate of PNB (3.05) has been greater than that of SBI Group (2.14).

The pattern of growth of spread as percentage of average working funds has been most volatile for ICICI Bank as depicted by its Coefficient of Variation (30.01%),followed by CBoP (27.26%),PNB (21.03%), while it has been quite smooth for SBI Group(19.88%).

On an average, the ratio of spread as a percentage of average working funds has been highest for PNB (2.97%), followed closely by CBoP (2.95%), SBI Group (2.78%) and ICICI Bank (1.89%).

6.7 BURDEN RATIOS

(a) **Non-Interest Expenditure as Percentage of Average Working Funds:** Table 6.16 depicts the ratio of non-interest expenditure to total assets of the four selected banks during the period under review.Non-Interest expenditure of commercial banks consists of manpower expenses like salaries, allowances, provident fund and other current and non-current expenses. This ratio improved from 2.99% in 1985 to 3.09% in 1995-96 for SBI Group.

Table 6.16: Trends in Non-Interest Expenditure/ Average Working Funds

Year	SBI Group	ICICI Bank	PNB	CBoP
1985	2.99	-	2.46	-
1995-96	3.09	2.32	3.24	2.57
2006-07	2.05	2.33	2.05	3.82
Average Rate	2.65	2.14	2.68	3.10
Trend GR Period I	-1.70	-	0.75	-
Period II	-3.61	0.66	-4.27	4.71
Period I&II	-1.80	-	-0.46	-
C.V.	15.16	29.96	14.17	26.15
T-value	5.26*	0.22	0.78	2.51*

Source: Performance Highlights of Private Sector and Public Sector Banks, IBA Mumbai, various years.

However, over the years, this ratio reduced due to the introduction of the Voluntary Retirement Scheme to downsize the size of staff and rationalize the staff cost and it was 2.05% in 2006-07. PNB also showed a similar pattern in this ratio, by improving from 2.46% in 1985 to 3.24% in 1995-96 and again reduced to 2.05% in 2006-07.

Non-Interest Expenditure as percentage of average working funds has shown a significant rise for SBI Group and CBoP at 5% level of significance.

During period I, from 1985 to 1994-95, the trend growth rate of Non-Interest Expenditure as percentage of average working funds has been (0.75) for PNB while SBI Group has suffered decline reflected by its negative growth rate (-1.70). During Period II, i.e. the post-reforms period (1995-96 to 2006-07) however, the trend growth rate has shown greater reduction for PNB (-4.27), than that of SBI Group (-3.61).The growth rate has risen for both the Private Sector Banks, the rise being greater for CBoP(4.71) than that of ICICI Bank(0.66).The Non-Interest Expenditure has reduced for the two Public Sector Banks due to the introduction of Voluntary Retirement Scheme in 2002.

The pattern of growth of Non-Interest Expenditure as percentage of average working funds has been most volatile for ICICI Bank as depicted by its Coefficient of Variation(29.96%),followed by CBoP (26.15%),SBI Group (15.16%), while it has been quite smooth for PNB (14.17%).

On an average, the highest ratio has been for CBoP (3.10%), followed by PNB (2.68%), SBI Group (2.65%) and ICICI Bank (2.14%).

Thus, the Private Sector Banks have displayed the most volatile behaviour in respect of manpower and operating expenses due to their use of technology. ICICI Bank, on the other hand, has controlled its non-interest expenditure most efficiently. Although after the introduction of VRS, the manpower expenses have reduced for both the Public Sector Banks, yet they need to be reduced more. The remedy lies in reducing the operating expenses by adopting technology-intensive methods.

(b) Non-Interest Income as Percentage of Average Working Funds

Other incomes of the bank constitute income by way of commission, exchange, brokerage, service charges and other miscellaneous receipts. Ratio of non-interest income as percentage of average working funds for the four selected banks is depicted during the period under study in Table 6.17.The Non-Interest Income has reduced for all the banks after the introduction of reforms due to intense competition among the banks to tap the fee-based sources of income.

Table 6.17: Trends in Non-Interest Income/Average Working Funds

Year	SBI Group	ICICI Bank	PNB	CBoP
1985	1.02	-	0.52	-
1995-96	1.83	2.15	1.04	1.07
2006-07	1.00	2.07	0.95	2.81
Average Rate	1.39	2.23	1.07	2.21
Trend GR Period I	4.94	-	5.96	-
Period II	-1.53	-0.12	-0.87	-1.60
Period I&II	1.29	-	4.80	-
C.V.	20.35	13.81	38.66	42.32
T-value	2.00	0.12	4.44*	0.59

Source: Performance Highlights of Private and Public Sector Banks, IBA Mumbai, Balance-sheets of banks, various years.

From 1985 to 1995-96, this ratio increased from 1.02% to 1.83% for SBI Group. For PNB, initially this ratio increased from 0.52% in 1985 to 1.04% in 1995-96.Later on, this ratio was 1.00% for SBI Group and 0.95% for PNB in 2006-07. ICICI Bank alone, suffered decline in this ratio from 2.15% in 1995-96 to 2.07% in 2006-07,while CBoP improved its share from 1.07% to 2.81%,during the same period.

On an average, the ratio of other income as percentage of average working funds has been the highest for ICICI Bank (2.23%), followed by CBoP (2.21%), SBI Group (1.39%) and PNB (1.07%). Non-Interest Income as percentage of average working funds has shown a significant rise only for PNB at 5% level of significance.

During period I, from 1985 to 1994-95, the trend growth rate of Non-Interest Income as percentage of average working funds has recorded higher a growth for PNB (5.96) than that of SBI Group(4.94).During Period II, i.e. the post-reforms period (1995-96 to 2006-07), however, the trend growth rate has shown reduction for all the four banks under study, the fall being maximum for CBoP(-1.60), followed by SBI Group (-1.53),PNB (-0.87) and ICICI Bank(-0.12).If we compare the overall trend growth rates of the two Public Sector Banks, then it is observed that PNB has a higher growth rate(4.80) than that of SBI Group(1.29).

The pattern of growth of Non-Interest Income as percentage of average working funds has been most volatile for CBoP as depicted by its Coefficient of Variation(42.32%),followed by PNB (38.66%),SBI Group (20.35%), while it has been quite smooth for ICICI Bank(13.81%). It is clear that both the selected private sector banks are leading in other incomes due to thrust on technology and ability to provide a plethora of services under one roof. They have blossomed as

253

financial boutiques providing all types of consumer-centric services to the urban elite.

Both the public sector banks, especially PNB are still relying on traditional sources of income. They need to redesign their financial products to match the varying needs of their customers. Another reason for low non-interest income is the high percentage of rural branches the banks cater, where scope of other income is limited. Private sector banks, in contrast have negligible social responsibility to the rural masses.

(c)Burden as percentage of Average working funds

The data pertaining to burden as percentage of Average working funds is depicted in Table 6.18. Burden as percentage of average working funds has declined for all the banks under study and the decline has been significant only for PNB.

Table 6.18: Trends in Burden/ Average Working Funds

Year	SBI Group	ICICI Bank	PNB	CBoP
1985	1.97	-	1.94	-
1995-96	1.26	0.17	2.20	1.50
2006-07	1.05	0.26	1.10	1.01
Average Rate	1.26	-0.09	1.60	0.89
Trend GR Period I	-3.59	-	-1.93	-
Period II	-6.06	-	-5.83	-
Period I&II	-4.56	-	-4.66	-
C.V.	52.85	-709.73	33.98	104.03
T-value	2.08	0.42	4.26*	1.23

Source: Performance Highlights of Private and Public Sector Banks, IBA, Mumbai, Balance-sheets of banks, various years.

This ratio reduced from 1.97% in 1985 to 1.26% in 1995-96 for SBI Group. For PNB, this ratio initially rose from 1.94% in 1985 to 2.20% in 1995-96, which declined to1.10% in 2006-07.In 2006-07, the ratio decreased to 1.05% for SBI Group.

In the post-VRS period, Public Sector Banks have tended to rationalize staff cost to contain non-interest expenses.

For both the Private Sector Banks, burden ratio has been negative, i.e. non-interest income has exceeded non-interest expenditure. It is remarkable as burden has diminished despite large expenditures incurred by these banks in installation and upgradation of information technology.

During period I, from 1985 to 1994-95, the trend growth rate of burden as percentage of average working funds has recorded greater reduction for SBI Group(-3.59) than that of PNB(-1.93).During Period II, i.e. the post-reforms period (1995-96 to 2006-07) however, the trend growth rate of CBoP and ICICI Bank could not be computed due to negative burden. However, for SBI Group, the fall has been greater (-6.06) than that of PNB (-5.83). If we compare the overall trend growth rates of both the Public Sector Banks, then it is observed that the rate of decline is almost similar. PNB and SBI Group have a negative growth rate of -4.66 and -4.56% respectively. The burden as percentage of average working funds has reduced for all the banks after the introduction of reforms due to intense competition among the banks to tap the fee-based sources of income.

The pattern of growth of burden as percentage of average working funds has been most volatile for ICICI Bank as depicted by its Coefficient of Variation(-709.73%),followed by CBoP (104.03%),SBI Group (52.85%),while it has been quite smooth for PNB(33.98%).

On an average, burden as a percentage of average working funds has been the least for ICICI Bank (-0.09%), followed by CBoP (0.89%), SBI Group (1.26%) and PNB (1.60%).

Better management of burden has also been possible due to the diversification by these banks into newer sources of revenue other than the conventional business of granting loans and advances. Thus, the key to profitability is increasing spread and reducing burden. In today's deregulated era, the scope of increasing spread is limited. So the remedy lies in reducing burden either by increasing the non-interest expenditure or by both. Both the Private Sector Banks have been more successful in the management of burden than their Public Sector counterparts as they have augmented their incomes by adopting newer strategies of earning incomes and have substantially reduced the operating expenditure by adopting technology intensive measures.

6.8 RATIOS OF PROFITABILITY

(1) Net profit as Percentage of Total Income

Profitability of banks can also be related to the total income of the banks. Total income includes both interest incomes and non- interest incomes of banks.

Table 6.19 portrays the ratio of Net profit to Total Income of the four selected banks over the period under study. A discernible feature of the growth in profits has been the remarkable increase in the post-reform period for both the Public Sector Banks. Profits in relation to Total Income improved from 1.03% in 1985 to 3.86% in 1995-96 for SBI Group, but reduced from 1.99% in 1985 to a position of net loss in 1995-96 for PNB possibly due to the introduction of the Capital Adequacy norms along with provisioning norms.

The ratio of Net Profit to Total Income reduced from 12.06% and 39.39% for ICICI Bank and CBoP respectively in 1995-96 to 10.75% and 7.23% for the two banks in 2006-07.

Year-wise analysis reveals that this ratio was highest for CBoP, i.e. 39.39% in 1995-96 and minimum for SBI Group, i.e. 1.03% in 1985.CBoP, being a Private Sector Bank earned high profits while SBI Group, because of its social obligations to the priority sector was less profitable prior to the reforms.

Table 6.19: Trends in Profit as Percentage of Total Income

Year	SBI Group	ICICI Bank	PNB	CBoP
1985	1.03	-	1.99	-
1995-96	3.86	12.06	#	39.39
2006-07	10.24	10.75	12.24	7.23
Average	5.34	12.33	6.10	12.40
Trend GR Period I	15.33	-	2.52	-
Period II	6.79	-0.78	9.91	-12.25
Period I&II	13.21	-	10.09	-
C.V.	68.19	22.15	65.25	72.69
T-value	11.40*	0.49	8.62*	3.87*

Source: Performance Highlights of Private and Public Sector Banks,
    IBA Mumbai,Balance-sheets of banks , various years.
Note: (i) # indicates loss in 1995-96 for PNB.

Bank-wise analysis indicates that on an average, this ratio has been maximum for CBoP(12.40%),followed by ICICI Bank (12.33%),PNB (6.10%)and SBI Group (5.34%).

Another noteworthy feature is the trend of this ratio. This ratio has decreased over the period for both the Private sector banks, and in contrast has risen for both the Public Sector Banks, because they were making handsome profits earlier. After the ushering in of competition, the Public Sector Banks have risen to the occasion and are giving their Private Sector counterparts a run for their money.

Thus, both the Private Sector Banks lead in profitability in relation to total income. Profits in relation to Total Income   have shown a significant rise for SBI Group and PNB, while it has shown a significant decline for CBoP (at 5% level of significance).

During period I, from 1985 to 1994-95, the trend growth rate of Profits in relation to Total Income has been greater for SBI Group(15.33) than that of PNB(2.52). During Period II, i.e. the post-reforms period (1995-96 to 2006-07), however, the trend growth rate was the highest for PNB (9.91), followed by SBI Group (6.79) ICICI Bank (-0.78), and least for CBoP(-12.25). If we compare the overall trend growth rates of the two Public Sector Banks, then it is observed that the rate of growth has been greater for SBI Group (13.21) than that of PNB (10.09).

The pattern of growth of Profits in relation to Total Income has been most volatile for CBoP as depicted by the Coefficient of Variation (72.69%),followed by SBI Group (68.19%),PNB (65.25%), while it has been quite smooth for ICICI Bank (22.15%).

(2) The ratio of Profit as Percentage of Total Deposits

The data shown in Table 6.20 reflects that profits in relation to deposits have increased for both the selected public sector banks, viz. SBI Group and PNB, whereas these have decreased in the case of private sector banks, viz. ICICI Bank and CBoP.

This ratio reveals profit per hundred rupee of total deposits. Total deposits consist of fixed, savings and current deposits both from public and banks. The ratio rose from 0.09%in 1985 to 0.62% in 1995-96 for SBI Group, while it reduced from 0.19% in 1985 to a position of net loss in 1995-96 for PNB. However, the ratio declined from 2.33% in 1995-96 to 1.35% in 2006-07 for ICICI Bank and from 4.67% in 1995-96 to 0.81% in 2006-07.

Table 6.20: Trends in   Profits as Percentage of Deposit

Year	SBI Group	ICICI Bank	PNB	CBoP
1985	0.09	-	0.19	-
1995-96	0.62	2.33	-	4.67
2006-07	1.04	1.35	1.10	0.81
Average	0.68	1.74	0.67	1.55
Trend GR Period I	24.10	-	6.83	-
Period ii	2.77	-1.15	4.27	-12.71
Period I&II	13.73	-	7.26	-
C.V.	65.29	41.75	65.99	74.62
T-value	8.35*	0.44	7.04*	4.01*

Source: Performance Highlights of Private and Public Sector Banks, IBA
       Mumbai, Balance-sheets of banks, various years.

However, this ratio improved for both SBI Group and PNB   to 1.04% and 1.10% for the respective banks in 2006-07.

Bank-wise analysis reveals that   on an average, this ratio has been the   highest for ICICI Bank (1.74%), followed by CBoP (1.55%), followed by SBI Group (0.68%) and PNB (0.67%). SBI Group and PNB have shown a significant rise in profits   as a percentage of deposits, while CBoP   has recorded a significant decline in this ratio   at 5% level of significance.

During period I, from 1985 to 1994-95, the trend   growth rate of profit as percentage of total deposits   has been higher   for SBI Group (24.10) than that of PNB (6.83). During Period II, i.e. the post-reforms period (1995-96 to 2006-07) however, the trend growth   rate of PNB has been higher (4.27) than   that of SBI Group (2.77).Both the private sector banks suffered a   decline in this   ratio, the reduction being greater for CBoP (-12.71) than of ICICI Bank(-1.15).If we compare the overall trend growth rates of both the Public Sector Banks, then it is observed that the rate of growth of SBI Group has been higher

(13.73) than that of PNB (7.26). The profit as percentage of total deposits has reduced for all the banks under study after the introduction of reforms due to intense competition among the banks to tap the fee-based sources of income.

The pattern of growth of profits as a percentage of deposits has been most volatile for CBoP as depicted by the Coefficient of Variation (74.62%),followed by PNB (65.99%),SBI Group (65.29%), while it has been quite smooth for ICICI Bank(41.75%).

With gradual deregulation of interest rates on deposits and advances, profits earned have somewhat been converged due to competition.

6.9 CONCLUSIONS

The major sources of other incomes, viz. income from sale of investment, income from commission, exchange and brokerage increased significantly for all the four banks under study.The trading income increased significantly only for except for ICICI Bank, while the foreign exchange income increased significantly for all the banks except SBI Group. As other sources of income have significantly helped to raise their incomes, the banks have been increasingly turning to them.

The public sector banks started Voluntary Retirement scheme in 2000-01 to downsize their staff. However, the establishment expenses increased due to liabilities on superannuation. A discernible feature of the trends in operating expenses has been the dominance of establishment expenses in total expenses of SBI Group and PNB, and the dominance of other operating expenses in the case of their private sector counterparts. This is attributed to the large size of the staff in the case of both the selected public sector banks initially, and later on due to VRS also, liability increased due to payment of liabilities on superannuation. The share of other operating expenses in the total operating expenses has been higher for both the private sector banks as they have been initially in the stage of branch expansion and are spending heavily on technology intensive systems, thereby reducing the need of manpower. These banks have installed ATMs and have been extending internet banking to their customers since the day of their inception.

All the four banks viz. SBI Group, PNB, ICICI Bank and CBoP have recorded a significant rise in all the sources of interest income, viz. interest/discount Income, Income on investment, income from balance with RBI and other inter-bank funds and other incomes, except PNB, for which, income from balance with RBI and inter-bank funds and other incomes did not increase significantly.

As far as interest expended is concerned, the interest expended on deposits has increased significantly for all the four selected banks during the period under study. The interest on RBI and other inter-bank borrowings increased significantly for both ICICI Bank and CBoP. However, for all the four banks, miscellaneous interest expenses increased significantly. The non-interest income of all the four banks scaled new heights to augment their total income.

Profits in relation to total income registered significant rise(at five percent level) for both the public sector banks, while CBoP suffered a significant decline in this ratio mainly due to the liquidity crisis suffered by it in the later years of the study. ICICI Bank which initially had a high ratio suffered some decline due to the competition posed by the public sector banks, which have geared up and are responding well to the challenge thrown by their counterparts.

Profits in relation to deposits increased significantly for both the public sector banks, while these declined alarmingly in the case of CBoP. ICICI Bank suffered a decline in this ratio. Thus, both ICICI Bank and SBI Group emerged strong on most of the major parameters of profitability. Initially, with the entry of private sector banks, the monopoly of the public sector banks was broken. Both the banks registered a remarkable rise in interest income, and non-interest income. Both the banks controlled the expenses due to the interest on balances with RBI and inter-bank borrowings effectively. ICICI Bank increased income from major non-fund activities, while SBI Group could not increase forex income significantly.

Burden, which influences profits, has been reduced substantially by both ICICI Bank and CBoP. Both the public sector banks have been plagued with heavy burden and they have never been able to control it effectively due to heavy manpower expenses and lesser dependence on technology. With the merger of ICICI Ltd. with ICICI Bank, economies of scale have been achieved by ICICI Bank, reflected in the efficient management of burden. Initially, Bank of Punjab recorded a remarkable progress, but due to an expansion over-drive it suffered liquidity crisis in the later years of study. However, after its merger with Centurion Bank, it has shown signs of improvement on all major parameters of profitability.

Initially, both the public sector banks suffered due to high priority sector advances, low technology base and rural orientation. In contrast, both the private sector banks have been banking heavily on technology; have negligible commitment to the rural masses or the priority sector, which has been responsible for their profitability. ICICI Bank has been able to consolidate its position after the merger as all the indicators of profitability responded in its favour. Bank of Punjab has reinvented itself by going in for merger with Centurion Bank to recoup its losses and regain its lost profitability.

SBI Group and PNB have gone for core banking solutions and have reduced their operating expenses greatly. The reforms have granted flexibility to banks in meeting their targets of priority sector lending. In the recent years, the profits of Public Sector Banks have become commensurate with their share of assets and are competing well with the private sector banks. The interest income and interest expenditure as proportion of total average funds and assets are declining. However, the decline in interest expenditure has been greater.

To sum up, profitability is an aggregate of various factors at play. With deregulation and soft interest schemes, the scope of intervention by RBI has reduced while the market forces are the key determinants. The C.R.R. and S.L.R have been reduced thus freeing more lendable resources for banking activities. The rates on deposits have also been freed and now only the rates on savings are mandatory. Only the efficient banks can survive as the spreads are thinning out putting tremendous pressures on profitability.

The banks have become dynamic and are devising new strategies to capture fee-based incomes and other non-traditional sources of income to supplement their income. Banks have become cost conscious as proper burden management can effectively reduce expenses and add to profits. The purpose of Asset-Liability Management is to increase profits by matching the maturity of liabilities in accordance with the assets so as to reduce the risks, which adversely affect the profitability.

REFERENCES

Ajit, D.;and Bangar, R.D.(2003)," Banks in Financial Intermediation," in A. Vasudevan (ed.)*Money Banking-Select Research Papers by the Economists of RBI*, Academic Foundation,p.253.

Amandeep(1993), *Profits & Profitability in Commercial Banks*, Deep & Deep Publications, New Delhi.

Anbumani, V.;and Niranjana, S.(2002),"Social Objectives and Priority Sector Lending," in Amalesh Banerjee and S.K.Singh (eds.) *Banking & Financial Sector Reforms in India*, Deep & Deep Publications Pvt. Ltd., New Delhi, p.231.

Arora, Usha;and Verma, Richa(2005),"Banking Sector Reforms & Performance Evaluation of Public Sector Banks in India," *Punjab Journal of Business Studies*, Vol. 1, No.1, April- September. p.12.

Chandan C.L.;and Rajput, P.K(2002),"Profitability Analysis of Banks in India: A Multiple Approach," *Indian Management Studies Journal*, Vol. 6,No.2,October, p.120.

Chandan C.L.;and Rajput, P.K.(2005),"Performance of Individual Commercial Banks –A 'Z' Score Analysis,"*Indian Management Studies Journal*, Vol. 9, No.2, October, p.72.

Das, Abhiman(2002),"Risk and Productivity change of Public Sector Banks,"*EPW*,Vol. XXXVII, No.5, February.2, p. 438.

Das, Abhiman; Nag Ashok;and Ray,C. Subash(2005),"Liberalisation Ownership and Efficiency in Indian Banking," *EPW*, Vol. XL, No. 12, March19-25, p.1191.

Deo, Malabika(2005), "Bancassurance A Win-Win Solution for Banks & Insurance," *Business & Economic Facts for You*, April,p.39.

Gurumoorthy, T.R. (2004),"'Analysis of Income and Expenditure in Banks,"*Business and Economic Facts For You*,June.

Jagirdar, Brinda(1991),"Profitability and Capital Adequacy,"*SBI Monthly Review*, Vol.XXXI,No.4,p.179.

Kannan, R.; Narain, Aditya.;and Ghosh, Saibal(2001),"Determinants of Net Interest Margin under Regulatory Requirements," *EPW*, Vol. XXXVI, No.4, Jan. 27- Feb. 2, p.338.

Mahadevan, K.(2002),"Non-Interest Income; Our Potential and Strategies to Increase its Share,"in P. Mohana Rao. and T.K Jain (eds.)*Management of Banking & Financial Institutions*' Deep and Deep Publications, New Delhi,p.59.

Mohan, Rakesh(2005),"Financial Sector Reforms in India-Policies & Performance Analysis," *EPW*, Vol. XL, No.12, March19-25, p.1112.

Mohan, Ram T.T.; and Ray, C. Subhash(2004),"Comparing Performance of Public and Private Sector Banks-A Revenue Maximisation Efficiency Approach,"*Economic and Political Weekly*,Vol. XXXIX,No. 12,March. 20-26.

N. Nettini;and G,Kuruba(2002),"Reforming Banking and Financial Sector Reforms in the context of Economic Restructuring," in Amalesh Banerjee and S.K. Singh (eds.),*Banking & Financial Sector Reforms in India*, Deep & Deep Publications Pvt. Ltd., New Delhi.

Padmavathi,A.;and Hemachandrika,G.(2006),*Public Sector Banks in India*, Global Research Publications Pvt.Ltd.,New Delhi.

Prasad, Umesh(2006),"Banking Sector Reforms: An Assessment and Future Version,"in Ravishankar Kumar Singh(ed.),*Indian Banking & Financial Sector Reforms-Realizing Global Aspirations*,"Vol. II

Abhijeet Publications, New Delhi, p.387.

Qamar, Furquan(2003),"Profitability & Resources Use Efficiency in Scheduled Commercial Banks in India: A Comparative Analysis of Foreign, New Private Sector , Old Private Sector and Public Sector Banks,"*Synthesis*, Vol.I, No. 1, July-Dec., p.1.

Ramasastri, A.S.;Samuel, Achamma.;and Gangadaran,S.(2004), "Income Stability of Scheduled Commercial Banks- Interest vis-a-vis Non-Interest Income, "*EPW*, Vol. XXXIX,No.12, March.20-26, p.1319.

Ramathilagam, G.;and Preethi, S.(2005),"Efficiency of Indian Commercial Banks in the Post-Reform Period," *Business & Economic Facts for You*, November, p.36.

Raut,C. Kishore.;and Das, K. Santosh(1996),"Commercial Banks in India-Profitability, Growth & Development,"Kanishka Publishers, Distributors, New Delhi.

RBI (2004-05),Operations & Performance of Commercial Banks, *Report on Trends & Progress of Banking in India*.

RBI(2005-06), Policy Developments in Commercial Banking,*Report on Trends & Progress of Banking in India*.

Reed, W. Edward.;and Gill, K. Edward(1989), *Commercial Banking*, Prentice Hall, New Jersey, Fourth Edition.

Sagar, Saveeta(2005),*Commercial Banks in India*,Deep & Deep Publications Pvt.Ltd.,New Delhi.

Sangwan, S.D.(2005),"Social Banking: An Assessment," *Vinimaya*, Vol. XXVI, Oct.-Dec., p.19.

Sehgal, Madhu;and Kher, Rajni(2002),"Asset Liability Management in the Indian Banks,"in P. Mohana Rao,and T.K Jain (eds.) *Management of Banking & Financial Institutions*,Deep & Deep

Publications Pvt. Ltd.,New Delhi ,p.91.

Singh, Kumar Shrawan(2002), " Banking Sector Reforms Some Issues with emphasis on problem of NPAs", in, Amalesh Banerjee & S.K Singh (eds.), *Banking & Financial Sector Reforms in India*, Deep & Deep Publications Pvt. Ltd., New Delhi.

Sinha, R.K.(2006), "Thinning Spreads Calls for Focused Interest Rate Risks Management by PSBs,'' *The Management Accountant*, November, p.895.

Sreekantaradya, B.S.(2004),*Banking & Finance-Perspective on Reforms*, Deep & Deep Publication Pvt. Ltd., New Delhi.

Srivastava, R.M.;and Nigam, Divya(2005*) Management of Indian Financial Institutions*,Himalaya Publishing House, Mumbai.

Subramanian, K.G.(2002)," Role of Branches in Asset Liability Management System,in P.Mohana Rao and T.K. Jain (eds.), *Management of Banking & Financial Institutions*, Deep and Deep Publications Pvt. Ltd., New Delhi,p.268.

Sundaram,Satya(1984),"Banks :Improving Productivity & Profitability,"*The Journal of the Indian Institute of Bankers*, Vol.55, No. 3, July-Sept., pp.155-156.

Uppal, R.K.;and Kaur, Rimpi(2007) ,"Falling Rate of Interest in the Banks: Bank Spreads, Profitability comes under Pressure,"in R.K Uppal, Rimpi Kaur (eds.),*Banking in the New Millennium*, Mahamaya Publishing House, New Delhi, p.356.

Varde, Varsha S.; and Singh, Sampat P.(1983),*Profitability of Commercial Banks*, NIBM ,Pune, p7.

Verma, Satish.;and Saveeta(2002),'Determinants of Profitability of SBI Group, other Nationalised and Foreign Banks in India," in Amalesh Banerjee and S.K. Singh (eds.).*Banking & Financial*

Sector Reforms in India', Deep & Deep publications Pvt. Ltd., New Delhi, pp. 320-321

Yeole, Arun(2006),"The Problem of NPAs,"in Sawalia B. Verma., Karmatma Panday and Narendra Sinha K. (eds.),*Economic Reforms*, Shree Publishers & Distributors, New Delhi, pp.221-222.

CHAPTER-7
LOAN PORTFOLIO MANAGEMENT

Lending is one of the two principal functions of commercial banks not only because of their social obligation to cater to the credit needs of different sections of the community but also because lending is the most profitable activity, for the interest rates realized on business loans have always been well above those realized on investments(Srivastava and Nigam,2005). Lending being done mainly from out of the funds mobilized by the banker from the public, it is required that the banker takes care to place his funds in customers who will repay the advance granted to them as undertaken, on time. Through lending, bank management strives to satisfy the legitimate credit needs of the community or credit markets that the bank serves or intends to serve.

Directed credit in the Indian banking system takes the form of priority sector credit, wherein the Reserve Bank of India (RBI) mandates a certain type of lending on the banks operating in India, including foreign banks. RBI sets targets in terms of percentages (of net bank credit lent by the banks) to be lent to certain sectors, which would not have had access to organized credit market in the normal course, without regulatory intervention and purely on commercial considerations (Roy,2006).

The scheme of social control over banks was introduced in 1968 with the main objective of achieving through management reforms, the wider spread of bank credit, preventing its misuse by the directors for their own benefits through hoarding and speculation, canalizing of credit to the priority and weaker sectors like agriculture, small scale industries, exports, retail trade etc. and making banks more effective

269

instruments of economic progress (Abrol, 1987). Thus, the banks were required to shift from security-oriented credit to purpose-oriented credit. This had the following disastrous effects for the commercial banking:

- Deterioration in the quality of the loan portfolio because of fixation of targets for specific sector lending;
- Inadequate attention to qualitative aspects of lending;
- No proper loan appraisal of credit applications;
- No insistence on collectable requirements;
- No post-credit supervision and monitoring;
- Growth of overdues and consequent erosion of profitability (Passah, 2002).

Political control of public sector banks and the consequent lobbying by various pressure groups has resulted in loans being given without adequate safeguards against default and a low attitude towards enforcing repayments (Nettimi and Kuruba, 2002). Before nationalization, banks had hardly paid any attention towards advances to agriculture, small industries, small borrowers, but were catering to the need of large business and industrial houses (Sangwan, 2005).

7.1 NEW NORMS OF BANK LENDING

After nationalization, the government of India undertook corrective measures for such lop-sided lending by the banks. Indian banks were expected to contribute towards economic development of the country by extending credit for the activities undertaken in the areas, which were considered to be "priority sectors."(Roy, 2006).

The Government and RBI have sponsored various schemes and taken other steps to help commercial banks in this regard, which are as follows:

- Lead Bank Scheme,
- Rural Oriented Branch Expansion Scheme,
- Village Adoption Scheme,
- Service Area Approach,
- Financing of Primary Agriculture Credit Societies,
- Farmer's Service Societies.

In 1991, the Narasimham Committee Report on the Financial System was tabled, which recommended an array of measures to revitalize the banking industry and give it a new strategic thrust- the fundamental change in the banking paradigm being the shift from resources mobilization to resource utilization(Agarwal,1998)."

The Narasimham Committee on Financial Sector Reforms (1991) has drawn attention to the problem of low and declining profitability and stated that "there is need for gradual phasing out of the directed credit programmes, i.e. the stipulation that 40 percent of all the credit should go to the priority sector should be scrapped. Priority Sector should be redefined and the proportion should be fixed at ten percent of the aggregate credit.''(Anbumani and Niranjana, 2002).

Despite the rejection of the recommendations of the Committee on the Financial System in respect of directed credit policy, some changes have taken place in respect of directed credit in the reforms era due to which the concept of directed credit is diluted. The definition of directed credit in the reforms era included agriculture, small scale industries, small road and water transport operators, small business, retail trade, state-sponsored organizations for SC/STs, educational loans granted to individuals by banks under their schemes and credit schemes for weaker sections. The definition of Priority Sector has been enlarged in the reforms era and now it includes:

- Loans to traditional plantation crops, viz. tea, coffee, cardamom.
- Loans for housing up to Rs. 5 lakh.
- Loans to transport operators up to ten vehicles.
- Advances to dealers of drip/sprinkler irrigation system and agricultural machinery.
- Investments made by bank in special bonds of SIDBI, NABARD , NHB, HUDCO, SFCs, SIDC and REC and contributions to Rural Infrastructure Fund.
- Banks' investment in bonds issued by Rural Electrification Corporation (REC) for financing its Systems Improvement Scheme under Special Project Agriculture.
- Advance to NBFC for on-lending to truck operators satisfying priority sector norms.
- Advance up to Rs.10 Million to software industry (Sreekantaradhya, 2004).

The Committee on Banking Sector Reforms, i.e. Second Narasimham Committee gave up the idea of phasing out the directed credit programme and recognized the need for its continuation. It said, "The Committee has noted the reasons why the Government could not accept the recommendation for reducing the scope of directed credit under priority sector from 40 percent to 10 percent. The Committee recognized that the small and marginal farmers and the tiny sector of industry and small business have problems with regard to obtaining credit and some earmarking may be necessary for this sector. Under the present dispensation, within the priority sector 10 percent of the bank credit is earmarked for lending to weaker sections. A major portion of this lending is on account of Government sponsored poverty alleviation and employment generation schemes. The Committee recommends that given the social needs of the sector, the current practice may continue.''(Sreekantaradhya, 2004).

The RBI introduced various measures to promote the effective use of credit. The credit delivery system has undergone major changes during the 1980s and also in the 1990s, after the economic reforms. In this process, the programme and sector specific prescriptions were discontinued except loans under DIR scheme, exports and priority sectors.

As a part of the reform measure, banks have been granted operational autonomy in fixation of inventory and receivable levels and setting the credit limits. A loan system for delivery of bank credit was introduced in 1995 to overcome the problems associated with cash credit and by large borrowers. Under this system, the maximum permissible bank finance (MPBF) has been worked out and a part is allocated under "loan" component and the remaining under "cash credit" (Rao et al.,2006).

The RBI prepared a 'Draft Technical Paper on Priority Sector Lending' in2005. This paper has recommended that only the financing of small-scale industry, small business, education agricultural activities and export activities should fall under the priority sector category, which aimed at undoing the dilution that the priority lending sector concept has suffered over the years on account of the induction of a wide range activities in the list of qualifying advances (Roy,2006).

The RBI issued the following instructions to the banks in respect of lending to the priority sector:

1. Forty percent of the priority sector advances should be earmarked for agriculture;

2. Advances to the rural artisans, village craftsmen and cottage

273

industries should constitute 12.5 percent of the total advances to small-scale industries;and

3. Direct advances to the weaker sections in agriculture and allied activities should reach a level of at least 60 percent of the total direct lending of agriculture(Jha,2002).

Today, the modern banker has to undertake lending on commercially viable terms as banking is not charity. In the era of globalization and competition, only the competent and profitable banks will be able to survive.

Thus, a bank has to strike on optimal balance between the three considerations of liquidity, solvency and income. The need for a balanced portfolio of advances acts as a constraint on lending operations and thus requires a policy decision regarding the extent of involvement in any area of advances.

7.2 REGULATORY FRAMEWORK FOR LENDING

The banks in the country are subject to the regulation of the Reserve Bank of India, which is the Central Bank of the country. Section 21 of the Banking Regulation Act 1949 empowers the Reserve Bank of India to determine the policy in relation to advances to be followed by banks generally or by any bank in particular and issue directions to Banks as regards the purpose of advances, the margins to be maintained in respect of the secured advances and also prescribe the rate of interest, maximum amounts of loans which may be given by any banking company to any borrower and other terms and conditions on which the advances can be made(Ramamurthy,2006).

Apart from the statutory framework, especially after the nationalization of Banks during 1969, the Reserve Bank of India has from time to time constituted various committees to study the operations of the banking industry and make recommendations to it. The recommendations of the following committees are as follows:

(1)   Tandon Committee recommendations

The Committee stipulated the norms for holding inventories and emphasized on better management of inventory and the concept of material management gained greater recognition

(2)   Chore Committee

The Committee observed that it would be difficult to replace the cash credit limits and streamlining the system was recommended. An annual review of all borrowers' accounts exceeding Rs. 10 lakh as working capital was suggested.

(3)   Narasimham Committee-I Recommendations

The Committee recommended the phase-wise reduction of SLR and CRR. It suggested that directed credit programmes should be phased out and priority sector be redefined.

(4)   Nayak Committee

The Committee suggested that 25% of the output value should be computed as working capital requirement of which 4/5 should be provided by the banking sector and the balance 1/5 should represent borrower's contribution towards margin for the working capital.

(5)   Narasimham Committee-II

The Second Report of Narasimham Committee recommended that the capital adequacy requirements should consider market risks alongwith credit risks. The duality of control over cooperative credit institutions by the State Government and RBI/NABARD should be eliminated and all the cooperative banking institutions should come under the discipline of Banking Regulation Act. It further suggested that banks should devise appropriate criteria suited to the small industrial

275

sector and be responsive to its genuine credit needs but this should not be done by sacrificing the canons of sound banking.

(6) Kannan Committee Report on MPBF

This group studied all the aspect of working capital assessment. According to it, the modality of working capital assessment of the borrowers should be left to the discretion of each bank which should devise a flexible system under the over all regulatory guidelines of the Reserve Bank of India, taking into account the size of the bank and what category of a bank it is, its prudential exposure limit and resources base, bank's Credit policy guidelines, credit skill management of the bank and the cadre of specialized credit officials and the thrust for business priorities.

(7) Kapoor Committee

This committee submitted its report in June 1998. The main recommendations of this committee are: delegation of more powers to branch managers to grant adhoc limits; freedom of banks to decide their own norms for assessment of credit requirements; Enhancement in the unit for composite loans to Rs. 5 lakh (since enhanced to Rs. 1 crore) and strengthening the recovery mechanism.

(8) Report or Working Group on Flow of Credit to SSI Sector (Ganguly Committee).

The recommendations of this Committee accepted by RBI are; adoption of cluster based approach for financing SME sector and sponsoring specific projects as well as widely publicizing successful working models of NGOs by Lead Banks, which service small and tiny industries and individual entrepreneurs and revision of tenure and interest rate structure of deposits kept by foreign banks with SIDBI for their shortfall in priority sector lending.

276

(9)   Internal Group to Review Guidelines on Credit Flow to SME Sector.

It recommended constitution of empowered committees at the regional office of RBI to periodically review the progress in SSI and Medium Enterprises financing and also to coordinate with other banks/financial institutions and the state government in removing bottlenecks, to ensure smooth flow of credit to the sector.

7.3 ISSUES IN LENDING POLICY

While bankers are quite familiar with the hazards of credit risk, and the related tools and techniques needed to assess and manage it in their portfolios, many are less prepared to deal with the myriad of new loan customer challenges that today's dynamic operating environment brings(Barsky and Catanach,2005). Two types of risks are typically greater for bank loans than for most other banking assets: Credit risk- that is, the possibility that promised payments will not be made and liquidity pressure often associated with bank loans. Thus, at the time of formulating a lending policy the following aspects have to be considered:

-What is to be financed?

-How is it to be financed?

-What is likely to happen after financing?

-What adjustments can be expected from the side of the borrower and the lender?

Thus, the major issues in bank lending are:

(1) Portfolio Considerations: Loans are generally the most profitable assets of banks as such they are tempted to increase the size of loan portfolio. However, loans generally are less liquid and carry more credit risk than most of the securities banks buy so the size of the loan portfolio must be limited. The need for a balanced portfolio of advances acts as a constraint on lending operations and thus requires a policy decision regarding the extent of involvement in any area of advances considering:

(a) the person, the activity and the region in which lending is being done;

(b) time roll-over of funds determining possibilities of withdrawal from the commitment as and when portfolio needs change;

(c) Income generated from various types of avenues for fund deployment; and

(d) Expected changes in environment affecting various persons, types of activity and regions(Hingorani,1983).

(2) Marketing of Funds: The reform process has awakened the management and staff to the need for marketing loans. The areas where policy decisions are needed would be: deciding on new activities, areas and types of borrowers: review of stagnating activities; over-saturated areas and borrowers with whom the bank is over-committed; and deciding on promotional costs to be incurred on cultivating additional worthwhile activities over a stipulated time horizon(Hingorani,1983).

(3) Loan Commitments: Many bank customers, especially large business borrowers, plan their borrowing needs with the bank well ahead of the time the funds will be needed. Therefore, banks adopt policies regarding the types of commitments that will be made, the types of enterprises to which they will be made, the amounts that will be made available, and the charge for such commitments.

(4) Terms and conditions: The terms and conditions have to be mutually acceptable and advantageous, encompassing the duties of the lender and the obligations of the borrower.

(5) Loan Pricing: The pricing of bank loans involves the setting of interest rates, the establishment of a compensating balance requirement-especially for business firms and in many cases, the imposition of loan fees.

Thus, the numerous factors that are considered in pricing loans include:

(1) The direct interest cost of funds;

(2) Bank overhead expenses;

(3) The costs of originating and administering the loan;

(4) The credit (default) of the loan;

(5) The maturity (interest rate) risk of the loan;

(6) Rates available to the borrower from competitive sources of funds including other lenders and the commercial paper and bond markets;

(7) The overall relationship between the bank and the borrower;

(8) The rates of return can be earned on alternative investments; and

(9) The desired return on stockholders' equity.

(6) Interest Rates: The range of rates that a bank may charge on various kinds of loans will be largely determined by the market rates influenced by the forces of competition. The rates that banks charge must be sufficiently high to cover: the cost of funds loaned; the cost of marketing and servicing different kinds of loans (including a proportionate share of the overhead expenses of the bank); a cost factor representing the probable losses that may be incurred over time; and a reasonable margin of profit.

7.4 CONSIDERATIONS IN FORMULATION OF BANK LOAN POLICY

Lending is a vital function to be performed by banks; hence, loan policies should be carefully framed.

The most crucial factors are:

(a) **Capital Position:** The capital of a bank serves as a cushion for the protection of the depositor's funds. Banks with a relatively large capital structure can make loans of longer maturities and greater credit risk.

(b) **Profitability of Various Types of Loans:** Profit making is an important objective for commercial banks as profits ensure the smooth flow of banking operations. Banks with greater need for earnings might adopt more aggressive lending policies than those that do not consider earnings to be paramount.

(c) **Stability of Deposits:** The variations in deposits and types of deposits are vital considerations for formulation of lending policy. Lending commences after providing adequately for primary and secondary reserves. Banks with rising deposits over the year can liberally grant loans and vice versa.

(d) **National Economic Scenario:** Stable economic conditions favour liberal lending policy, while economic variations act as a deterrent in lending.

(e) **Monetary and Fiscal Policy:** The monetary policy and fiscal policy are powerful instruments of credit control. Thus, when credit has to be created aggressive lending is encouraged and when credit has to be controlled restrictive lending policy is followed.

(f) **Expertise of Banks' Personnel:** The skill and competency of loan officers greatly affects the lending policy of a bank.

(g) **Credit Requirements of the Area Served:** The credit requirements of the local borrowers has to be met by banks,

280

which influence their lending policy accordingly. Banks have to fulfil their social commitments in the area they serve and thus lending policy has to be formulated in the light of the credit needs of the area of their operation.

(h) **Portfolio Consideration:** Aggregate deployment of funds has to be done in such a manner that any gradual as well as sudden changes in environment should not affect the funds adversely.

7.5 CONSTITUENTS OF LOAN POLICY

Loan policy of a bank should be comprehensive to encompass the various dimensions of lending. The contents of loan policy are:

- **Composition of Loan Portfolio:** A decision has to be taken with regard to the types of loans to be made by the bank. Some of the more important considerations in making this decision are the risks associated with various kinds of loans, the types of customers the bank wants to serve, the capabilities of banks' personnel, and certainly, the relative profitability of various kinds of loans (Reed and Gill,1989). The more liquid the loan portfolio, the less the need for large amounts of traditional liquid assets, such as cash and securities, to act as buffer reserves against unexpected liability withdrawals.

- **Credit Needs of the Area Served by the Bank:** Information about the credit needs of the bank's actual and potential customers for the present and foreseeable future is essential not only for the establishment of lending policies but for the determination of liquidity needs and investment policies as well. Need for credit should be determined realistically, fairly and accurately only on the basis of the operations of the borrowers, business as translated into cash flows during the period (Singh, 1983).

- **Acceptable Security and Creditworthiness:** In lending, the reduction of risk to an acceptable level is the main purpose of security. The RBI has, of late, prescribed a uniform margin of 40% for guarantees and advances (w.e.f. 11.5.2001) extended by Banks against shares including a minimum cash margin of 20 %(Srivastava and Nigam,2005).

- **Size of the Loan Portfolio:** The decision regarding the proportion of a bank's assets to be in the form of loans is a matter of overall bank policy. The credit demands of the community, the depositors' demands for funds, capitals funds, the abilities of bank personnel and the liquidity needs are all different for different banks. Apart from these considerations, a banker has to reconcile between the mutually conflicting objectives of liquidity and profitability.

- **Types of Loans to be made:** A bank's lending policies are, in effect, screening devices by which the directors and bank managers seek to limit the bank's loans to the type and character that they think appropriate, particularly when loan demand is pressing hard against a bank's available funds. Some of the more important considerations in making this decision are: the risks associated with various kinds of loans; the need for diversification to spread the risk; the need for liquidity; the types of customers the bank wants to serve; the capabilities of bank personnel; and certainly, the relative profitability of various kinds of loans(Reed and Gill,1989). Typically, bankers classify loans into risk categories based upon multiple criteria including loan type, the financial strength and character of borrowers, the nature and condition of assets pledged as collateral, borrowers' payment histories and both general and industry specific economic conditions (Janson,2004).

- **Maturities:** The maturity of a bank's loan portfolio affects its liquidity and risk exposure. Loan policy should cover the extent to which a bank will make and hold intermediate and long-term loans so that a consistent approach to protecting against the interest rate risk of such loans can be followed. With an increase in the maturities of loans the money and credit risk associated with them would tend to increase.

- **Compensating Balances:** The term compensating balances is used to describe a deposit balance primarily of a business firm that is required and is part of the consideration for the extension of credit. The policy statement on the compensating balance should include, among other things a statement on the manner of computing the compensatory balance, the type of borrowers to whom the compensating requirement would apply and the specific percentages of the loans that different borrowers would be required to hold as deposits in the bank.

- **Consortium Lending:** When the need of a borrower or a project for funds is so large that it is beyond the capacity of a bank or financial institution to provide, then three or four banks combine to form a consortium of banks which provides the funds to the borrower.

7.6 FACTORS INFLUENCING THE PRICE OF LOAN PRODUCTS

The pricing of bank loans involves the setting of interest rates, the establishment of a compensating balance requirement especially for business firms and in many cases, the imposition of loan fees (Reed and Gill,1989).

The rates that banks charge must be sufficiently high to cover:

-the cost of funds loaned;

-the cost of making and servicing different kinds of loans (including proportionate share of the overhead expenses of the bank);

-a cost factor representing the probable losses that may be incurred over time; and

-a reasonable margin of profit.

- **Demand for the Product:** Banks must be conscious of the extent to which demand will change for any material movement in the price of the product they offer.

  - **Extent of Risk:** A risk premium needs to be attached to the various risks faced by banks, viz. credit risk, liquidity risk, interest rate risk and foreign currency risk.

    -The cost of originating and administering the loan.

    -Rates available to the borrower from competitive sources of funds.

7.7 TYPES OF LOANS

(1) Commercial Loans: Loans intended to fulfil the credit needs of business enterprises, including farm operations, are commercial loans. On the basis of security, commercial loans may be secured or unsecured. In addition, loans can be made at either fixed rates of interest or floating rates. Commercial loans can be further classified as:

(a)Seasonal Loans: In its pure form, the seasonal loan is taken out only for seasonal needs and is repaid when inventory and receivables are partially converted into cash at the end of the seasonal upsurge.

(b)Working Capital Loans: The commonest type of business loan is the working capital advance which is needed for financing current assets: inventories, receivables and debtors (credit sales) and for other operational expenses. Current/ short term financial needs for working capital may arise for many purposes but the most common cases are.

- To finance increasing level of sales;
- To finance the provision of longer credit terms to customers;
- To finance large stock holdings a retailer wishing to offer more lines (leading hopefully to increased sales).

(c) Term Loans: Terms loans are defined as:

1) Loans sanctioned for a period exceeding one year with specific schedule repayment;

2) Interim cash credit/ bridge loans pending disbursements of sanctioned term loans and;

3) Installment credit where repayment is spread over more than one year.

Banks provide term loans primarily to finance purchase of fixed assets such as plant and machinery, constructions of factory building, purchase of factory land etc, for selling up new industrial enterprises and also for expansion, modernization, replacement or diversification of existing ones.

(2) Consumer Loans: These are the loans granted by Banks to individuals who may feel inclined to purchase articles to improve their standard of living. In broad usage, short and intermediate term consumer loans include both installment credit and non-installment.

(3) Real Estate Lending Mortgage Loans: Mortgage loans are a specialized form of consumer and commercial lending. Two considerations dominate a financial institution's decision of whether to approve a mortgage loan application:

- The applicant's ability and willingness to make timely interest and principal payments; and
- The value of the collateral underlying the loan.

The type of construction and location are extremely important since they influence the marketability of the property.

7.8 CREDIT EXPOSURES TO INDIVIDUALS/GROUP BORROWERS' CEIILINGS

The exposure limit needs to be fixed in relation to bank's capital funds, which is as follows:

- The exposure ceiling limits applicable from April 1, 2002, would be 15 per cent of capital funds in case of single borrower and 40 per cent in the case of a borrower group.

- Credit exposure to borrowers belonging to a group may exceed the exposure norm of 40 percent of the bank's capital funds but an additional credit exposure is due to extension of credit to the infrastructure projects.

- In addition to these limits, banks may, in exceptional situations, consider enhancement of the exposure to a borrower up to a further 5 per cent of capital funds.

7.8.1 Exemptions:

(i) **Rehabilitation of Sick/Weak Industrial Units:** The group exposure limits will not be applicable to weak/sick industrial units under rehabilitation.

(ii) **Food Credit:** Borrowers to whom limits are allocated directly by the Reserve Bank, for food credit will be exempt.

(iii)**Guarantee by the Government of India:** Where principal and interests are fully guaranteed by the Government of India the ceilings on single/group exposure limits will not be applicable.

(iv)**Loans against own Term Deposits:** Loans and advances granted against the security of Bank's own term deposits is excluded from the purview of exposure ceiling.

7.8.2 Credit Exposure to Industry and Certain Sectors

Internal Exposure Limits:

(1)Sectoral Limits: The banks may also consider fixing internal limits for aggregate commitments to specific sectors, e.g. textiles, jute, tea so that they are evenly spread over various sectors.

(2)Exposure to Real Estate: Banks need to frame comprehensive prudential norms relating to the ceiling on the total amount of real estate loans, single group exposure limits for such margins, security, repayment schedule and availability of supplementary finance. The guidelines of RBI need to be considered by the bank.

(3)Unhedged Foreign Currency Exposures of Corporates: The policy for hedging should exclude:

- At the time of extending forex loans to finance exports banks may not insist on hedging but ensure that such customers have uncovered receivables to cover the loan amount.
- Foreign exchange loans extended for meeting foreign exchange expenditure.

7.8.3 Exposure to Indian Joint Ventures/Wholly owned Subsidiaries Abroad:

- Banks are permitted to grant credit/ non-credit facilities to Indian Joint venture/Wholly-owned subsidiaries abroad,
  - Certain considerations have to be borne by the banks;

Loan will be granted only to those joint ventures where the holding by the Indian company is more than 51%.

(a)Banks will have to comply with the provisions of Section 25 of The Banking Regulation Act, 1949 under which the assets of every banking company in India at the close of business on last Friday at every quarter shall not be less than 75 per cent of its demand and time liabilities in India.

(b)All existing prudential guidelines relating to capital adequacy, exposure norms applicable to domestic credit/non-credit exposures are complied with.

The loan policy should ensure that the extension of such loans is based on proper appraisal and commercial viability of the projects.

7.8.4 Banks' Exposure to the Capital Markets

The detailed guidelines on Bank Finance against Shares and Debentures are given separately in the circular DBOD. No. DIR. BC. 90/13.07.05/98, dated 28th August, 1998 on Bank Finance against shares and debentures. The guidelines consist of:

- **Statutory Limit on Share Holding in Companies:** Under section 19(2) of the Banking Regulation Act, 1949, no banking company shall hold shares in any company (whether as pledgee, mortgagee, owner) of an amount greater than 30 per cent of its own paid-up capital and reserves, whichever is less.

- **Regulatory Restriction:** The bank's aggregate exposure to the capital markets covering direct investment by a bank in equity shares, convertible bonds and debentures, units of equity-oriented mutual funds, advances against shares to individuals for investment in equity shares and secured and unsecured advances to stock brokers should not exceed 5 percent of their total outstanding advances.

- **Advances against Shares to Individuals:** Loans against the security of shares, debentures and PSU bonds to individuals held in physical form should not exceed Rs. 10 lakh per individual

288

borrower (Rs. 20 lakh per individual borrower, if the securities are held in demat form.

- **Advances against Shares to Stock Brokers and Market Makers:** Banks can provide credit facilities to stock brokers and market makers, within the overall ceiling of 5 percent of their total advances.

- **Arbitrage Operations:** Banks are not permitted to undertake arbitrage operations against themselves or extend credit facilities directly or indirectly to stock brokers for arbitrage operations in Stock Exchanges.

- **Margins on Advances against Shares/Issue of Guarantees:** A uniform margin of 40 percent shall be applied on all advances/financing of IPOs' issues of guarantees.

7.8.5 Restrictions on Loans and Advances against Shares and Debentures

These are as under:

- No loans to be granted against partly paid shares;
- Advances against Money Market Mutual Funds to be regulated by SEBI;
- Advances not to be granted against Fixed Deposit Receipts (FDRs) issued by other banks;
- Advances not to be granted to Agents/ Intermediaries based on consideration of Deposit Mobilization;
- Loans not to be granted against Certificate of Deposits.

7.9 LOAN PORTFOLIO OF BANKS

The major objective of bank nationalization was to make banks more responsive to the needs of national development. The hitherto neglected sectors of the economy like agriculture, small scale industry, small business and economically weaker sections were brought within the ambit of commercial banking and declared as "priority sectors" for bank lending (Padmavathi and Hemachandrika, 2006).Thus, with the enlargement of the scope of the priority sector, the share also increased. However, with the initiation of the reforms, the Narasimham Committee suggested the reduction of the share of priority sector in the total share as majority of the advances to the priority sector were not granted on commercially viable terms.

The Narasimham Committee had observed that the asset quality has suffered due to the directed credit programme. Thus, the objective of social banking and the canons of sound banking were conflicting. However, both the objectives can be served if the credit to the directed sectors were made the basis of supervised credit to emphasize the nexus between production and to ensure that credit is made available to credit-needy borrowers for productive purposes. (Narasimham Committee Report) Hence, after the reforms, the banks have become cautious in granting advances to the priority sector.

7.9.1 Priority Sector Lending

The Narasimham Committees' recommendation that advances to the priority sector should be fixed at 10% of the total advances has not been accepted by the Government. But, banks have been given operational autonomy in meeting the priority sector targets.

Since the initiation of reforms, there has been a decline in priority sector lending due to greater flexibility provided by to banks to meet such targets. The stipulation that 40 percent of total bank credit should go to the priority sector continues, the target is not rigid. If the target is not achieved, an amount equal to the shortfall can be invested in NABARD/SIDBI. Now, banks have several profitable avenues included in the priority sector to extend loans on commercially viable terms and have increased lending to it as is evident in Table7.1.

Table7.1 Trends in Priority Sector Lending

(Amount in Rs.crore)

Year	SBI Group	ICICI Bank	PNB	CBoP
1985	8,646 (40.46)	-	1,493 (44.45)	-
1995-96	21,393 (27.38)	76 (11.69)	4,092 (32.37)	42 (19.00)
2006-07	1,57,583 (32.66)	55,277 (28.22)	36,528 (37.81)	3505 (31.23)
Trend GR Period I	7.34	-	14.36	-
Period II	19.04	84.37	24.30	39.97
Period I&II	13.37	-	16.40	-
C.V.	100.10	152.36	109.07	157.91
T-value	6.67*	4.72*	7.23*	3.33*
Average Share	31.65	21.04	39.87	19.27

Source: Performance Highlights of Public Sector and Private Sector Banks, IBA Mumbai, Various Issues.

Note: (i)GR stands for growth rate in all the tables.

(ii)*denotes significance at 5%level in all the tables.

(iii)Figures given in parentheses indicate percentage share in   total advances in all the tables.

(iv) C.V. stands for Coefficient of Variation in all the tables.

All the four banks have shown significant rise in priority sector advances   in absolute terms (at 5% level of significance).

During period I, from 1985 to 1994-95, the trend   growth rate of priority sector advances   have recorded   greater   rise   for PNB(14.36)than   SBI Group (7.34) .During Period II, i.e. the post-reforms period (1995-96 to 2006-07),the maximum rise in priority sector advances has been for ICICI Bank(84.37),followed by CBoP(39.97),PNB(24.30) and   SBI Group(19.04).If we compare the overall growth, then the rise has been greater for PNB(16.40) than that for SBI Group(13.37). Priority sector advances have increased for the two Public Sector banks in absolute terms after the introduction of reforms, which is a healthy outcome of the reforms.

The pattern of growth of priority sector advances has been most volatile for CBoP as depicted by the Coefficient of Variation (157.91%),followed by ICICI Bank (152.36%),PNB (109.07%),while it has been the most smooth for SBI Group(100.10%).

Thus, for the two selected public sector banks, initially after the advent of reforms, the share of priority sector advances reduced in the total advances. Towards the later years of the study, the share rose for all the four banks. This rise has been due to the flexibility provided to banks in meeting the priority sector targets. Though the stipulation that 40 percent of total bank credit should go to priority sector continues, the target is not a rigid one. The requirement is that if the target is not reached, an amount equivalent to the shortfall should be invested in NABARD/SIDBI and that means banks need not lend to commercially non-viable activities.

A discernible feature of the advances to the priority sector has been the reluctance of the two Private Sector Banks in making advances to the priority sector. Their share has been lesser as compared to their Public Sector counterparts. This is due to the fact that the Private Sector Banks are solely motivated by profits and avoid areas lacking infrastructure. However, over the years, both ICICI Bank and CBoP have progressively increased their share in the priority sector advances.

7.9.2 Trends in Cash Credit, Overdraft and loans

Table 7.2 depicts that the trends in cash credit, overdraft and loans payable on demand for all the banks under study have increased significantly (at five per cent level of significance). The share of cash credit, overdraft and loans payable on demand decreased from 93.52% in 1985 to 63.60% in 1995-96 for SBI Group and from 89.99% to 64.75%

292

for PNB, during the same period.

The share further declined drastically to 37.45% for SBI Group and to 44.68% for PNB in 2006-07.

Table 7.2: Trends in Cash Credit, Overdraft and Loans Payable on Demand

(Amount in Rs. crore)

Year	SBI Group	ICICI Bank	PNB	CBoP
1985	19,985 (93.52)	-	3,023 (89.99)	-
1995-96	49,689 (63.60)	4992 (76.65)	8,210 (64.75)	102 (46.15)
2006-07	1,80,696 (37.45)	32,864 (16.78)	43,161 (44.68)	2,712 (24.17)
Trend GR Period I	7.45	-	11.75	-
Period II	12.39	44.46	16.03	27.98
Period I&II	9.56	-	13.13	-
C.V.	63.54	136.68	84.96	93.31
T-value	9.99*	4.36*	8.68*	4.71*
Average Share	64.08	42.12	63.62	37.61

Source: Performance Highlights of Public Sector and Private Sector Banks, IBA Mumbai, Various Issues.

Similarly, this share decreased for both the Private Sector Banks from 76.65% in 1995-96 to 16.78% in 2006-07 for SBI Group and from 46.15% to 24.17% for CBoP during the same period.

During period I, from 1985 to 1994-95, cash credit, overdraft and loans payable on demand have recorded a growth rate of 11.75 for PNB while for SBI Group, the growth rate has been 7.45 only. During Period II, i.e. the post-reforms period (1995-96 to 2006-07) the growth rate has been the maximum for ICICI Bank (44.46), followed by CBoP(27.98), PNB(16.03) and SBI Group(12.39). If we compare the overall trend growth rates of the two Public Sector Banks, i.e. from 1985 to 2006-

07,then the growth rate has been higher for PNB(13.13) than that of SBI Group(9.56).

The rise in cash credit, overdraft and loans payable on demand has been most volatile for ICICI Bank as shown by its Coefficient of Variation (136.68%), followed by CBoP(93.31%),PNB(84.96%), while the growth has been quite steady for SBI Group(63.54%).

7.9.3 Trends in Bills Purchased & Discounted

Table7.3 exhibits the trends in another vital component of loans and advances, i.e. bills purchased & discounted. During Period I, the trend growth rate of SBI Group (22.87) has been greater than that of PNB(17.76) for this component of advances.

The share of Bills purchased and discounted was 6.48% and 10.00% for SBI Group and PNB respectively in 1985,which increased to 13.31% and 10.88% in 1995-96 for the two banks respectively in 1995-96.However,the share decreased to 7.69% and 4.79% for both the banks in 2006-07.

Table 7.3: Trends in Bills purchased & discounted

(Amount in Rs.crore)

Year	SBI Group	ICICI Bank	PNB	CBoP
1985	1384 (6.48)	-	336 (10.00)	-
1995-96	10,403 (13.31)	66 (10.14)	1379 (10.88)	54 (24.43)
2006-07	37,087 (7.69)	11,746 (5.99)	4,631 (4.79)	244 (2.17)
Trend GR Period I	22.87	-	17.76	-
Period II	14.18	56.70	12.32	4.65
Period I&II	15.20	-	10.55	-
C.V.	83.92	150.27	63.09	42.98
T-value	10.36*	4.05*	11.19*	1.05
Average Share	9.58	9.73	10.44	14.07

Source: Performance Highlights of Public Sector and Private Sector Banks, IBA Mumbai, Various Issues.

This share decreased for both the Private Sector Banks from 10.14% in 1995-96 to 5.99% in 2006-07 for ICICI Bank and from 24.43% to 2.17% for CBoP during the same period.

During Period II, i.e. the post-reforms period (1995-96 to 2006-07) the growth rate has been the maximum for ICICI Bank (56.70), followed by SBI Group(14.18),PNB (12.32) and CBoP (4.65). If we compare the overall trend growth rates of both the selected Public Sector Banks, i.e. from 1985 to 2006-07,then the growth rate has been higher for SBI Group(15.20) than that of PNB(10.55).

The rise in bills purchased and discounted has been most volatile for ICICI Bank as shown by its Coefficient of Variation i.e.150.27%, followed by SBI Group (83.92%),PNB(63.09%), while the growth has been quite steady for CBoP, its Coefficient of Variation being only 42.98%.The growth in bills purchased and discounted has been statistically significant at five per cent level of significance for all the banks except CBoP.

7.9.4 Trends in Term Loans

Table 7.4 indicates the trends in term loans of the four banks under study. All the banks have registered a significant increase in term loans,in absolute terms (at five per cent level) throughout the period under study.

Table 7.4: Trends in Term Loans

(Amount in Rs. crore)

Year	SBI Group	ICICI Bank	PNB	CBoP
1985	N.A.	-	N.A.	-
1995-96	18,033 (23.09)	85 (13.21)	3,090 (24.37)	66 (29.42)
2006-07	2,64,643 (54.86)	1,51,255 (77.23)	48,804 (30.46)	8,265 (73.66)
Trend GR Period I	-	-	-	-
Period II	27.03	127.27	28.69	50.25
Period I&II	-	-	-	-
C.V.	108.95	126.31	104.86	143.55
T-value	6.02*	6.58*	6.82*	3.82*
Average share	34.71	48.32	36.20	48.33

Source: Performance Highlights of Public Sector and Private Sector Banks,
IBA Mumbai, Various Issues.
Note: (i) N.A. stands for not available.

The share of Term Loans in total advances have risen from 23.09% in 1995-96 to 54.86% in 2006-07 for SBI Group and from 24.37% to 30.46% for PNB during the same period.

Both the selected Private Sector Banks also improved their share of Term Loans stupendously, from 13.21% in 1995-96 to 77.23% in 2006-07 for ICICI Bank and from 29.42% to 73.66% for CBoP during the same period. During period I, from 1985 to 1994-95, the growth rates of SBI Group and PNB could not be computed as the data was not available. During Period II, i.e. the post-reforms period(1995-96 to 2006-07)ICICI Bank has registered maximum rise in Term Loans, the trend growth rate being (127.27),followed by CBoP (50.25),PNB (28.69) and SBI Group (27.03).The rise in Term Loans has been most spontaneous for CBoP as reflected by its Coefficient of Variation i.e.143.55%,followed   by ICICI Bank(126.31%),SBI Group(108.95%), while the growth has been most steady for PNB (104.86%).

7.9.5   Trends in Secured Advances /Total Advances

Secured advances to total advances ratio indicates the proportion of advances granted after securing them. Table 7.5 highlights the trends in this ratio.   The growth in Secured Advances/Total Advances ratio has not been significant for any of the banks under study. After the reforms,   these advances have shown a declining trend for both the Public Sector Banks.

The share of secured advances initially increased for both the Public Sector Banks, viz. SBI Group and PNB from 78.67% and 91.28% in 1985 to 96.60% and 98.60% in 1995-96 respectively.

Table   7.5: Trends in Secured advances /Total advances

Year	SBI Group	ICICI Bank	PNB	CBoP
1985	78.67	-	91.28	-
1995-96	96.60	89.25	98.60	78.37
2006-07	78.59	79.76	85.38	81.29
Trend GR Period I	2.48	-	0.77	-
Period II	-2.20	-0.77	-1.61	0.39
Period I&II	-0.01	-	-0.12	-
C.V.	8.34	8.33	5.02	8.08
T-value	0.06	1.11	0.66	0.51
Average share	88.07	88.44	93.11	86.55

Source: Performance Highlights of Public Sector and Private Sector Banks,
IBA Mumbai, Various Issues.

However, later on, the share declined to 78.59% for SBI Group and 85.38% for PNB in 2006-07.The share of secured advances decreased from 89.25% in 1995-96 to 79.76% in 2006-07 for ICICI Bank, but increased from 78.37% to   81.29% for CBoP   during the same period.

During period I, from 1985 to 1994-95, this ratio recorded growth rate of 2.48 for SBI Group, while for PNB, the rate has been 0.77. However, during Period II, i.e. the post-reforms period (1995-96 to 2006-07) all the banks suffered a fall in this ratio except CBoP, which recorded a trend growth rate of 0.39. The maximum decline has been observed for SBI Group (-2.20), followed by PNB (-1.61) and ICICI Bank(-0.77). If we compare the overall trend growth rates of both the selected Public Sector Banks, i.e.from1985 to 2006-07,then the growth rate has improved for both SBI Group (-0.01) and PNB (-0.12).

The rise in Secured Advances/Total Advances has been most volatile for SBI Group, ICICI Bank and CBoP as shown by their Coefficients of Variation, i.e. 8.34%, 8.33% and 8.08% respectively, while the growth has been quite steady for PNB, its Coefficient of Variation being only 5.02%.On an average, this ratio has been the highest for PNB (93.11%) ,followed by ICICI Bank(88.44%),SBI Group (88.07%)and minimum for CBoP (86.55%).

7.9.6 Trends inRatio of Term Loans to Total Advances

Ratio of term loans to advances indicates the proportion of term loans granted by a bank in the entire advances, which is depicted in Table 7.6. Ratio of Term Loans to Total Advances has recorded a significant rise (at five percent level) for all the banks during the period of study.

The share of term loans in total advances increased from 23.08% and 24.37% in 1995-96 to 54.86% and 50.52% in 2006-07 for SBI Group and PNB respectively. The two Private Sector Banks experienced dramatic rise in the share from 13.05% to 77.22% for ICICI Bank and from 29.86% to 73.65% for CBoP during the same period.

During period I, from 1985 to 1994-95, the growth rates of SBI Group and PNB could not be computed as the data was not available. During Period II, i.e. the post-reforms period (1995-96 to 2006-07) ICICI Bank has registered a maximum rise in Term Loans/Total Advances, the trend growth rate being (26.75), followed by CBoP (11.45), SBI Group (8.29) and PNB (6.88).

Table7.6: Trends in Term loan to Total Advances

(Amount in Rs. crore)

Year	SBI Group	ICICI Bank	PNB	CBoP
1985	N.A.	-	N.A.	-
1995-96	23.08	13.05	24.37	29.86
2006-07	54.86	77.22	50.52	73.65
Average share	34.71	48.20	36.20	48.33
Trend GR Period I	-	-	-	-
Period II	8.29	26.75	6.88	11.45
Period I&II	-	-	-	-
C.V.	32.06	78.27	25.11	38.00
T-value	8.76*	4.60*	7.76*	10.31*

Source: Performance Highlights of Public Sector and Private Sector Banks, IBA Mumbai, Various Issues.
Note: (i) N.A. stands for not available.

The rise in Term Loans/Total Advances has been most spontaneous for ICICI Bank as reflected by its Coefficient of Variation(78.27%), followed by CBoP (38.00%),SBI Group (32.06%), while the growth has been quite steady for PNB, its Coefficient of Variation being (25.11%) only.

On an average, the share of term loans in the total advances has been the highest for CBoP (48.33%), followed by ICICI Bank(48.20%), PNB(36.20%) and SBI Group(34.71%).

The rising proportion of term loans in the total advances shows that it is the preferred mode of financing by banks. This ratio has been almost the same for both the Private Sector Banks. The Public Sector

Banks also showed a similar   trend.

7.10 CONCLUSIONS

After the introduction of the banking sector reforms, both SBI Group and PNB reduced lending to the priority sector. However, with flexibility provided to banks to invest in apex institutions on failure to meet the priority sector targets, the banks have started lending on commercially viable terms. As such, in the later years of the study, again, lending to the priority sectors has increased for all the four banks under study.

The various constituents of loans and advances, viz. cash credit, overdraft and loans payable on demand; and term loans have shown a significant rise for all the four banks under study. The exception has been bills purchased and discounted; in which CBoP did not register significant growth. Initially, cash credit, overdraft and loans repayable on demand constituted the major share in total loans and advances of all the four banks. However, in the later years of the study, term loans dominated the   loans and advances. For all the selected banks, term loans constituted the largest proportion of advances, followed by cash credit, overdraft and loans repayable on demand and bills purchased and discounted. PNB is granting   more advances on the basis of security than SBI Group, while ICICI Bank is ahead of CBoP in this regard.

The share of secured advances in the total loans and advances has decreased for all the banks, except CBoP, which recorded a   rise in the   share. This alarming feature of loan portfolio management   can prove counter-productive for the banks.

REFERENCES

Abrol, Premnath(1987)*Commercial Banking*, Anmol Publications, New Delhi.

Agarwal, Som(1998)," Management of Assets and Liabilities of Indian Banks-The long and short of credit ," *The Economic Times*, Monday 28,September, p. 9 .

Anbumani,V.;and Niranjana, S.(2002),''Social Objectives and Priority Sector Lendings,'' in Amalesh Banerjee and S.K. Singh(eds.), *Banking and Financial Sector Reforms in India*, Deep & Deep Publications Pvt. Ltd., New Delhi,p.232.

Barsky, P. Noah.;and Catanach, H. Anthony(2005)," Evaluating Business Risk in the Commercial Lending Decision,'' *Commercial Lending Review*, Vol. 20, No. 3, May –June p.3.

Cornett & Saunders(1999),*Fundamentals of Financial Institutions Management*, Irwin McGrawHill International Edition, Finance Series, Singapore.

Hingorani, N.L.(1983)," Major Issues in Lending Policy," in Sampat P. Singh. (ed.), *Bank Lending-Some Controversial Issues*, NIBM, Pune.

Indian Institute of Bankers (2004),*Indian Financial System and Commercial Banking,* Macmillan Publications,New Delhi.

Janson, R. Kenneth(2004)," Estimating Loan-Loss exposure ," A Comparison of Traditional and Markov Models", *Commercial Lending Review*, Vol. 19, No. 6, Nov-Dec, p.25.

Jha, Tarakant(2002), "Priority Sector Lending: A Case Study in Mithila Region," in Amalesh Banerjee and S.K. Singh(eds.), *Banking and Financial Sector Reforms in India*, Deep & Deep Publications Pvt. Ltd., New Delhi, p.270.

Lucia,De,R.D.;and   Peters,J.   (1993)   *Commercial   Bank Management*
:*Functions and Objectives*, Serendip Publications,Wahroonga.

Management Policies for Commercial Banks(1980), Prentice Hall Englewoods, New Jersey, 3rd Edition.

Mohan Rakesh (2006),"Agricultural Credit in India-Status, Issues   and Future Agenda," *EPW*, Vol. XLI, No.11, p. 1015.

N. Nettimi;and G, Kuruba (2002), "Reforming Banking and Financial sector in the Context of Economic Restructuring," in Amalesh Banerjee, S.K Singh (eds.), *Banking and Financial Sector Reforms in India*, Deep & Deep Publications Pvt. Ltd., New Delhi, pp. 43-44.

Padamavathi,A;and HemaChandrika,G.(2006), *Public Sector Banks in India*, Global Research Publications, New Delhi.

Passah P.M (2002) "Banking and Financial Sector reforms in India-Rationale, Progress, Efficacy and Future Agenda, "in Amalesh Banerjee, S.K Singh (eds.), *Banking and financial sector reforms in India*, Deep& Deep Publication Pvt. Ltd., New Delhi, p21.

Ramamurthy, T.R.(2006), *How to Borrow from Banks & Financial Institutions*, Bharat Law House Pvt. Ltd., New Delhi.

Rao, Ramachandra K.S.; Das, Abhiman; Singh, Kumar Arvind (2006)," Commercial Bank Lending to Small Scale Industry," *EPW* Mar18 Vol. XL1, No.11, p.1028.

Reed, W. Edward;and Gill, K. Edward(1989), *Commercial Banking,* Prentice Hall, New Jersey, Fourth Edition.

Roy, Mohua (2006), "A Review of Bank Lending to Priority and Retail Sectors," *Economic and Political Weekly*, Mar 18, EPW, Vol XLI, pp. 1035-1037.

Sandhu, Ranjit(2002), "Quality Lending," in P.Mohana Rao and T.K Jain (eds.), *Management of Banking and Financial Institutions,* Deep & Deep Publishers Pvt. Ltd., New Delhi.

Sangwan S.D. (2005)" Social Banking An Assessment," Vinimaya. Oct- Dec Issue, Vol xxvi No3, p 19.

Saunders, Anthony(2002),*Financial Institutions Management– Modern Perspective*,McGrawHill International Edition, Finance Series, Third Edition,Singapore.

Seetapathi, K; Sivaram, Y.G ;and RamaKrishna,T.S.(2003), *Loan Portfolio -Key Issues,* ICFAI Press, Hyderabad.

SenGupta, A.K.(1994)," Study of Credit Policy and Decision systems in Banks, " April, *Project Report*, NIBM ,Pune.

Singh, P. Sampat(1983)," Credit Appraisal, Review and follow up: A Framework for Decisional Analysis," in Sampat P. Singh (ed.), *Bank Lending –Some Controversial Issues,*" NIBM, Pune, p.138.

Srivastava, R.M.;and Nigam, Divya(2005), *Management of Indian Financial nstitutions*, Himalaya Publishers, Mumbai.

Suneja, H.R.(1992), *Management of Bank Credit*, Himalaya Publishing House, Mumbai.

CHAPTER-8

FINDINGS AND SUGGESTIONS

The introduction of Financial and Banking Sector Reforms has brought some major policy measures like disintermediation, deregulation, decontrol, liberalizing of control in trade/foreign exchange etc. Deregulation and integration have led Indian Banks and financial institutions into competition both on Assets side as well as Liabilities side of the Balance-sheet, forcing them to assume greater and newer risks in their quest for higher returns.

The Narasimham Committee Reports on the Banking Sector Reforms highlighted the weaknesses in the Indian banking system and suggested reforms based on the Basel norms.

Recognizing the need for a strong and sound banking system, the Reserve Bank of India came out with its guidelines on Asset Liability Management System in banks in February 1999. These guidelines were to be implemented with effect from April 1, 1999. Asset Liability Management (ALM) has grown up as a response to the problem of managing modern day business which is subject to a wider range of risks in an environment where interest rates, exchange rates and economic conditions are subject to changes. The maturity mismatches and disproportionate changes in the levels of assets and liabilities cause both liquidity risk and interest-rate risk.

Though the ALM process is too complex to practice, it is perhaps the only solution for banks to survive in this rapidly changing environment where the composition, duration and risk profile of their assets and liabilities have an important bearing on their growth and profitability.

8.1 OBJECTIVES OF THE STUDY

The present research attempts to undertake a comprehensive study on the various areas of asset liability management and their impact on the profitability performance of banks. The specific objectives of the study are:

- To analyse the growth and development of banks over the last two decades since consolidation started.
- To study the extent to which banks have effectively managed their Assets and Liabilities during the period under study.
- To examine the profitability trends in the light of changed policies after privatisation.
- To examine the change in lending policies of Banks.
- To suggest the future strategy for assets and liabilities of banks.

The present study relates to the impact of Asset Liability Management as part of the Banking Sector Reforms, on the profitability and performance of the selected banks.RBI implemented Asset Liability Management in the year 1999 and its impact may be studied in two ways. Firstly, to analyse the change in the pattern of development of all those activities which banks had been pursuing prior to the reforms, e.g. branch expansion, deposit mobilization, credit deployment and profitability. This would require a study of the performance of the banking activities prior to the reforms.Secondly, to probe the performance of banks in the light of the objectives of the reforms, viz. ensuring capital adequacy of banks, improved profitability, lending on commercial considerations and avoidance of mismatch between assets and liabilities.

The study aims at analyzing the pattern and profitability of banking from the period of consolidation of banks, i.e. from 1985 to 2007, so as to compare the performance of banks during the pre and post-reforms era.

8.1.1 RESEARCH METHODOLOGY

Scope

The study titled,''Management of Assets & Liabilities in Relation to Performance & Profitability of Commercial Banks,''covers State Bank of India Group, Punjab National Bank, ICICI Bank and Centurion Bank of Punjab. These banks have been selected with the purpose to concentrate on two largest banks, one each from public and private sector and two banks having strong presence in Punjab, one each from both the sectors.

Database

For the purpose of this study, secondary data has been collected from the following sources, viz. RBI Bulletins, IBA Bulletins, Economic Surveys, Various Reports on RBI's Trends and Progress of Banking in India, RBI's Basic Statistical Returns of Scheduled Commercial Banks,Performance Highlights of Public Sector and Private Sector Banks published by IBA,Annual Reports of the banks and Websites of RBI,IBA and the banks under study.

Period of Study

The study covers the period from December 1985 to March 2007.

Data Analysis and Interpretation

The data collected from the secondary sources has been tabulated and anlaysed.Various statistical techniques have been applied on the collected data to reach meaningful conclusions. In the course of analysis, besides using percentages and averages, the performance on various parameters has been recorded in terms of trend growth rates and t-test has also been applied to test their significance.The coefficient of variation has also been calculated to find the variation of various parmeters.

8.2 MAIN FINDINGS OF THE STUDY

The findings are presented chapter-wise as under:

8.2.1 PROGRESS AND DEVELOPMENT OF COMMERCIAL BANKING

The public as well as private sector banks have grown enormously since their nationalisation, especially in unbanked and under-banked areas, in terms of the number of branches, volume of deposits, credit and priority sector advances.

- All the four selected banks have registered a significant rise in deposits during the period of study.The growth rate of deposits has been higher for the private sector banks as compared to that of public sector banks and ICICI Bank has recorded the highest growth rate.

- The banks under study have registered a significant rise in investments. In the case of both the private sector banks, the growth rate of investments has been higher than that of the public sector banks and ICICI Bank, again, has recorded the highest growth rate.

- All the four selected banks have registered a significant rise in loans and advances. The growth rate of loans and advances has been higher for the private sector banks as compared to the public sector banks and ICICI Bank again leads as far as growth rate is concerned.

- The Credit-Deposit ratio, on an average, has been the highest for ICICI Bank, followed by SBI Group, CBoP and least for PNB.
- After the expiry of the five year Branch expansion programme (1990-95), the subject of opening rural branches was left to the commercial judgement of banks. Banks were allowed to convert their non-viable rural branches into satellite offices or even closure of bank branches at rural centres served by two commercial banks. The number of urban and metropolitan branches has increased rapidly, more so for ICICI Bank and CBoP. Thus, for SBI Group and PNB, the share of rural and semi-urban branches has been the highest while for CBoP and ICICI Bank, the share of metropolitan and urban branches has been the highest.

8.2.2 ASSETS MANAGEMENT

Reserves Position Management

As far as primary reserves are concerned, on an average, SBI Group(14.36%), CBoP(14.28%) PNB (14.17%), have maintained similar amount in the form of primary reserves as a proportion of total deposits, while ICICI Bank (12.68%) has the least primary reserves in relation to deposits.However, the situation in the case of Secondary Reserves is different. Secondary Reserves as a percentage of total deposits have decreased for all the four banks under study. These Reserves as a percentage of total deposits, on an average, have been maximum for SBI Group (86.99%), followed by ICICI Bank (86.45%), CBoP (71.40%)and PNB(69.91%).

Investment Management

The Investment Portfolio of the selected four banks has shown that:

- The government securities form a major chunk of the investment portfolio of all the four banks under study.
- PNB and SBI Group have a wide portfolio of investments ranging from government and approved securities to subsidiaries & joint ventures.
- Both the selected private sector banks have been reluctant to invest in approved securities probably due to their lesser marketability.
- All the banks have increased investment in shares and subsidiaries and joint ventures over the years, except CBoP, as it has never invested in subsidiaries and joint ventures.
- The share of investment in debentures has reduced over the period for all the selected banks. The decline in investment in debentures has been due to the lack of development of corporate bond market. The secondary market has not developed commensurately and market liquidity remains an issue.

Liquidity Management

Various liquidity ratios have been calculated to ascertain the liquidity position of the four banks:

- Liquid Assets/Total Assets ratio has declined for all the banks under study, the decline being the most for ICICI Bank, followed by SBI Group, CBoP and PNB. However, Liquid Assets/Total Assets ratio has been well above the Prudential Limit of 5% for all the four banks. On an average, the ratio has been the highest for SBI Group (13.36%), followed closely by ICICI Bank (13.01%), PNB (12.30%) and CBoP (8.43%).

- Current Ratio has declined for both ICICI Bank and PNB and increased for SBI Group and CBoP, over the period under study. On an average, the ratio has been the highest for PNB (5.39%), followed by ICICI Bank (4.94%), CBoP (4.67%) and SBI Group (2.36%).

- Purchased Funds/Total Assets ratio has reduced for PNB and CBoP, indicating dependence on external sources for funds, while it has increased for ICICI Bank and SBI Group. However, on an average, Purchased Funds/Total Assets ratio has been the least for SBI Group(47.57%), followed by PNB(50.80%), CBoP(58.23%) and ICICI Bank(67.41%).

- Loan/Deposits ratio has increased for all the banks. On an average, it has been the most for ICICI Bank(46.25%), followed by CBoP (29.80%), SBIGroup (14.78%)and PNB(14.01%).Thus, on an average, Loan/Deposits ratio has been above the Prudential Limit of 65% only for ICICI Bank, in the later years of the study.

o As per RBI Guidelines, banks are preparing Gap Statements to find out the extent of asset liability mismatch and take remedial measures. From the year 2000 to 2007 the gap statements indicate that SBI Group and ICICI Bank have maintained their assets and liabilities according to the interest rate scenarioin most of the years. PNB and CBoP have had adverse gap for a couple of years. On an average, banks have become cautious with regard to their asset liability mismatch and are making efforts to reduce the magnitude of gap to avoid financial crisis because liquidity shortfall in a single institution can have significant repercussions for the entire banking sector.Thus, as far as liquidity management is concerned, both ICICI Bank and SBI Group are effectively

310

managing it.

The various aspects of asset management viz. Reserve position management, Investment management and Liquidity management of the four selected banks have been studied. Thus, in all the areas of asset management, ICICI Bank and SBI Group have more or less similar position and are giving each other tough competition. PNB has been conservative and consistent towards lending funds, over the years.

8.2.3 LIABILITIES MANAGEMENT

Liabilities management has become a vital area of concern for banks today as assets have to be managed in tandem with liability for commercial banks.

o   Capital is the most important constituent of the liabilities of a bank; hence its adequacy needs to be attained by the banks at all costs. Over the period under review, from 1995-96 to 2006-07, the Capital Adequacy Ratio has increased significantly only for PNB, while it has declined alarmingly for both the private sector banks, viz. ICICI Bank and CBoP. This is a matter of grave concern for the two banks and needs to be looked into for assuring the confidence of the investors especially for CBoP. Moreover, with the introduction of Basel-II norms, the operational risk has also come into focus along with credit risk and market risk for which more capital has to be provided for.

o Reserves and surplus complement the capital of a bank and have risen significantly for all the four banks under study.

o   Deposits form the major source of funds for banks. Deposits from public provide the funds for lending to banks. All the types of deposits from public, viz. Fixed, Savings and Current deposits have increased significantly for all the four banks under study during the

311

period under review. Deposits from banks; fixed and current have also grown significantly for all the four banks under study. A discernible feature of the various types of deposits from the public has been the rising dominance of fixed deposits and declining share of current deposits in the total deposits of all the four banks under study.Thus, fixed deposits constitute the major share of deposits for all the banks under study, followed by savings deposits and current deposits. The chief reason for this has been the deregulation of interest rates on deposits. Only the rates on the savings deposits are regulated by RBI. Savings deposits, which reflect the strength of the retail liability franchise, are the focus of the banks' customer acquisition efforts.

o Commercial banks have to depend on external sources to meet their financial commitments.The banks have rarely relied on RBI for funds due to availability of cheaper sources of funds.Borrowings from other banks have increased significantly for SBI Group and ICICI Bank. Borrowings from institutions and agencies have grown significantly only for SBI Group while it has decreased for PNB. Borrowings from abroad have increased significantly for all the banks under study. Borrowing funds from RBI has been the most unpopular form of borrowings for all the four banks during the period of study.Borrowings from abroad forms the major share of borrowings for all the four banks followed by Borrowings from institutions and agencies.

o Among the other liabilities and provisions of banks, bills payable have increased significantly for all the four banks under study. The rise in liability due to inter-office adjustments has risen significantly for both SBI Group and PNB.Interest accrued has risen

312

significantly for ICICI Bank and CBoP, while other liabilities (including provisions) have grown significantly for all the four banks under study. Provisions have risen for all the four banks due to the introduction of asset classification and provisioning norms adopted by all the banks as a result of the economic reforms. Bills seem to be most popular among banks to even out short-term liquidity within the perimeter of the banking system. The share of other liabilities (including provisions) has been the highest for all the four banks under study, followed by Bills payable.

o On the liability side, there has not been much compositional change since the initiation of forms as deposits continue to account for the major share of the total liabilities. This is also due to the fact that after the reduction in cash reserve ratio and statutory reserve ratio, banks are concentrating on deposits mobilization with greater vigour as banks have more lendable resources at their disposal. Deposits are, thus the key to banks' profitability as they provide credit for lending which enables the banks to attain profits.

8.2.4 TRENDS IN PROFITABILITY

Spread in relation to Assets, also known as Net Interest Margin (NIM) has increased significantly for both the Public Sector Banks, while it has reduced for both the Private Sector Banks. A system of benchmark Prime Lending Rate (PLR) has been adopted by Indian banks since 2004 to afford flexibility to banks in pricing loans and advances based on market benchmarks. Thus, with falling interest rates, the lending rates are also declining, thereby reducing the interest earnings of banks. On an average, NIM has been the highest for PNB (2.92%), followed by CBoP (2.79%), SBI Group (2.73%) and ICICI Bank (1.89%). Competition has reduced the divergence in income from this source.

- The Public Sector Banks started Voluntary Retirement scheme in 2000-01 to downsize their staff. However, the establishment expenses increased due to liabilities on superannuation. A discernible feature of the trends in operating expenses has been the dominance of establishment expenses in total expenses of SBI Group and PNB and the dominance of other operating expenses in the case of their private sector counterparts.This is due to the fact that Private Sector banks have been investing heavily in technology upgradation to provide consumer-centric services.

- All the four banks, viz. SBI Group, PNB, ICICI Bank and CBoP recorded significant rise in all the sources of interest income, viz. interest/discount income, income on investment, income from balance with RBI and other inter-bank funds and other miscellaneous sources, except PNB, for which, income from balance with RBI & inter-bank funds and other interest sources did not increase significantly. Interest and discount income constituted the major source of interest income for all the four banks under study, followed by income on investment and interest on Balances with RBI & other Inter-bank funds and other interest income.

- As far as interest expended is concerned, the interest expended on deposits has increased significantly and constitutes the major share among interest expenses for all the four banks during the period under study. The interest on RBI and other inter-bank borrowings increased significantly for both the private sector banks, viz. ICICI Bank and CBoP. However, for all the four banks, miscellaneous interest expenses increased significantly.

- The non-interest income of banks scaled new heights with all the four banks recording a significant increase in it.This is due to the fact that non-interest income is not dependent on the banks' capital adequacy and thus, the potential to increase these transactions is tremendous. All the four banks registered a significant rise in income from commission,exchange and brokerage.ICICI Bank alone, has recorded significant rise in income from sale of investment.All the banks,except SBI Group,have recorded significant rise in income from foreign exchange transactions.For all the banks under study, income from commission,exchange and brokerage forms the major share of Other income. The other sources of income have become very important for banks and banks are increasingly turning towards them to raise their incomes. These sources of income have the added advantage of not requiring capital. Share of income from other sources is also rising indicating greater diversification of banks into non-traditional activities. Foreign exchange business, trading income and income from brokerage and commission have become potential profit cells for banks.However,the share of non-interest income in the total income,on an average has been highest for ICICI Bank(20.84%), followed closely by CBoP(20.53%), SBI Group(14.09%) and least for PNB(10.58%). Hence, as compared to interest income, the share of non-interest income is quite small.
- The non-interest expenses (establishment and operating) have increased significantly for all the banks under study.On an average, for SBI Group (22.38%) and PNB(22.01%) ,the share of Establishment expenses has been higher than other operating

expenses,which has been 9.49% and 9.38% respectively.This is attributed to the large size of the staff in the case of the two Public Sector Banks initially, and later on due to VRS also, liability increased due to payment of liabilities on superannuation. Moreover,technology has put pressure on the Public Sector Banks to restrict the branch network and employ better skilled workforce resulting in large manpower expenses.On the contrary,the share of other operating expenses has been higher for CBoP(32.61%) and ICICI Bank(20.28%) than Establishment expenses,which has been 5.28% and 6.76% respectively. The share of other operating expenses in the total operating expenses, on an average, has been high for both the Private Sector Banks as they have been initially in the stage of branch expansion and are spending heavily on technology intensive systems, thereby reducing the need of manpower. These banks have installed ATMs and are extending internet banking since their inception.

- The share of Profits in Total Income has increased significantly for both the Public Sector Banks,while ICICI Bank and CBoP,recorded a decline, the reduction being alarming for the latter. Initially, the two PSBs suffered due to high priority sector advances, low technology base and rural orientation. In contrast, the two Private Sector Banks have been banking heavily on technology and have negligible commitment to the rural masses or the priority sector, which added to their profitability. ICICI Bank has been able to consolidate its position after the merger as all the indicators of profitability responded favourably to it.

- Initially, with the entry of private sector banks, the monopoly of the Public Sector Banks was broken. Both the banks registered a remarkable rise in interest income, and non-interest income. For all the four banks, the share of Interest Expenses has been the largest, being the most for ICICI Bank(74.45%),followed by PNB (68.61%), SBI Group(68.13%)and CBoP(60.63%). ICICI Bank increased income from major non-fund activities, while SBI Group could not increase forex income significantly. Both the PSBs have been plagued with heavy burden and they have never been able to control it effectively due to large manpower expenses and lesser dependence on technology. With the merger of ICICI Ltd. with ICICI Bank, economies of scale have been achieved by ICICI Bank, reflected in the efficient management of burden. Initially, Bank of Punjab recorded a remarkable progress, but due to an expansion over-drive, it suffered liquidity crisis in the later years of study. However, after its merger with Centurion Bank, the new entity, Centurion Bank of Punjab has shown signs of improvement on all major parameters of profitability.CBoP recently merged with HDFC Bank in April 2008, which will go a long way in increasing the market power and revenue generation of HDFC Bank.

8.2.5   LOAN PORTFOLIO   MANAGEMENT

The rise in priority sector lending since the initiation of reforms reflects greater flexibility provided to banks to meet such targets. Currently, if a bank fails to meet the priority sector lending target through direct lending, the bank can invest the shortfall amount with the apex organizations dealing with the flow of funds towards agriculture and small scale industries. While adherence of banks to the norms on priority sector is desirable, the current arrangement reflects the operational flexibility that the reform process has provided while attaining social objectives.

Initially after the advent of reforms, the share of priority sector advances reduced in the total advances for the two selected public sector banks. Towards the later years of the study, the share rose for all the four banks. This rise has been due to the flexibility provided to banks in meeting the priority sector targets. The stipulation that 40 percent of total bank credit should go to the priority sector continues, the target is not rigid. If the target is not achieved, an amount equal to the shortfall can be invested in NABARD/SIDBI.

As far as Loan Portfolio Management is concerned, all the selected four banks have experienced a significant growth in total loans and advances over the period under study. The various constituents of loans and advances, viz. Cash credit, overdraft and loans payable on demand and term loans have also shown significant rises. The exception has been bills purchased and discounted; in which CBoP did not register significant growth. In the later years of the study,Term Loans have formed the major chunk of loans and advances granted by all the four banks under study, followed by Cash credit,Overdraft and loans payable on demand and Bills purchased & discounted.Thus,Term loans have been the most preferred mode of financing by banks and demanded by customers also.

8.3 SUGGESTIONS

1. Both the selected Public Sector Banks, viz. SBI Group and PNB have initiated the process of implementing their core banking solutions and networking their branches. Inter-bank connectivity among the subsidiaries of SBI Group still remains to be achieved.The banks need to update their technology and increase

318

their fee-based incomes by providing consumer-centric services to be at par with their private sector counterparts. The focus needs to be shifted to the customer and his needs and providing products and service.

2. While providing credit to the priority sector, sound principles of lending should be followed by the public sector banks to avoid NPAs.

3. Both the selected public sector banks, viz. SBI Group and PNB need to explore the unconventional sources of income especially income from foreign exchange transactions.

4. All the banks should follow the essentials of Basel Committee regarding the management of interest rate risk to avoid reduction in spread.

5. Off-Balance-Sheet (OBS) activities should be undertaken as they generate fee-income and increase the non-interest revenues of banks.

6. Both the Public Sector Banks need to manage their burden effectively because spreads are thinning due to deregulation of interest rates. The only hope of increasing profitability lies in reducing burden by reducing the manpower and operating expenses. VRS has been effective in reducing manpower expenses and now operating expenses need to be curtailed.

7. Marketing of banking services, cross-selling of other non-banking financial products to enhance fee-based incomes needs to be done extensively by the Public Sector Banks. The strategy of offering 'the right kind of products in the right markets' rather than providing everything everywhere is essential for having competitive edge over rival banks.

8. All the banks need to move from deposit orientation to profit orientation. However, the shift in focus to profitability rather than the balance-sheet does not mean that targeted resource mobilization and asset build up should take a back seat.

9. PNB needs to be cautious about its Secondary Reserves. ICICI Bank is in a dubious position of having maximum Secondary reserves and minimum Primary Reserves.

10. The decline in investment in debentures has been due to the lack of development of corporate bond market. The secondary market has not developed commensurately and market liquidity remains an issue. The Government constituted a High Level Committee on Corporate Bonds and Securitisation (Patil Committee) to identify the factors inhibiting the development of an active corporate debt market in India. The Committee recommended two important measures to be initiated by the Government, viz. rationalisation of stamp duty and abolition of tax deduction at source, as in the case of government securities. The implementation of the recommendations of the Committee can go a long way in removing the lacunae that prevail in the bonds market and making the banking sector more vibrant.

11. CBoP needs to explore new horizons for investment to become a force to reckon with though its liquidity position has improved remarkably after the merger.

12. All the four banks under study need to increase loans commensurately so that the Loan/Assets ratio reaches the Prudential Limit of 50%.Only ICICI Bank attained the Prudential Limit of 65% in respect of Loan/Deposits ratio. PNB, CBoP and SBI Group need to enhance their loans in relation to deposits to

achieve this Limit in respect of Loan/Deposits ratio.

13. The deposits insurance cover needs to be raised from the present cover of one lakh. The private sector banks need to tap rural areas for deposits. They need to open up branches in rural areas.

14. The Capital Adequacy of the two Private Sector Banks has declined over the period of study.This is a matter of grave concern for the two banks and needs to be looked into for assuring the confidence of the investors especially for CBoP. The Basel accord aims to provide a healthy and competitive financial system through risk based supervision and attainment of capital adequacy. This, in turn, will propel the banks towards better capital management through asset-liability management. Moreover, with the introduction of Basel-II norms, the operational risk has also come into focus along with credit risk and market risk for which more capital has to be provided for.

15. Private Sector Banks are not bound by the objectives of social banking and are solely motivated by commercial considerations. ICICI Bank, which is the largest in private sector, needs to increase lending to the priority sector as its lending is short of the stipulated target. Even CBoP is also short of the stipulated target of lending to the priority sector. The private sector banks need to work in tandem with the public sector banks so as to provide greater financial inclusion for the masses. It is highly imperative that the private sector banks also shoulder their responsibility towards the priority sector. Only then the socio-economic goals can be achieved and banking system will become harbinger of growth and development.

16. Unsecured advances carry the risk of repayment, thus leading to high loan losses, which adversely affect the profitability of banks.

All the four selected   banks need to be cautious and should rely on adequate securities before granting advances. Moreover, with securitisation becoming a practice, asking for security should be the norm rather than an exception.

17. The software to implement ALM system is very complex and needs to be developed in the light of the Basel-II recommendations by all the banks.The availability of the required software is a hurdle in the effective implementation of ALM system.

To conclude, profitability is an aggregate of various factors at play. With deregulation and soft interest schemes, the scope of intervention by RBI has reduced while the market forces are the key determinants. The CRR and SLR have been reduced, thus freeing more lendable resources for banking activities. The rates on deposits have also been freed and now only the rates on savings are mandated. Only the efficient banks can survive as the spreads are thinning out putting tremendous pressure on profitability. The banks have become dynamic and are devising new strategies to capture fee-based incomes and other non-traditional sources of income to supplement their income. Banks have become cost conscious as proper burden management can effectively reduce expenses and add to their profits. This is the purpose of Asset-Liability Management, i.e. to increase profits by matching the maturity of liabilities in accordance with the assets so as to reduce risks, which adversely affect profitability.

8.4 SCOPE FOR FURTHER RESEARCH

- The efficacy of derivatives to hedge the asset liability mismatch can be a related area of research.
- The impact of Off-Balance-Sheet activities on the profitability of banks can be studied.
- The impact of Capital Adequacy, in the light of Basel-II, on profitability can be an interesting topic of research.

BIBLIOGRAPHY

Books

Abrol, Prem Nath (1987), *Commercial Banking,* Anupma Publishers, Distributors, New Delhi.

Banerjee, Amalesh; and Singh, S.K.(eds.)(2002),*Banking and Financial Sector Reforms in India*, Deep & Deep Publications   Pvt. Ltd., New Delhi.

Bhasin, Niti(2006), *Banking Developments in India- 1947 to 2007, Growth Reforms and Outlook*,"New Century Publications, New Delhi.

Cornett & Saunders(1999), *Fundamentals of Financial Institutions Management*, Irwin McGrawHill International Edition, Finance Series, Singapore.

Franks,Julian;Mayer Colin;and Correia, Da Silva Luis(2003),*Asset Management and Investor Protection-An International Analysis,*Oxford University Press,U.K.

Hudson, Robert; Colley, Alan;and Largan, Mark(2000), *Capital Markets & Financial Management in Banking*, Glen Lake Publishing Co. Ltd, Fitzroy Dearborn Publishers, Chicago & London.

Indian Institute of Banking (2004),*Indian Financial System and Commercial Banking,* Macmillan Publications,New Delhi.

Joshi, C. Vasant;and Joshi, C. Vinay(2002),*Managing Indian Banks-The Challenges Ahead*, Response Books Pvt. Ltd., New Delhi. Khurana, S.K.(2000),*Asset Liability Management*, Skylark Publications, New Delhi.

Kumar, Parmod(2006),*Banking Sector Efficiency in Globalised Economy*,Deep &Deep Publications,New Delhi.

Kumar, Pawan (2005), *Indian Banking Today- Impact of Reforms*, Kanishka Publishers & Distributors, New Delhi.

Kumar, Ravi T. (1996) *Indian Banking System in Transition- Issues and Challenges*, ICFAI Vision Series, Finance,Hyderabad.

Kumar, Ravi. T. (2000),*Asset Liability Management*,Vision Books Pvt.Ltd.,New Delhi.

Lucia, De,R.D.;and Peters, J.(1993)*Commercial Bank Management-Functions and Objectives*, Serendip Publications,Wahroonga.

Machiraju, H.R.(2002), *Indian Financial System*, Vikas Publishing House Pvt. Ltd., New Delhi.

Mithani, D.M.(2004), *Money, Banking, International Trade and Public Finance*, Himalaya Publishing House, Mumbai.

N.,RajShekhar(ed.)(2004),*Banking in the New Millennium*,The ICFAI University Press, Hyderabad.

Ong,K. Michael(1998) "Integrating the Role of Risk Management in ALM,'' in *Asset & Liability Management- A Synthesis of New Methodologies*, KamaKura Corporation, London.

Padmavathi, A.; Hemachandrika, G.;and Prasad, Siva(2006), *Efficiency of Public Sector Banks in India*,Global Research Publications, NewDelhi .

Padmavathi, A;and Hemachandrika, G.(2006),*Public Sector Banks in India*, Global Research Publications, New Delhi.

Patheja, Anju(1994) , *Financial Management of Commercial Banks*, South Asia Publications, New Delhi.

Ramamurthy, T.R. (2006), *How to Borrow From Banks & Financial Institutions*, Bharat Law House Pvt. Ltd., New Delhi,

Rao, Mohana. P; and Jain, T.K.(eds.)(2002), *Management of Banking and Financial Institutions*, Deep & Deep Publications Pvt. Ltd., New Delhi.

Raut,C. Kishore;and Das, K. Santosh(1996),*Commercial Banks in India-Profitability, Growth and Development*, Kanishka Publishers Distributors, New Delhi.

Reed, W. Edward.;and Gill, Edward(1989), *Commercial Banking*, Prentice Hall, New Jersey, Fourth Edition.

Sagar,Saveeta(2005),*Commercial Banks in India*,Deep & Deep Publications,Pvt.Ltd.,New Delhi.

Saunders,Anthony(2002), *Financial Institutions Management-A Modern Perspective*,Third Edition, Irwin Mc- Graw Hill Series in Finance, International Edition, Singapore.

Seetapathi, K; Sivaram, Y. G; and Rao Rama Krishna T.S.(2003),*Loan Portfolio-Key Issues*, ICFAI University Press,Hyderabad.

Sen, Amiya Kumar.; Gupta, Malay.;and Chakrabarti, Swapen (eds.)(1990), *Banking* in the 1990s, Himalaya Publishing House, Mumbai.

Sharma,Manoranjan (ed.)(2005), *Studies in Money, Finance and Banking*, Atlantic Publishers & Distributors,New Delhi.

Shekhar, K.C.;and Shekhar, Lekshmy(1998), *Banking Theory and Practice*, Vikas Publishing House Pvt. Ltd, New Delhi, 18th Edition.

Shrivastava, M.P;and Singh, S.R.(eds.)(2004),*Indian Banking in the New Millenium*,Anmol Publications,New Delhi.

Shrivastava,MohanPrasad;Pandey,Pradeep;andVidyarthi,V.P.(eds.) *Banking Reforms and Globalisation*,A.P.H. Publishing Corporation,New Delhi.

Singh, Kumar Ravishankar(ed.)(2006), *Indian Banking and Financial Sector Reforms: Realising Global Aspirations*, Abhijeet Publications Pvt. Ltd, New Delhi, Vol. I & II.

Singh, P. Sampat(ed.)(1983),*Bank Lending-Some Controversial Issues*, NIBM, Pune.

Sinkey, Jr. F. Joseph(1992),*Commercial Banks' Financial Management in the Financial Services Industry*,MacMillan Publishing Co.,Nu York.

Sreekantaradhya, B.S.(2004), *Banking and Finance-Perspectives on Reforms,* Deep & Deep Publications Pvt. Ltd., New Delhi.

Srivastava, R.M.;and Nigam, Divya(2005),*Management of Indian Financial Institutions*, Himalaya Publishing House, Mumbai.

Thamare,Thomas(1988),*Banker's Guide to New Growth Oppurtunities*,Prentice Hall,New Jersey.

Tripathy,Nalini Prava (ed.)(2005),*Emerging Scenario of Indian Banking Industry*,Mahamaya Publishing House,New Delhi.

Uppal,R.K;and Kaur, Rimpi(eds.)(2007),*Banking in the New Millennium*,Mahamaya Publishing House,New Delhi

Vashisht, A.K. (1991),*Public Sector Banks in India*, H.K. Publishers & Distributors , New Delhi.

Vasudevan,A. (ed.),(2003), *Money and Banking-Select Research Papers by the Economists of Reserve Bank of India*,Academic Foundation, New Delhi.

Verma,S.B.(ed.)(2005), *Risk Management*, Deep & Deep Publications Pvt. Ltd., New Delhi.

Vij, Madhu(1991),*Management of Financial Institutions in India*, Anmol Publication Pvt. Ltd., New Delhi.

Vinayakam,N. (ed.),(1995) *Indian Banking by 2000 A.D.*, Kanishka Publishers, Distributors, New Delhi.

Reports

RBI (2001-02),Financial Regulation and Supervision, Annual Report.

RBI (2004-05),Operations & Performance of Commercial Banks, Report on Trends & Progress of Banking in India.

RBI (2005-06),Policy Developments in Commercial Banking, Report on Trends & Progress of Banking in India.

RBI (2005-06),Operations & Performance of Commercial Banks, Report on Trends & Progress of Banking in India.

RBI (2006-07),Policy Developments in Commercial Banking, Report on Trends & Progress of Banking in India.

RBI's Basic Statistical Returns of Scheduled Commercial banks in India,Various Years.

Articles

Ammannya, K.K. (1996), "Asset Liability Management Strategy for Banks,"*The Banker*,Vol.43.No.8,October, 1996.

Arora, Usha;and Verma, Richa(2005),"Banking Sector Reforms & Performance Evaluation of Public Sector Banks in India." *Punjab Journal of Business Studies*, Vol. 1, No.1, April- September.

Bagchi, S.K.(2005),''BaseI II:Operational Risk Management need for a Structured Operational Risk policy for banks,*''The Management Accountant*, Vol.40, No.1, January.

Barsky, P. Noah;and Catanach, H. Anthony(2005),"Evaluating Business Risk in the Commercial Lending Decision," *Commercial Lending Review*, Vol. 20, No. 3, May –June .

Bhalerao, Asha(1988), "Post-Nationalisation Trends in profitability of Commercial Banks in India," *Banking Finance*, Vol. 1,No. 4, April.

Bhasin, Aastha(2007),"Understanding Risks in Banking: A Note,"*Vinimaya*,Vol.XXVII,No.4,January-March.

Bhatt, K.A.(2003), "Total Quality Banking: Panacea for Competitiveness of PSBs," *The Business Review*,Vol. 9,No. 2,March.

Bhattacharya, Indernil;and Ray, Partha(2007), "How do we Assess Monetary Policy Stance ?" *EPW*, Vol. XLII, No. 13.

Bhide, M.G.;Prasad, A.;and Ghosh, Saibal(2002),"Banking Sector Reforms-A Critical Overview,"*EPW*,Vol. XXXVII,No.5,Feb 2.

Bhushan,Sanjay;Mani, Saurabh;and Sharma, S.K.(2002),"Strategic Focus on Executive Development-Genesis of Banking Sector Reforms: A Study of Selected Commercial Banks of India," *South Asian Journal of Socio-Political Studies*, Vol. 3, No. 1, July-December.

Chandan, C.L.;and Rajput, P.K.(2005),"Performance of Individual Commercial Banks-A 'Z' Score Analysis,"*Indian Management Studies Journal*,Vol. 9,No.2, October.

Chandan,C.L.;and Rajput, Pawan Kumar(2002),"Profitability Analysis of Banks in India: A Multiple Regression Approach,"*Indian Management Studies Journal,Vol.6,*No 2,October issue.

Chaplin, Graeme.; Emblow, Alison.;and Michael, Ian(2002)," Banking System Liquidity-Development & Issues," in K. Seetapathi(ed.), *Risk Management in Banks,* ICFAI Banking Series, ICFAI Press, Hyderabad.

Cheema, C.S.;and Agarwal, Monika(2002),''Productivity in Commercial Banks: A DEA Approach,''*The Business Review*,Vol. 8,No. 1&2.

Das, Abhiman; Nag, Ashok; and, Ray, Subhash C.(2005), "Liberalisation, Ownership and Efficiency in Indian Banking- A Non-Parametric Analysis, " *EPW*, Vol. XL, No. 12, March 19.

Das, Abhiman(1996),''Structural Changes and Asset-Liability Mismatch of Scheduled Commercial Banks,''*Reserve Bank of India Occasional Papers*,Vol.17,No.4,December.

Das, Abhiman(2002)," Risk and Productivity change of Public Sector Banks,"*EPW*,Vol. XXXVII, No.5, Feb.2

Das,M.R.;and Singh, Balwant(2001),''Maturity Pattern of Assets and Liabilities of Public Sector Banks: An Empirical Investigation,''*SBI Monthly Review*, Vol. 40,No.7, July.

Datar,M.K.;and Banerjee, Saumya Sankar(2007),''Simultaneity Between Bank Profitability and Regulatory Capital,'' *Prajnan*,Vol.XXXVI, No.1,April-June .

Debasish, Satya Swaroop(2004),''Investigating the Evidence of Market Discipline in the Banking Sector,''*Journal of Management Studies and Research*,Vol. II,No. 2,April –September.

Deo, Malabika(2005), " Bancassurance A Win-Win Solution for Banks & Insurance," *Business & Economic Facts for You*, April.

Dharmarajan, S. (2004)," ALM model for Managing Liquidity and Interest Rate Risks in Cooperative Banks," *Vinimaya*, Vol. XXV, No.1, April- June.

Diercks, Lee A.(2004),''Identifying and Managing Troubled Borrowers in Asset-Based Lending Scenarios,'' *Commercial Lending Review*,Vol. 19,No.3,May.

EPW Research Foundation (2005), "Metamorphic Changes in the Financial System, " March 19, Vol. XL, No. 1,.

EPW Research Foundation (2006), "Increasing Concentration of Banking Operations-Top Centers & Retail Loans," March 18, Vol. XLI, No. 11,.

EPW Research Foundation(2004),''Corporate Bond Market-Need for a Revamp,'' July, 24, Vol. XXXIX, No. 30.

EPW Research Foundation(2004),''Scheduled Commercial Banks in India," March 20, Vol. XXXIX, No. 12.

Ghosh, Saibal;and Das, Abhiman(2005),''Market Discipline,Capital Adequacy and Bank Behaviour,''*Economic and Political Weekly*,Vol.XL,No.12,March.19.

Gurumoorthy, T.R. (2004),''Analysis of Income and Expenditure in Banks,'' *Business and Economic Facts For You*, June.

Jagirdar, Brinda(1991),"Profitability and Capital Adequacy," *SBI Monthly Review,Vol.XXXI,No.4*.

Jain, A.K.(2003),''Challenges before the Banking and Financial Sectors in the context of Globalisation,'' *Indian Journal of Economics*,Vol.XXXIV,No.332,July.

Jain, Paras Mal(2005), "Consolidation in Banking Industry through Mergers and Acquisitions, " *IBA Bulletin Special Issue*, Jan, Vol. XXVII, No. 1.

Jha, Kumar Pramod(1986), "Commercial Banking and Economic Growth in. S. Subrahmanya (ed.), *Trends and Progress of Banking in India,* Deep & Deep Publications Pvt. Ltd., New Delhi.

Jha, Tarakant(2002), "Priority Sector Lending: A Case Study in Mithila Region," in Amalesh Banerjee and S.K. Singh(eds.), *Banking and Financial Sector Reforms in India*, Deep & Deep Publications Pvt. Ltd., New Delhi.

Kamath, M.V. (1996) " ALM in Banks, " *CanBank Quarterly Review*, Vol. VI No. 4 & Vol. VII No. 1, October- March.

Kanagasabapathy, K.(2001),"Monetary Policy Underpinnings: A Perspective," *Economic and Political Weekly*, Vol. XXXVI, No. 4 Jan 27-Feb 2.

Kannan, R.;Narain, Aditya;and Ghosh, Saibal(2001),''Determinants of Net Interest Margin under Regulatory Requirements-An Econometric Study,'' *Economic and Political Weekly*, Vol.XXXXVI,No. 4,January 27.

Kapil, Sheeba; Kapil, Kanwal Nayan; and Nagar Kailash (2003),''Benchmarking Performance of Indian Public Sector Banks,'' *Indian Journal of Accounting*, Vol.XXXIV, December.

Kidder, Lee A.(2004),''Straight-Through Processing in Commercial Banking Industry: A Solution Waiting for Awareness of the Problem,'' *Commercial Lending Review*,Vol.19,No.6,Nov.-Dec.

Kumar, Birendra(2005),"Consolidation in the Indian Banking Industry: Market Segmentation for success," *IBA Bulletin Special Issue,* Jan Vol XXVII, No. 1.

Kumar, Ranjana(2003),''Move Towards Risk Based Supervision of Banks:The Role of the Central Banker and the Market Players,'' *Vinimaya*,Vol.XXIV,No.1.

Leeladhar,V.(2007),''Basel-II Implementation in Indian Banks:Challenges Ahead,''*Vinimaya*,Vol. XXVII, No.4, January-March.

Mariappan, V.(2005)," Changing the way of Banking in India: Technology as a Driver, What is the Trigger?" *Vinimaya,* NIBM, July-September, Vol. XXVI, No. 2.

Mazumdar,Tanusree(1996),"*Profitability and Productivity Indian Banking in Transition:Issues & Challenges*, ICFAI Vision Series.

Mohan, Rakesh (2005),''Financial Sector Reforms in India-Policies and Performance Analysis,'' *EPW*,Vol. XL,No.12,March 19-25,

Mohan, Ram T.T.(2002),''Deregulation and Performance of Public Sector Banks,''*EPW* Vol XXXVII,No.5,February 2.

Mohan, Ram T.T.; and   Ray, Subhash C.(2004),''Comparing Performance of Public and Private Sector Banks-A Revenue Maximisation Efficiency Approach,''*Economic and Political Weekly*,Vol. XXXIX,No. 12,March 20.

Mohanty, A.K.(2005),''An Overview of Operational Risk Management in Banks,''*Vinimaya*, Vol XXVI, No. 1,April-June.

Nitsure, Rupa Rege (2007),''Corrective Steps towards Sound Banking,'' *EPW* Vol. XL, No.13, March. 31.

Qamar, Furquan(2003), " Profitability and Resources Use Efficiency in Scheduled Commercial Banks in India: A Comparative Analysis of Foreign, New Private Sector, Old Private Sector & Public Sector Banks," *Synthesis* Vol. 1, No.1, July- December.

Raghuraman, K.(2006), "Corporate Social Responsibilities," The Indian Banks, *IBA Bulletin*, August. Vol. 1 No. 8.

Rajwade,A.V.(2002),"Issues   in   Asset-Liability   Management-I" *Economic and Political Weekly*, Vol. XXVII, No.5, February 2.

Ramachandra, Rao K.S.; Das, Abhiman.;and Singh, Kumar Arvind (2006)," Commercial Bank Lending to Small Scale Industry," *EPW* March.18 Vol. XLI, No.11.

Ramasastri, A.S.; Samuel, Achamma.; and Gangadaran,S. (2004), "Income Stability of Scheduled Commercial Banks: Interest vis-a-visNon-Interest Income,"*EPW*,Vol.XXXIX,No.12,Mar 20.

Ramathilagam, G;and Preethi, S. (2005),''Efficiency of Indian Commercial Banks in the Post-Reform Period,'' *Business and Economic Facts For You*,November,

Rao,Ramachandra K.S.; Das, Abhiman; Singh, Kumar Arvind (2006)," Commercial Bank Lending to Small Scale Industry," *EPW,* March18 Vol. XL1, No.11.

Reddy,Y.V.(2002),''Public Sector Banks and the Governance Challenge-the Indian Experience,'' *http//www.rbi.org.in.*

Roy, Mohua(2006),''A Review of Bank Lending   to   Priority   and Retail Sectors,''*EPW* ,March 18,Vol.XLI,No.11.

Sangwan, S.D. (2005)" Social Banking An Assessment," *Vinimaya,* October- December Issue, Vol. XXVI, No.3.

Satyamurthy(1987),''Profitability and Productivity in Banks-Concepts and Evaluation,'' *IBA Bulletin*,Vol.9,No.11,Nov.

Sen Gupta, A.K.(1994)" Study of Credit Policy and Decision systems in Banks, " *Project Report*, NIBM , April.

Sharma, Kapil.;and Kulkarni, P.R.(2006),'' Asset Liability Management Approach in Indian Banks:A Review and Suggestions,'' *The Journal of Accounting and Finance*,''Vol. 20,No. 2,April-September.

Shetty, V.P. (2005),''Interest rate risk in Investment Portfolio and its impact on the Profitability of Banks,'' *IBA Bulletin*,Vol. XXVII.No. 2,February.

Singh, Dalbir.(2005),"Consolidation in the Banking Industry: HR Challenges, Consequences & Solutions," *IBA Bulletin, Special Issue* , Vol. XXVII, No. 1.

Sinha, R.K(2006), "Thinning Spreads Calls for Focused Interest Rate Risks Management by PSBs,*"The Management Accountant*, November.

Sinha, R.K(2006),''A Need for Fine-Tuning Interest Rate Risk Management by Banks,''*Vinimaya*,Vol.XXVII,No.2,July-September.

Sinha, R.P(2005),''Asset Liability Management :Relevance for Indian Banks,''in Sugan C.Jain; Priti Gupta;and N.P Agarwal (eds.), *Accounting and Finance for B*anks, Raj Publishing House,Jaipur.

Sinha, Ram Pratap(2008),'' Priority Sector Lending of Indian Commercial Banks: Some Empirical Results,''*Prajnan*, Vol. XXXVI, No. 4,January-March.

Sooden, Meenakshi;and Bali, Manju(2004),"Profitability in the Public Sector Banks in India in the Pre and Post-Reform Period," *Indian Management Studies Journal*, Vol. 8 No. 2, October.

Srivastava, R.M. (2006),''Indian Commercial Banks on Path Towards Competitive Efficiency,''*Vinimaya*,Vol.XXVII,No.3.

Subrahmanyam, Ganti(1995)," Asset Liability Management, for Banks in a Deregulated Environment, " *Prajnan*, Vol.XXIII, No.1.

Sundaram,Satya(1984),''Banks:Improving Productivity and Profitability,''*The Journal of Indian Institute of Bankers,*Vol.1,No. 55(30),July-September.

Sy, Amadou(2007),''Indian Banks' Diminishing Apetite for Government Securities,''*Economic and Political Weekly*, Vol.XLII,No.13.

Thimmaiah, G.(2004),"Asset Liability Management in Post Indian Banking Sector Reforms,"in M.P. Shrivastava and S.R. Singh (eds.) *Indian Banking in the New Millennium*,Anmol Publications,New Delhi.

Upadhyay, Saroj(2003),"Financial Sector Reforms:New Norms have reduced Credit Supply to Commercial Sector,*"The Management Accountant*,Vol.38,No.3.

Uppal, R.K.;and Kaur, Rimpi (2007),"Falling Rate of Interest in the Banks:Bank Spreads,Profitability Comes Under Pressure,"in R.K.Uppal and Rimpi Kaur (eds.)*Banking in the New Millennium*,Mahamaya Publishing House,New Delhi.

Vij, Madhu(2005)," Asset Liability Management,"in *Management Mosaic*, S.K.Tuteja (ed.)Excel Books,New Delhi.

Newspaper Articles

Agarwal, Som(1998),"Aseets & Liabilities of Indian Banks- The Long and Short of Credit," *The Economic Times,*September 28.

Bhat,PrasannaV.(1999),"A System for Asset-Liability Management,"*Hindustan Business Line*,August 19.

Bhat, Prasanna ,V. (1999),"Asset Liability Management-System for Match-making," *Hindustan Business Line*,August 26.

Bhat, PrasannaV.(2000),"Asset-liability matching-Time-tested Concepts Still Best," *Hindustan Business Line*,March 16.

Bhusunurmath, Mythili(1998),"Teaching old dogs new tricks,*"The Economic Times*,September.21.

Chawla, O.P. (1998)"Asset Liability Management in banks," The *Financial Express* February 7.

Devarajan, P. (1998),"For better ALM, buckets are useful," *Hindustan Business Line*,October 7.

Devarajan P. (1998),''Q is for quality, C is for caution,'' *Hindustan Business Line*,October 10.

KrishnaMurty, V. (1999),''Asset-liability Mismatch,''*OBP*, July 19.

Mehta, Sangita(1998),''Defusing Time Bombs Ticking in the Books,'' *Business Standard*,September 24.

Nag, Anirban(1998),"RBI asks Banks to set up System for Asset-Liability Management," *The Financial Express*, September 16.

Websites

www.rbi.org.in

www.iba.org.in

www.epw.org.in

www.bankers india.com

www.banknet india.com

Lightning Source UK Ltd.
Milton Keynes UK
UKOW04f2319270913

218092UK00001B/55/P